WE HAVE UNDERGONE AN EVOLUTION IN
WHICH, 'LITTLE BY LITTLE, THE DEAD CEASE
TO EXIST,'...CAST OUT OF OUR SYSTEM OF
SOCIAL AND CULTURAL EXCHANGE, 'NO
LONGER BEINGS WITH A FULL ROLE TO PLAY.'

PAUL KOULOURIS, THE EMPIRE OF DEATH

OTHER BOOKS BY APRIL SLAUGHTER

* REACHING BEYOND THE VEIL
* GHOSTHUNTING TEXAS

OTHER BOOKS BY TROY TAYLOR

* AMERICAN HAUNTINGS
* DEAD MEN DO TELL TALES SERIES
* CABINET OF CURIOSITIES SERIES
* WEIRD HIGHWAY SERIES
* THE DEVIL CAME TO ST. LOUIS
* AND OTHERS

Disconnected from Death

The Evolution of Funerary Customs
& the Unmasking of Death in America

by

April Slaughter & Troy Taylor

ORIGINAL COVER ARTWORK DESIGNED BY

© Copyright 2018 by April Slaughter & Troy Taylor

THIS BOOK IS PUBLISHED BY:

American Hauntings Ink
Jacksonville, Illinois | 217.791.7859
Visit us on the Internet at
http://www.americanhauntingsink.com

First Edition — June 2018
ISBN: 978-1-7324079-0-9

Printed in the United States of America

ACKNOWLEDGEMENTS

For Madison & Jordyn,
Now and Always.

With every new project comes a litany of inevitable obstacles, some seemingly insurmountable. From the birth of the idea, to the numerous outlines, drafts, and never-ending edits, this book has been an absolute labor of love. Without the patience, knowledge, and support of so many, it might never have come to be.

Troy Taylor, my prolific co-author and friend, has continually encouraged and inspired me, despite the many setbacks he has had to guide me through. I could not be more grateful for the breadth of his knowledge or the depth of his dedication. The co-creation of this book has meant a great deal more to me than he will ever realize.

I am fortunate to know and work with yet another amazing author, Rosemary Ellen Guiley. Such a strong and inspiring female presence in my life, she has consistently supported me in my efforts to become a knowledgeable researcher and writer. There are few women like her in the world, and far fewer who have made such a meaningful impact on my professional pursuits.

While my choice in career has often mystified my parents, I would not have had the courage to work as hard as I have to reach my goals without their continued praise and encouragement. I couldn't have asked for more beautiful and loving parents than Brad and Cheri Page, even if I had been able to hand-pick them myself. The path I have chosen has always been fraught with difficulty, but without them, the road set out in front of me would have been quite impossible to travel. I pray they remain as proud of me as I am of them.

To the following individuals, I owe my love and sincere gratitude. They are the individuals who have brought true friendship into my life, and without whom I could never have succeeded in all that I have strived to accomplish. Thank you, Rene Kruse, John Alleman, Anthony and Teirney Armstrong, Matthew and

Courtney Lewandowski, Daniel Knauf, Kris Kuksi, Ed Kosary, Wade Burwell, John Melchior, Steve Mangin, Bill Alsing, Tamera Bovyer, Sarah Soderlund, James and Mary Hampton, David C. Cowan, Denver Robbins, Lauren T. Hart, Scotty Roberts, Jerry Bowers, and so many more. I am blessed to know and love such genuinely kind and caring people.

The dead cannot go unmentioned, for they have always been the driving force behind all my creative endeavors. I have such admiration and respect for those who have come and gone before me, and it is my sincere hope that I have always represented them well, with the remembrance and honor they deserve.

Thank you all.
April Slaughter

I won't attempt to compete with the well-written and thoughtful things that April had to say here. I'll simply say thank you to April for all the hard work, care, and diligence that she has put into this book. It's been a pleasure to have her as a friend for so many years and now she's a co-author, too. There are few people who would be insane enough to want to work on a book with me, so I've been lucky to have this chance. Her passion for the subject matter inspired me to want to deliver her the best material that I could, and I hope it all turned out the way that she wanted. It's been a long, strange trip but I'm proud to put this book in the readers' hands with both of our names on the cover.

I also want to say thank you to my partner (and co-author) Lisa Taylor Horton for helping me to keep this project moving and making sure that the words that came out of my head were corrected before they made it onto paper. Not many people would dare to dig around in this overcrowded brain to make sure that happened, so thank you!

Thanks also to the usual suspects: Rene Kruse, Rachael Horath, Elyse and Thomas Reihner, John Winterbauer, Kaylan Schardan, Len Adams, Luke Naliborski, Steve Mangin, Mary DeLong, Julie Warren, Julie Ringering, Sandy Guire, Bill Alsing, Dave Goodwin, Cody Beck, Chris and Robyn Waterston, Maggie Walsh, and Lux Eisley.

Thanks!
Troy Taylor

INTRODUCTION

There has always existed some measure of connection and disconnection between the living and the dead, but in delving into the annals of American history, it is apparent that we began as a nation both terrified and unified by death and have evolved into a culture largely in denial of it. When it occurs, we submit ourselves (as well as our dead) to routines defined as necessary by the thriving business that death has become... and it *is* a business.

Presently, dealing with the dead is a duty we most commonly assign to strangers, but it wasn't always so. Caring for and preparing a deceased loved one prior to burial was once a familial responsibility; one that many today would find repugnant. Traditions that once held emotional significance for the bereaved are now seen as macabre reminders of the reality of death.

Take, for instance, the late nineteenth century photograph of a young boy, eyes wide, hands placed neatly on his lap (cover image.) At first glance, it is an unremarkable and even somewhat pleasant image. Upon closer inspection, however, there is apparent lividity - or discoloration - of the child's hands. When I first obtained this photograph, my initial thought was that it was taken posthumously, as such discoloration is common among the recently deceased, but I could not be sure without a professional opinion. Having long been a fan of Stanley B. Burns, M.D. and his various publications on postmortem photography, I sought his expertise. Dr. Burns was kind enough to respond and confirm that this picture was indeed an authentic postmortem image.

Your first question might be why anyone would want such a photograph, or why this child was posed to appear alive and well. While a much more detailed explanation of the practice is included in the later chapters of this book, I will tell you that this image - as well as thousands of others like it -

once brought some measure of peace to those who possessed it. These photographs were often the only visual representation a family had of those they'd loved and lost.

Put yourself in your ancestor's shoes and imagine being a family of limited means that did not have easy access to an expensive process like photography. Family photos – especially photos of children – were not seen as a priority. But when your child dies unexpectedly, a postmortem photograph would be the only chance that you might have to capture their likeness and keep a memento of their life. These photos were never meant to be macabre – they are another example of how life in America existed hand-in-hand with death.

Several times in this book, we will mention that the people of America's past had death as a next-door neighbor. In hindsight, after all the writing was completed, this statement may not have been totally accurate. It might be more precise to say that death was a lodger in our ancestor's home, perhaps renting out a back bedroom as a necessary –but unwelcome—part of daily life.

Adults and children died young. Life expectancy was short. Death came easily on the streets, the highways, on farms, in factories, mills, and mines, and from diseases that are easily treated today. Unlike now, people expected to die. They saw family and friends perish at a young age and simply assumed they would be next. In many cases, they were right, and they learned to accept this outcome because they had been exposed to death for their entire existence. Children watched – and participated – in the rituals of death, from washing a corpse with water from the kitchen sink to sitting up next to the body when it was laid out in the parlor.

Americans of the past were connected to death.

Today, a very large percentage of Americans – especially children – have never seen a dead body. If they have, it was likely in the sterile conditions of a hospital or after being carefully prepared for viewing by representatives from the local funeral establishment. Our society knows little about the subject of death because most of us have never been exposed to it. We don't understand the traditions of the past or how our ancestors coped with an inevitable situation from which they could not escape. We have been disconnected from the final thing that makes us all human. And for that reason, we believe that this makes our experience here on Earth less fulfilling that it could be. How do we enjoy every second of the life that we have if we don't possess an understanding of what it means when it's all over?

This is not a book about religion, or what happens to us after we die. This is a book that tries to connect our modern lives to the lives of those who had more than a passing acquaintance with death. Far too often, the traditions and rituals of the past have been presented as "spooky" or "strange" and, while some of them were unusual, all of them served a purpose. No matter how bizarre they might seem, they served to present a vivid portrait of how we are all connected to death.

Death is – and always will be – a part of life and we hope this book will shed some light on the funeral customs, practices, and traditions of the past and how they have been changed, softened, and sterilized to make death seem like a distant stranger.

We can assure you that it is not.

Death may not be renting out our back bedroom anymore, but it's still with us, waiting to take us by the hand and lead us into the unknown.

April Slaughter
Troy Taylor
Spring 2018

THE KING OF TERRORS

Death and Burial Among the Puritans

Remember me as you pass by,
As you are now so once was I.
As I am now you soon must be.
Prepare for death and follow me.

-Puritan Epitaph

Puritanism arose as a separatist movement, a split from the Church of England over dissatisfaction with the Church's absorption and modification of Catholic rites. The roots of the movement go back to 1536, when King Henry VIII, enraged over the Catholic Church's refusal to grant him a divorce from Catherine of Aragon, split from Catholicism as the religion of the land. Henry established the Church of England, a Protestant church, and from 1536 to 1542 he carried out a brutal campaign to shut down the Catholic monasteries, priories, convents and friaries. Many were not just shut down – they were destroyed. Thus began the English Reformation, a tumultuous time politically and socially.

In the century following Henry's split, religious turmoil also prevailed. Catholicism was not going to vanish without a fight. Within the Church of England, a great deal of disagreement led to separatist movements.

The Puritans were never a defined sect, nor did they name themselves such; "Puritan" was a derogatory term, along with "precisionists." Both terms were used to describe a wide range of separatists, who eventually formed various Protestant denominations, such as the Calvinists and the Quakers. The Puritans were derisively called such because many of them did not consider the Church of England to be pure enough, but too muddled with Catholicism. By the mid-16th century the term "Puritan" stuck, and separatism in its various expressions grew in force. The Puritans attracted upper levels of society – the educated and intelligent, and the upwardly mobile merchant class.

Many Puritans were persecuted, and under the reign of Queen Mary (1553-58), who was a staunch Catholic, some clerics were exiled and even executed. The persecutions forced many separatists underground. Groups of them, including entire families, emigrated to other countries in search of religious freedom. Many of them became colonists in America, a land that represented a difficult but fresh start, a blank slate devoid of religious history.

The small band of Pilgrims who landed at Plymouth, Massachusetts in 1620 were separatists. Massachusetts Bay Colony was formed in 1628 and granted a charter by England in 1629. In 1630, a group of about 1,000 English Puritans arrived in Massachusetts Bay Colony, led by John Winthrop, who was intended to be governor. That role went to Thomas Dudley in 1634, but Winthrop remained one of the most influential figures in New England until his death in 1649 at age 61.

The Puritans established a theocratic government and limited full citizenship in the colony to church members. Though they had fled repression in England, the Puritans now became just as repressive in America, opposing any religious views not sanctioned by government. Discipline was harsh and rigid, and laws were strict – and punishments were strictly enforced.

There were even separatists among the separatists. Not long after the establishment of Plymouth Colony, a group unhappy that Plymouth was not strict enough split away and settled in Salem, Massachusetts, on land the natives said was cursed. Life in Salem was bleak. There were laws against wearing colorful clothing, displaying affection in public, and even against celebrating Christmas, which was supposed to be a somber day of prayer. Church attendance was mandatory and involved a day of sitting on hard wooden benches listening to a preacher drone on about sin. Those who broke laws could be pilloried, fined, have their ears cut off, be banished from the community, or even sentenced to death. Adultery was one of the sins that carried a death sentence.

Puritans in Massachusetts Bay Colony and elsewhere in New England had similar oppressive laws and practices.

EARLY COLONIAL PURITAN FUNERAL AND BURIAL CUSTOMS

Treatment of the dead mirrored the harsh, restrictive daily life. Early Puritans eschewed anything resembling the elaborate rites of Catholicism, including burial. To pray for the souls of the dead was to engage in a superstitious act.

The Puritans held that death is inevitable and is God's punishment for the original sin of Adam. A chosen few will be rewarded with eternal salvation, but the majority of people are doomed to eternal damnation in hell, a place of "unspeakable terrors."

Many of them accepted the teaching of Protestant reformist Jean Calvin, that every person's life is determined by predestination. One's eternal fate was sealed long before death, and so there was nothing that could be done to alter it.

This fate was constantly reinforced by severe fire and brimstone preaching. Cotton Mather, one of the leading ministers of New England, stated, "Shall they that are faithful to death, receive a crown of life? Then the faithful have no cause to be afraid of death."

However, a person, no matter how faithful and righteous, could not be confidant that he or she was among the saved. One had to be religiously diligent to the last breath and then hope for the best. This uncertainty created a tremendous fear of death, and it is no wonder that people on their deathbeds clung to the last possible breath.

John Winthrop, in his journal *The History of New England* (1630-1649), dealt with these fears, which sometimes caused overwrought individuals to take drastic action. He described a man in his fifties who led a "loose and dissolute" life. One Sunday in church, the man was greatly upset by the sermon, which evidently caused him to do a great deal of self-reflection upon his supposedly wicked and hopeless life. Shortly after that, he went out one Sunday night and drowned himself in a pit filled with two feet of water.

Winthrop also related a bizarre account of a woman so distraught over her eternal fate of likely damnation that she threw her child into a well and let it drown. For her, this sealed her damnation; it was no longer an uncertainty and she did not have to worry about it.

The Puritans lived daily with death as a constant companion. Many children died of diseases, and few adults living into old age as well. One in 10 infants in rural areas was expected to die within a year of birth, and three in 10 in more populated areas, where there was greater exposure to contagious

PURITAN DEATH ANNOUNCEMENT ARTWORK.

disease. Only half of all those born could be expected to reach adulthood, and many of those would die in their twenties.

The early colonial Puritans considered funerals as ceremonies for showy Catholics. They went to great lengths to be at the complete opposite end of the spectrum. The dead, who were not embalmed, were conveyed to the graveyard in a silent procession, and then buried without benefit of graveside prayers or benedictions. Since one's fate was predestined, there was no point to offering prayers for the dead – their afterlife situation could not be altered or alleviated. To pray for the souls of the dead was superstitious. For the same reason, there were no death anniversary services or memorials. The grave was not a place for remembrance.

Some people were not even buried in coffins but were cast straight into the earth like animals. Grave markers, if placed, were usually simple, with only an individual's name, birth and death dates, and age.

The Pilgrims of Plymouth Colony especially followed these practices. They often left graves unmarked – but there was a practical reason for it. They did not wish the Native Americans to take note of how many of their numbers died, for the colony could then appear weakened and vulnerable. It was not until the 1650s that stone markers were put on graves.

Thomas Lechford (1590-1644) of Boston traveled to Plymouth in the 1630s and 1640s and wrote in his diary:

At Burials, nothing is read, nor any Funeral Sermon made, but all the neighborhood, or a good company of them, come together by tolling of the bell, and carry the dead solemnly to his grave, and there stand by him while he is buried.

Even when William Bradford, the governor of Plymouth Colony, died in 1657, there was little in the way of extra ceremony, except for the firing of volleys and a bit of band music.

LATER PURITAN FUNERARY AND BURIAL PRACTICES

In stark contrast to the stiffness and bleakness of Pilgrim funerals, the Puritans of Massachusetts Bay Colony and elsewhere in New England began indulging in increasingly extravagant funerals, especially among the wealthy, by mid-17th century (John Winthrop died in 1649). The 1740s ushered in "the great Puritan Awakening." Death was no longer seen as a dismal end to life and the beginning of a grim afterlife, but rather a rite of passage to a better place.

Perhaps human beings have an innate hope for a pleasant afterlife, and a deep feeling that the dead must be honored and given a good send-off. The bleakness of early Puritan burial rites surely must have seemed to many an inadequate way to mark the end of a life.

The wealthy merchant class was eager to show off its prosperity in homes, dress and possessions, an attitude that extended to burying the dead. Gone were the solemn and stark burials without benefit of sermon or graveside prayers, and simple interment in unmarked and poorly marked graves. Attitudes toward death, including send-offs for the dead, changed significantly.

Funerals and burials became increasingly ritualized, turning into drawn-out social occasions with their own sets of etiquette. There were rules for invitations to the service, clothing, events, home decorations and even gifts to be given to mourners. A family could be considerably set back financially by a funeral and burial, and some had special savings for just such events. With the frequent deaths of adults and children, the living could spend their entire lives paying for the dead. The lavishness indulged by the Puritans paved the way for increasingly elaborate funerals and burials of the Victorian age.

Funerals were not seen as something under the provenance of the church. Rather, they were civic affairs. Ministers were not to be "burthened with the execution of Civil affaires, as the celebration of marriage, burying the dead, which things belong as well to those without as within the Church," as one writing of the time declared. This view was part of the anti-Catholic sentiment that still prevailed.

A plaque at the King's chapel Burial Ground in Boston provides a description:

In late 17th century Boston, funerals were often elaborate rituals. Samuel Sewall noted Capt. Clap's death in his famous diary and we can imagine the ritual as described in other entries and accounts.

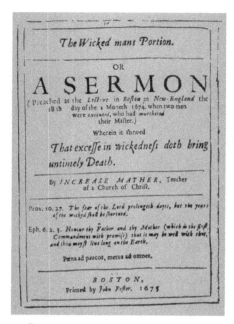

The Wicked mans Portion.

OR

A SERMON

Preached at the Lecture in Boston in New-England the 18th day of the 1 Moneth 1674. when two men were executed, who had murthered their Master.)

Wherein is shewed

That excesse in wickednefs doth bring untimely Death.

By INCREASE MATHER, Teacher of a Church of Christ.

Prov. 10. 27. The fear of the Lord prolongeth dayes, but the years of the wicked shall be shortned.

Eph. 6. 2, 3. Honour thy Father and thy Mother (which is the first Commandment with promise) that it may be well with thee, and thou mayst live long on the Earth.

Pœna ad paucos, metus ad omnes.

BOSTON,

Printed by John Foster. 1675

PURITAN SERMON LITERATURE BY
BOSTON CONGREGATIONAL MINISTER
INCREASE MATHER.

Relatives and friends sent white gloves to invited guests and ordered a coffin and gravestone. An elegy broadside was printed and later pinned to the carriage of coffin. The funeral notice recorded the deceased name and death date and often a discourse on death and salvation. Mourners received the broadside and usually, a gold ring inscribed with the name of the deceased. By the 1720's, the ritual had become so extravagant that the colony prohibited the excessive gifts and expenses.

On the day of the burial the mourning carriage carried the coffin slowly toward the burying ground, as the bell tolled. The horses were draped in mourning clothes painted with "Scutcheons of death"; winged deaths head and crossbones, while mourners, dressed in black, followed. Once the coffin had been lowered into the ground, the mourners meditated in silence. Later the party usually gathered for a funeral dinner and the ministers delivered the funeral sermon on the next day.

Invitations to funerals were accompanied by gifts called "tokens." Gloves were given out, to be worn at the event. The more important the guest, the more expensive the gloves. For the funerals of prominent persons, hundreds, even thousands of pairs of gloves would be given out. Scarves were also given.

An especially popular token was a mourning or burial ring, usually made of gold and enameled white or black. Some were embellished with winged death's heads, coffins and skeletons, and were inscribed with the dead person's name and date of death. Many included locks of hair of the dead.

Mourning and burial rings were big business for jewelers, who kept supplies on hand, ready to be engraved with personal information at a moment's notice.

Rings and bits of hair were ways the living could remain close to the dead. There were no photographs, and only the very wealthy could afford to have portraits done.

Tokens became social collectibles, and some recipients sold theirs, much like people sell personal valuables to collectors today. One minister, Andrew

Eliot of North Church in Boston, recorded in his diary the number of rings and gloves he received – his gloves alone amounted to 2,940 pairs. He sold many of them – a nice side income. For others, tokens were cherished and handed down through generations.

Puritan families spent substantial amounts of money on the trappings, food and liquor for funeral events, with liquor accounting for the biggest bills of all. Gallons of rum, wine and spirits would be consumed at a funeral, along with lavish amounts of food. Feasting and drinking much like an Irish wake would take place before the procession to the burying ground. Corpses were laid out at home in coffins, and prior to burial, guests arrived to view the corpse, and then proceeded to the food and well-stocked bar. The eating drinking recommended afterwards.

Bell-ringing to announce deaths and burials was standard practice. Traditionally, three bells would be rung by undertakers around the time of a death. For the dying, a "passing bell" would be rung to announce impending death. That would be followed by the "death knell" to announce the death, and then a "corpse bell" that was rung at the funeral. As funerals became more elaborate, the undertakers became more zealous with their bell-ringing.

Thus, death galvanized entire families into social action. The men of a household arranged for the logistics, the undertakers and the pall-bearers, and acquisition of provisions and drink. The women prepared the food and decorated the house with black crepe and ribbons. Windows were shuttered. Mirrors were covered, an accommodation to an old superstition that held that the dead, who lingered by their bodies until burial, should not see their reflections, lest they become confused and not leave the house with their body when the funeral procession to the gravesite commenced. The black decorations were left in place for a year, the expected mourning period.

Multiple sets of bearers of the coffin were required to escort the dead from the home to the grave. The "underbearers" were young men who bore the weight of the coffin. The pallbearers were older men who held the corners of the pall, a cloth (owned by the city or town), which was draped over the coffin and covered the heads of the underbearers. If the journey to the graveyard was a long one, relief sets of bearers had to be hired. In some cases, the family hired a carriage to carry the coffin – in which case the carriage and the horses had to be properly decorated too. Palls were used to decorate the hearse carriage too. Many were made of the best velvet.

The use of palls has left its influence on language today. To "cast a pall" means to dampen, depress, discourage or make something hopeless.

PURITAN HEADSTONE RUBBING

Prayer and sermon customs changed as well. Whereas the early Puritans and Pilgrims made none, but buried people in silence, later Puritans enjoyed the addition of both. Typically, prayers were not said at graveside but at the home prior to the procession. Funeral sermons were given at other times, not on the day of the funeral; exceptions were made for prominent people, with sermons offered on the funeral day, and prayers said at graveside.

Sermons were printed on black-bordered paper decorated with death's heads and crossbones. Copies were given to participants and sent to others who, because of distance, could not attend.

Families added their own personal touches with printed epitaphs, elegies and mourning broadsheets, a large piece of paper with information about the deceased and the funeral. The broadsheets would be fastened to the coffin or carriage in a funeral procession.

As time went on, more prayers were given at graveside regardless of prominence of the dead, a custom still widely practiced today.

Grave markers also became more elaborate with the later Puritans. The Pilgrims wanted little to nothing to mark a grave. Aside from the practical reasons cited earlier, graves were not a place of remembrance of the dead. The later Puritans felt differently. They wanted the grave to be a place for the living to return to, to remember the dead and grieve.

The Puritans had prohibitions against the use of images in religious practices, but funerals and burials were considered civic affairs and cemeteries were under secular control, so the use of images there was considered acceptable. The Puritans created elaborate headstones and monuments carved with the symbols of death and the afterlife, such as angels and cherubs, weeping willow trees, death's heads, crossbones, hourglasses and urns. Skeletons, symbolizing death, and shells, symbolizing the pilgrimage of life, death and new life, were often used together to represent the pilgrimage from death to the afterlife. Many markers carried short epitaphs.

The Puritans avoided crosses, which had a Catholic symbolism.

The trend toward showy and elaborate funerals – something the early Puritan had rigorously avoided – offended some Puritan leaders. Efforts were made to dampen practices, but without lasting success. For example, in 1741, Massachusetts attempted to fine people 50 pounds for distributing wine or rum and funeral rings, and restricted gloves to pall bearers and the clergy, thus slighting the family and friends who were mourners.

Salem government tried to limit excessive bell ringing by limiting what undertakers could charge for it, as well as the number of times a bell could be rung. Limits also were placed on the costs of funerals.

Such sanctions lost over time to the swell of desire for celebrating death.

The customs of the Puritans extended into the Romantic Era and were absorbed into Victorian times. Many of them are still in use today.

GONE ARE THE LIVING, BUT THE DEAD REMAIN

THE RISE OF THE AMERICAN CEMETERY

"I told you I was sick."
Epitaph on the grave of B.P. Roberts
Key West, Florida

Death is the final darkness at the end of life. It has been both feared and worshipped since the beginning of history. For this reason, our civilization has dreamed up countless practices and rituals to deal with and perhaps understand it. We have even personified this great unknown with a semi-human figure, the "Grim Reaper," and have given him a menacing scythe to harvest human souls with. Yet, death remains a mystery.

Maybe because of this mystery, we have chosen to immortalize death with stones and markers that tell about the people who are buried beneath them. We take the bodies of those whose spirits have departed and place them in the ground, or in the enclosure of the tomb, and place a monument over these remains that speaks of the life once lived. This is not only out of respect for the dead because it also serves as a reminder for the living. It reminds us of the person who has died -- and it also reminds us that someday, it will be our bodies that lie moldering below the earth.

In America's ancient past, our ancestors had their own rituals for burying the dead. Long before the European explorers crossed the Atlantic and set foot on the soil of the New World, lofty burial mounds could be found scattered across the American landscape. Concentrated in the Mississippi River region, as far south as today's Florida, as far west as Texas, and as far north as Illinois and Ohio, they were built by Native Americans who lived in settled communities and interred their dead in mounds that were meant to be permanent. In contrast, nomadic societies of the Plains and Pacific Northwest, always wandering, exposed their dead to their elements using trees, scaffolds, and boxes on raised poles, all of which were meant to be ephemeral.

Most of the mounds were conical-shaped, some roughly rectangular and others in the shapes of animals, reptiles and birds. All were built from earth that had been carried in baskets and then piled over the dead, the mounds increasing in size as the new bodies were added. Some were low, no more than two of three feet high, while others soared to the heavens. Although most of the mounds have long since vanished, flattened by successive generations of farmers and urban developers, a few can still be found in the South and Midwest.

In time, the great cities that surrounded the mounds disappeared. No one knows why these civilizations abandoned their homes in the mid-sixteenth century, but historians have surmised war, famine, or disease. As the years passed, the Native Americans who resettled the regions lost all memory of the significance of the mounds that were once such a major part of their destiny.

When the Spanish explorers arrived in America in the sixteenth century, they buried their dead the best they could in the wilderness. Hasty disposal of the body, a few ritual words from the Catholic liturgy, no coffin, and a wooden cross were the most the dead could expect. But with the founding of St. Augustine on the eastern coast of Florida in 1565, and the establishment of a colony in New Mexico in 1598, the Spanish began to build Catholic churches with adjacent churchyards, just as it had been done in Europe.

When the British and French settlers began arriving on American shores, they also brought with them the customs, traditions, and cemeteries of the Old World. Those cemeteries, the repositories of the dead, where the living could come and feel some small connection with the one that passed on, were an ancient custom. But the old churchyards were anything but peaceful. The modern version of what became the "garden cemetery" began in Europe in the nineteenth century, but prior to that, burial grounds were hellish and often frightening places.

For centuries, churchyards were the only burial grounds for the dead. For the rich, burial within the church itself was preferred. Princes, clerics, and rich benefactors of the church came to regard such entombment as a right rather than a privilege and soon the buildings began to fill. The Church tried

WITH SO FEW RECOGNIZED PLACES TO BURY THE DEAD, THE CHURCHYARDS BECAME OVERCROWDED

hard to limit such burials but the abuse of the arrangements -- usually after a large sum of money had changed hands -- soon had the churches packed with the bodies of the dead. The accompanying health risks for the living forced officials to stop the practice. From that point on, only bishops, abbots, and "laymen of the first distinction" could be entombed within the church building. The interpretation of "first distinction" was left to the local clergy to decide upon and this decision was normally influenced by a large donation to the church funds. Most considered the extorted cash to be a small price to pay for the security of an interior tomb and a place safe from the elements.

For those who could not be buried inside of the church, the churchyard became the next best thing. Even here, one's social status depended on the section of the ground where you were buried. The most favored sites were those to the east, as close as possible to the church. In such a location, the dead would be assured the best view of the rising sun on the Day of Judgment. People of lesser distinction were buried on the south side, while the north corner of the graveyard was considered the Devil's domain. It was reserved for stillborn babies, bastards, and strangers unfortunate enough to die while passing through the local parish.

Suicides, if they were buried in consecrated ground at all, were usually deposited in the north end, although their corpses were not allowed to pass through the cemetery gates to enter. They had to be passed over the top of the stone wall. During the late Middle Ages, the lack of much-needed space finally "exorcized" the Devil from the north end of the churchyard to make way for more burials.

As expected, it soon became nearly impossible for the churchyards to hold the bodies of the dead. As towns and cities swelled in population during the eighteenth century, a chronic shortage of space began to develop. The first solution to the problem was simply to pack the coffins more closely together. Later, coffins were stacked atop one another and the earth was piled over them to the extent that some churchyards rose 20 feet or more above that of the church floor. Another solution was to grant only limited occupation of a grave site. You had a certain number of days to be buried and then your time was up to make way for the next person. Eventually, though, it got to the point that occupancy of a plot was measured in only days, or even hours, before the coffin was removed and another was put in its place.

Not surprisingly, with so many bodies crammed into the churchyards, a protest began to arise from the people who lived nearby. The decaying bodies and the vile stench coming from the graveyard were considered a great risk to local health and doctors began penning stern warnings about the unsanitary conditions. One solution to this was to begin "cycling" the bodies through the cemetery, whereby fresh corpses were deposited on top of coffins long since rotted away by natural decomposition. The burial cycle would begin and then 10 or 20-year gaps would take place between subsequent burials at the same site. Two factors continued this cycling for some time: population and profit. The death rate had stripped the land available for burial and now the churches needed income from whatever space they could create.

It became impossible for the churchyards to hold the dead and by the middle 1700s, the situation had reached crisis proportions in France. Dirt and stone walls had been added around the graveyards to hold back the bodies, but they often collapsed, leaving human remains scattered about the streets of Paris. The government was finally forced into taking action. All the

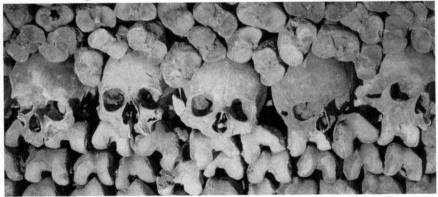

THE CATACOMBS OF PARIS PROVED TO BE A PARTIAL SOLUTION TO THE CITY'S OVERCROWDED CHURCHYARDS

PERE LACHAISE OUTSIDE OF PARIS, THE FIRST "GARDEN" CEMETERY

churchyards in Paris were closed for at least five years and cemeteries were established outside of the city to serve the needs of the parishes within the city itself.

Closure of the city graveyards was still not enough, though. In 1786, it was decided to move all the bodies from the Cemetery of the Innocents and transport them to catacombs that had been carved beneath the southern part of the city. It was a massive undertaking. On the night of April 7, a long procession of funeral carts, carrying the bones of tens of thousands of people, made its way to the catacombs. The wagons were escorted by torchlight and buoyed by the chanting of priests. There was no way to identify the individual remains, so it was decided to arrange the bones into rows of skulls, femurs, and so on. It has been estimated that the Paris catacombs contain the bodies of between three and six million people.

In addition to the catacombs, four cemeteries were built within the confines of the city. They were Montmartre, Vaugiard, Montparnasse, and Pere-Lachaise, the latter of which has become known as the first of the "garden" cemeteries. It was named after the confessor priest of Louis XIV and is probably the most celebrated burial ground in the world. As it was, the cemetery began in debt and caused a great amount of concern for the investors who created it. If Napoleon had been buried there, as he originally planned, the businessmen would have rested much easier, but they weren't that lucky. Instead, they were forced to mount a huge publicity campaign to persuade Parisians to be buried there. They even dug up the bones of famous Frenchmen who had been buried elsewhere and moved them to Pere-Lachaise.

Ironically, it was the burial of people who never lived at all that managed to make the cemetery popular. The novelist Honore de Balzac began burying many of the fictional characters in his books in Pere-Lachaise. On Sunday afternoons, readers from all over Paris would come to the cemetery to see the tombs that Balzac described so eloquently in his novels. Soon, business was booming and today, the walls of this graveyard hold the bodies of the most illustrious people in France, and a number of other celebrities as well. The dead include Balzac, Victor Hugo, Colette, Marcel Proust, Chopin, Oscar Wilde, Sarah Bernhardt, and Jim Morrison of the Doors -- if you believe he's dead, that is.

Pere-Lachaise became known around the world for its size and beauty. It covered hundreds of acres and was landscaped and fashioned with pathways for carriages. It reflected the new creative age where art and nature could combine to celebrate the lives of those buried there.

Paris set the standard and America followed, but London was slow to adopt the new ways. The risks to public health came not only from the dank odors of the churchyards but from the very water the people drank. In many cases, the springs for the drinking supply tracked right through the graveyards. Throughout the early 1800s, the citizens of London still continued to be buried in the overflowing churchyards or in privately owned burial grounds within the city limits. The call for the establishment of cemeteries away from the population center became louder.

In 1832, the London Cemetery Company opened the first public cemetery at Kensal Green. It was made up of 54 acres of open ground and was far from the crowded conditions of the city. From the very beginning, it was a fashionable place to be buried and in fact, was so prestigious that it can still boast the greatest number of royal burials outside of Windsor and Westminster Abbey. The dead also include novelists Wilkie Collins, James Makepeace Thackery, Anthony Trollope, and George Eliot. Other notables include Karl Marx, Sir Ralph Richardson, and several members of the Charles Dickens and Dante Rossetti families.

But if Kensal Green is London's most fashionable cemetery, then Highgate is its most romantic -- and its most legendary. Over time, the cemetery has crumbled and has fallen into gothic disrepair but for many years, it was considered the "Victorian Valhalla."

Highgate did not start out as a cemetery. In fact, in the late 1600s, the grounds were part of an estate owned by Sir William Ashhurst, who had built his home on the outskirts of a small, isolated hilltop community called

Highgate. By 1836, the mansion had been sold, demolished, and then replaced by a church. The grounds themselves were turned into a cemetery that was consecrated in 1839.

For years, it was a fashionable and desirable place to be buried, but as the decades passed, hard times came to Highgate. The owners steadily lost money and the monuments, statues, crypts, and markers soon became covered with undergrowth and began to fall into disrepair. By the end of World War II, which saw an occasional German bomb landing on the burial ground, the deterioration of the place was out of control.

If there was ever a location that was perfect for a Gothic thriller, Highgate was the place. Dark visions were created from the crumbling stone angels, lost graves, and the tombs ravaged by both time and the elements. As the cemetery continued to fall apart, trees grew slowly through the graves, uprooting the headstones. Dense foliage and growth gave the place the look of a lost city. Although paths were eventually cleared, nature still maintained its hold on Highgate and in such a setting, occultists and thrill-seekers began to appear.

In the early 1970s, Hammer Films discovered Highgate's moody setting and used it as a location for several of their horror films. Other companies began using the setting as well, attracting public interest to a place that had been largely forgotten. Soon, stories of grave robbing and desecration began to appear in local news reports.

Not long after, rumors circulated that Highgate was a haven for real vampires, as many claimed to see a peculiar creature among the graves. Scores of "vampire hunters" regularly converged on the graveyard in the dead of night. Tombs were broken open and bodies were mutilated with wooden stakes driven into their chests. Bizarre activity reached its peak with the 1974 trial of David Farrant, who the press called the "High Priest and President of the Occult Society." He was tried on five charges connected with activity inside the cemetery. Stories of weird rituals and naked women cavorting on desecrated graves filled the newspapers. When he was arrested, photographs of the nude women lying in open graves were found. He had also placed salt around all the doors and windows of his house and slept with a large, wooden cross under his pillow. Possible witnesses against him in the trial were sent dolls with pins stuck through their chests. Farrant acted as his own defense at trial. He admitted to occasionally visiting the cemetery but denied ever damaging any of the graves. He was eventually convicted on two criminal counts and sentenced to two-and-a-half years in prison.

Highgate Cemetery continues to hold a fascination for visitors. Thankfully today, the cemetery is under restoration by a group called the Friends of Highgate. They have been working hard to preserve this historic spot and tours are regularly conducted of the grounds.

In America, the churchyard remained the most common burial place through the end of the eighteenth century. While these spots are regarded as picturesque today, years ago, they varied little from their European counterparts. The colonists viewed them as foul-smelling, unattractive eyesores and in 1800, Timothy Dwight described the local burial ground as "an unkempt section of the town common where the graves and fallen markers were daily trampled upon by people and cattle." This view of the local churchyard intensified by the middle 1800s, when public health reformers began to regard graveyards as a source of disease. As a result, most burials were prohibited from taking place within city limits after the Civil War.

After the founding of the Pere-Lachaise Cemetery in Paris, the movement toward creating "garden" cemeteries spread to America. The first of these was Mount Auburn Cemetery in Cambridge, Massachusetts, which was consecrated in 1831. Proposed by Dr. Jacob Bigelow in 1825 and laid out by Henry A.S. Dearborn, it featured an Egyptian style gate and fence, a Norman tower and a granite chapel. It was planned as an "oasis" on the outskirts of the city and defined a new romantic kind of cemetery with winding paths and

a forested setting. It was the opposite of the crowded churchyard and it became an immediate success, giving rise to many other similar burial grounds in cities across America. In fact, they became very popular as not only burial grounds, but as public recreation areas, too. In such settings, people could enjoy the shaded walkways and even picnic on weekend afternoons. The Garden cemetery would go on to inspire the American Park movement and virtually create the field of landscape architecture.

The idea of the Garden cemetery spread across America and by the late 1800s was the perfect answer to the old, overcrowded burial grounds. Many of the early cemeteries had been established closer to the center of town and were soon in the way of urban growth. Small towns and large ones across the country were soon hurrying to move the graves of those buried in years past to the new cemeteries, which were always located outside of town.

There are several examples of wonderful Garden cemeteries scattered across America, but two of them are located virtually side-by-side in St. Louis, Missouri. They were created in 1849 for one simple reason – people were dying in the city that year, by the thousands.

The dead from numerous cholera epidemics were overflowing the cemeteries. And since nothing could be done to slow the spread of the disease, city leaders had more bodies to deal with after each passing day and no place to put them.

A search began for a new graveyard – one that was far outside the city limits. It needed room to expand and it needed to be far from where people lived so that the dead would not spread any kind of disease to the living. In March 1849, St. Louis Mayor John Darby and a banker named William McPherson found just the place for the new cemetery. A group of men from all different religious affiliations purchased land far north of the city limits and called it the Rural Cemetery Association. The name was later changed to Bellefontaine Cemetery.

The cemetery was given a peaceful, park-like setting by Almerin Hotchkiss, the same landscape artist who had created famous Greenwood Cemetery in Brooklyn, New York. He remained at Bellefontaine for the next 46 years, carving a burial ground with more than 14 miles of roads out of the prairie that surrounded the city.

Attempting to create a peaceful place, he had his work cut out for him in the early years. The cemetery's initial growth came from the epidemics that were claiming so many lives in the late 1840s. There were often as many as 30 burials each day. After a law went into effect that forced all cemeteries to be located outside of city limits for health reasons, Bellefontaine began to receive internments from every church in St. Louis. Over the next decade, as the city grew and encroached on the small graveyards that were scattered throughout downtown, graves began to be unearthed and the dead were reburied at Bellefontaine.

Later in the nineteenth century, Bellefontaine became a showplace for the excess of Victorian death movement. It is filled with statues, monuments, elaborate mausoleums, and unusual markers. It was the burial place of choice for city leaders, governors, war heroes, writers, celebrities, and the social elite. Under the trees and across the cemetery's rolling hills, a visitor can find the graves of William Clark – of Lewis and Clark fame – Sara Teasdale, William S. Burroughs, Adolphus Busch, the Lemp family, and scores of others.

The burial ground is also home to a very famous bullet. On August 2, 1876, famous gunfighter "Wild Bill" Hickock was killed while playing cards at a saloon in Deadwood, Dakota Territory. The bullet that killed Hickock passed through his back and ended up in the arm of a riverboat captain from St. Louis. He never had it removed. When he died, he was buried in Bellefontaine Cemetery. Today, under a tree in the southeast part of the cemetery is the final resting place of the bullet that killed Wild Bill.

One of my favorite monuments in the cemetery rests over the grave of St. Louis druggist Herman Luyties. It is a 12-foot marble statue of a young woman that has been placed in a glass case to keep it from being worn away by the weather. The story goes that Luyties was on a tour of Italy in the late 1800s and met and fell in love with a sculptor's model. The beautiful woman wanted nothing to do with him and he returned heartbroken to St. Louis. Before he left Italy, though, he commissioned a copy of one of the model's statues. The statue was crated and shipped to St. Louis, where Luyties had it installed in the foyer of his home – where he lived with his wife and children. Not surprisingly, his wife did not approve. When Luyties died, the statue was moved to Bellefontaine Cemetery and placed over his grave.

THE LUYTIES MONUMENT IN ST. LOUIS' BELLEFONTAINE CEMETERY

As a side note, I wanted to be sure and mention that Luyties' wife was buried elsewhere in the cemetery, in her family's plot. She did not want to spend eternity at the feet of a woman that her husband had fallen in love with.

Located across the road from Bellefontaine is Calvary Cemetery, which was started by the Catholic Church in 1857. It was also started because of the cholera epidemics and the shortage of space in the city's Catholic cemeteries.

It was started six miles beyond the city limits on land that belonged to famous Kentucky politician Henry Clay. He had been a popular figure in St. Louis. He had helped Missouri become a state and ran for president in 1844. He visited St. Louis a few years after his failed candidacy and was warmly welcomed by city and business leaders, but his main reason for the visit was to sell off a large piece of land called Old Orchard Farm. A big crowd came for the auction, but none of them came to bid – they just wanted to get a look at the famous statesman. Clay hung onto the farm and built a large home there. It had its own heating plant and indoor bathrooms, which was rare at the time. Despite the luxuries, he didn't stay long. His wife, Susanna, found the farm to be too isolated and didn't like St. Louis. Clay did what his wife wanted – he took her home to Kentucky.

When the land came up for sale again, the Catholic archdiocese realized it had an answer to its cemetery problem. Archbishop Peter Kenrick bought the land in 1853, established a farm on one half and set aside the other for a burial ground. Kenrick lived in the Clay mansion for many years, even after the cemetery was incorporated. Like Bellefontaine, the cemetery saw many burials in its early years. All the smaller Catholic cemeteries in the city exhumed their dead and moved them to Calvary. In addition, Native Americans and soldiers who had been buried at nearby Fort Bellefontaine were exhumed and moved to a mass grave on the property.

CALVARY CEMETERY IN ST. LOUIS

Calvary takes advantage of its natural wooded setting and rolling hills and is filled with amazing displays of cemetery artwork, like Egyptian-themed mausoleums, angelic statues, and more. It's also the final resting place of St. Louis notables like Dred Scott, General William Tecumseh Sherman, Tennessee Williams, author Kate Chopin, who died from a brain aneurysm at the 1904 World's Fair, and many others.

In Chicago, Illinois, one burial ground created several garden cemeteries, although the most spectacular of them is undoubtedly Graceland Cemetery. Graceland, along with Rosehill Cemetery and several others came about thanks to the closure of the old Chicago City Cemetery around 1870.

The City Cemetery was located exactly where Chicago's Lincoln Park is located today. Before its establishment, most of the early pioneers simply buried their dead on their immediate property, leading to many gruesome discoveries as the downtown was developed years later. Two cemeteries were later set aside for both Protestants and Catholics, but both of them were located along the lake shore, leading to the frequent unearthing of caskets whenever the water was high. Finally, the city set aside land at Clark Street and North Avenue for the Chicago City Cemetery. Soon, bodies were moved from the other sites to the new cemetery.

"ETERNAL SILENCE," WHICH MARKS THE BURIAL SITE OF DEXTER GRAVES IN
CHICAGO'S GRACELAND CEMETERY. ACCORDING TO LEGEND, PHOTOGRAPHS
CANNOT BE TAKEN OF THE STATUE – WHICH IS CLEARLY SEEN HERE.
SOMETIMES, CEMETERY MARKERS TAKE ON A LIFE ALL THEIR OWN.

Within 10 years of the opening of the burial ground, it became the subject of much criticism. Not only was it severely overcrowded from both population growth and cholera epidemics, but many also felt that poorly organized burials were creating health problems and contaminating the water supply. To make matters worse, both the city morgue and the local Pest House, a quarantine building for epidemic victims, were located on the cemetery grounds. Soon, local families and churches were moving their loved ones to burial grounds considered to be safer and the City Cemetery was closed.

One cemetery that benefited from the closure of the graveyard was Graceland, located on North Clark Street. When it was started in 1860 by real estate developer Thomas B. Bryan, it was located far away from the city and over the years, a number of different architects have worked to preserve the natural setting of its 120 acres. Two of the men largely responsible for the beauty of the place were architects William Le Baron Jenney and Ossian Cole Simonds, who became so fascinated with the site that he ended up turning his entire business to landscape design. In addition to the natural landscape, the cemetery boasts many wonderful monuments and buildings, including the cemetery chapel, which holds the city's oldest crematorium, built in 1893.

There are scores of Chicago notables buried in Graceland, including John Kinzie, one of the earliest residents of Chicago, Marshall Field of department store fame, Phillip Armour, the meat packing magnate, George Pullman, the much-maligned railroad car manufacturer, Potter Palmer, dry goods millionaire, Allan Pinkerton, of the Pinkerton National Detective Agency, author Vincent Starrett, architect Louis Sullivan, and many others.

America's great garden cemeteries saw their rise come about in the middle nineteenth century and into the waning years of the Victorian era. In funerary history, we think of this as the "Victorian Celebration of Death," a period when most of the mourning rituals that we think of today came about. It was a time of intricate customs and etiquette and a time that saw an explosion in ornate cemetery art and architecture. This period changed the face of America's garden cemeteries forever.

The mourning rituals of this period were extravagant (and will be looked at in more detail in a later chapter) and extended beyond things like clothing and custom to the cemeteries where the dead were buried. The burial grounds became a showplace of monuments, statuary, and tombs, incorporating every conceivable era of architecture in an attempt to overwhelm the living with how much attention and wealth could be lavished on the dead.

But this period would not last. After the death of Queen Victoria, fashion changed and ushered in the Edwardian Era, followed later by the Great Depression, which would largely bring an end to the kind of excess that had been seen in cemeteries in years past. By the later years of the twentieth century, hospitals, funeral parlors, and traditional cemeteries began following uniform procedures to distance the dead from the living. The garden cemeteries of yesterday had become the memorial parks of the modern age – boring, easily avoided, and failing to attract attention, repositories of the soon-to-be-forgotten.

The living had moved on, but the dead – no matter how troublesome – remained.

STORIES TOLD IN STONE

AMERICAN GRAVE MARKERS AND TOMBSTONES

Marking the grave of the dead reflects our need for a hallowed site of remembrance – a place to which we return, alone or with others, to renew the ties with someone who is now "gone, but not forgotten." Many of us return to the grave of a love one – a wife, husband, parent or child, especially in the first months after a death. Bringing flowers, a token of life, can soften the pain of death. Some will talk to the dead in the belief that the spirit still lingers near the corpse.

A grave marker is meant to be a touchstone of good memories and a life well-lived – but it was not always that way. Tombstones started out as crude items that were used more because of superstition than for remembrance of the dead. The earliest grave markers were literally stones and rocks that were used to keep the dead from rising out of their graves. It was thought, in primitive times, that if heavy rocks were placed on the grave sites of the deceased, they would not be able to climb out from underneath them.

But as time went on, a need developed for the living to mark the graves of the dead with a reminder of the person who was buried there. Humans have a great desire to know where their loved ones are buried, even though many early American settlers were buried in unmarked graves. Some were buried hastily during times of famine and epidemics. The remains of others who fell to nature – floods, storms and blizzards – were never found. Even under normal circumstances, or because of a shortage of natural stone, many families could not afford a tombstone. Many simple markers were made from wood, which did not last long in the elements.

Early stone monuments in New England copied motifs from Europe and were carved with frightening motifs like winged skulls, skeletons, and angels of death. The idea was to frighten the living with the very idea of death. In this way, they were apt to live a more righteous life after seeing the images of decay and horror on the markers of the dead. It would not be until the latter part of the 1800s that scenes of eternal peace would replace those of damnation.

EARLY AMERICAN GRAVE MARKERS WERE MEANT TO FRIGHTEN THE LIVING WITH SKULLS, BONES, AND MORBID IMAGES.

Eventually, making grave markers, monuments and tombs became a craft, as well as an art form. In those days, many brick layers and masons began to take up side jobs as gravestone carvers but soon demand became so great that companies formed to meet the needs of this new trade. Stone work companies started all over the country, especially in Vermont, where a huge supply of granite was readily available. Many stones and monuments that were carved and cut in Vermont were done by Scottish and Italian immigrants. The most delicate carving was done by the Italians, though. As children, many of them had trained in Milan, going to school at night to be carvers. Despite the thousands of statues and mausoleums that were created, only a few dozen carvers could handle the most intricate work.

The peak for the new funeral industry and for graveyard art and mausoleums came during the Victorian era. During those years, American cemeteries were packed with massive, ornate and beautiful statues and tombs. This was a time when maudlin excess and ornamentation was greatly in fashion. Funerals were extremely important to the Victorians, as were fashionable graves and mausoleums. The skull and crossbones tombstones had all but vanished by this time and now cemeteries had become very survivor-friendly and, of course, heartbreakingly sad. Scantily dressed mourners carved from stone now guarded the doors of the tombs and angels draped themselves over monuments in agonizing despair. The excessive

ornamentation turned the graveyards into a showplace for the rich and the prestigious. Many of them became inundated with artwork and crowded with crypts as society figures attempted to outdo one another with how much of their wealth could be spent celebrating death.

Gaudy and maudlin artwork like furniture, carved flowers, and life-size (and larger) statues dominated the landscape. Realistic representations of the dead began to appear, as did novelty monuments that told entire life stories or would spin on a round dais to be seen easily from any direction.

There was nothing as elaborate in the Victorian cemetery as the mausoleum, however. Tombs for the dead had already been around for thousands of years. The pyramids are the largest and most famous but even ancient man entombed their leaders and chieftains in subterranean and aboveground structures. Most of these were domed chambers created from circular mounds of earth, although some of the stone structures still exist today.

The word mausoleum comes from the name of Mausolus, who was the king of Halicarnassus, a great harbor city in Asia. When Mausolus died in 353 B.C., his grief-stricken wife, Artemisia, constructed a huge fortress to serve as his tomb. Inspiration for what would become the world's first mausoleum is believed to have come from the Nereid Temple, which boasted statues and friezes of battling warriors and female statues standing between Ionic columns. The tomb at Halicarnassus was similar to the temple, but much larger, standing a full five stories and having hundreds of statues decorating all quarters. It was said to be surrounded by a colonnade of 36 columns and a pyramid-like structure that climbed 24 steps to the summit. At the top was a four-horse chariot, cut from marble.

Nothing remains of the tomb today save for a few stones from the foundation. It was most likely damaged during earthquakes and by the Knights of St. John of Jerusalem, who plundered the structure in the late fifteenth and early sixteenth centuries. They took the stones to strengthen their own castles and destroyed the underground tomb chambers. During its heyday, though, the tomb attracted many sightseers, including Alexander the Great, who conquered Halicarnassus. The tomb is still considered one of the

Seven Wonders of the Ancient World. The Greeks adopted the tomb of Mausolus as the new standard and began building their own "mausoleums" and coining the word. The Romans emulated the Greeks and influenced the modern styles of the nineteenth century, thanks to the fact that many great archaeological finds were uncovered during this period.

The rise of the American mausoleum came with the founding of Mount Auburn, the first American garden cemetery, near Boston. The creation of this cemetery meant the end of the horrifying graveyards of the past and a new era for burial grounds. Although grave markers dominated the cemeteries, mausoleums experienced a Golden Age, starting in the mid-nineteenth century and ending

THE BUSCH FAMILY MAUSOLEUM IN ST. LOUIS – AN EXAMPLE OF THE KIND OF TOMB THAT A LOT OF MONEY COULD BUY IN THE VICTORIAN ERA

around the time of the Great Depression. They became the most desired burial spots in any cemetery and bankers, industrialists, robber barons, entrepreneurs, and anyone else with plenty of money to spend committed their mortal remains to a mausoleum. They became like the pharaohs of Ancient Egypt, who if they were not remembered for their accomplishments, would be remembered for their tombs.

The best architects were hired, and extravagant amounts of money were spent. Most mausoleums of the era were made from granite, marble, and various types of stone and often the imaginations of the designers ran wild. They created everything from gothic cathedrals to classic temples to even Egyptian pyramids. One can find just about everything imaginable decorating the tombs of the period, from nude women to macabre animals and the sphinx. They have been constructed in every architectural style imaginable and can only be classed as "uniquely funerary."

For cemetery enthusiasts, the gravestones have proven to be just as fascinating as the even the most eccentric tombs. The earliest American stones were copies of the old European ones with skulls, crossbones, and death's heads decorating their surfaces. Later, carvings on the stone began to represent the grief of the family and began to make a statement about the life of the person buried beneath it. A variety of different images were used to symbolize both death and life, like angels, who were seen as the emissaries between this world and the next. In some cases, they appeared as mourners and on other graves, as an offer of comfort for those who are left behind. As time passed, even the plainest of illustrations began to take on a new significance – a sort of code that could be read by those who visited the cemetery and knew what the motifs and illustrations actually meant.

PLANTS AND FLOWERS

Plants, especially flowers, were common symbols that represented love and purity or that life is beautiful, brief and never meant to be permanent. They have served as a symbol of remembrance since man began memorializing the dead. The Egyptians were the first culture to use flowers during funeral rites, believing their subtle scent contained divine powers. In America, flowers first began to be used for funerals after the death of President Abraham Lincoln. During the national state of mourning that followed, people searched for the proper symbol to pay tribute and flowers were chosen. As Lincoln's Funeral Train traveled across the country, the flowers served another purpose – to mask the scent of his decomposing body. This was an attractive additional use for undertakers and mourners in the nineteenth century, when embalming was still in its infancy.

The heyday of flower symbolism, though, occurred during the Victorian era, which coincided with the rise of the garden cemetery. The Victorians took great pains to give special attributes to flowers, adapting many of the ancient myths to Christian symbolism. Lovers passed flowers to each other to convey a special message, and in the cemetery, specific flowers were assigned proper funereal attributes.

Acanthus: This is one of the most popular architectural flowers, mostly because it adorns the tops of Corinthian columns. The use of acanthus in funerary architecture derives from the fact that the leaves are thorny and have often been used as a symbol of the prickly journey from life to death and, ultimately, to eternal life. Acanthus leaves decorate hearses, tombstones, and funerary garments, as well as column capitals.

Buds and seedpods: Seeds and small buds serve to remind the graveyard visitor of the fragile beginnings of life, all too often tragically cut short. Buds, especially those that are broken, often decorate the grave of a child. The buds can be almost any flower, but rosebuds are the most commonly used.

Calla Lily: With its broad leaves and large, vase-like flowers, the calla lily is one of the most stunning of flowers. On tombstones, it symbolizes beauty and marriage. This South American plant was introduced to the United States during the second half of the nineteenth century, which coincided with the beginning of the golden age of the American cemetery. Soon after it was imported, it began to appear in American art, including in funerary art.

Clover: Thanks to its three leaves, the clover has become the traditional symbol of the Holy Trinity. It is in this matter that it is usually used in funerary art. An Irish legend says that St. Patrick brought it to Ireland to be an enduring symbol of the Trinity, hence the clover, renamed the shamrock, has become the symbol of Ireland. Even before the arrival of Christianity, the Celts used the clover as a symbol of virility because of its abundant growth. The four-leaf clover is rare and has long been a symbol of good luck.

Daisy: In the cemetery, daisies and lambs often indicate the graves of children. Because of the unassuming simplicity of the daisy, many artists used

the flower in scenes of the Adoration to symbolize the innocence of the Christ child. Soon thereafter, wishful lovers started plucking daisy petals in the now familiar refrain, "he loves me, he loves me not." The daisy is also the symbol of the Virgin Mary because, like Mary's love, it can grow almost anywhere. And, lest we forget, a popular term to describe the dead is "pushing up daisies."

Ferns: Generally found deep in the forest, only by those who have honestly searched, the fern has come to symbolize humility, frankness, and sincerity in the cemetery.

Laurel: Usually found in the form of a wreath in funerary art, the laurel can represent victory, eternity, immortality, and chastity. Its association with eternity and immortality comes from its leaves, which do not wilt or fade. Its link with victory comes from ancient contests where winners were crowned with laurel wreaths, which was supposed to bestow immortality. In the Roman world, the laurel wreath was a symbol of both military and intellectual victory and was also thought to cleanse the soul of any guilt over the slaying of enemies. It was also a symbol of chastity because it was consecrated to the Vestal Virgins.

Lily of the Valley: All lilies, particularly the lily of the valley, are found in funerary art. They are symbols of innocence, purity, and virginity and are commonly found on the gravestones of children, especially young girls. The lily of the valley also has particular significance since it is one of the first flowers to bloom in the spring, thus symbolizing renewal and resurrection.

Rose: The rose has long been considered the queen of flowers because of its longevity, beauty, and fragrance. It has inspired lovers, poets, and dreamers for thousands of years. Venus, the goddess of love, claimed the rose as her own. Cleopatra stuffed pillowcases with rose petals. Nero arranged for rose petals to rain down on his guests. But, the early Christians were reluctant to use the rose as a religious symbol due to his association with

decadence. However, people's love of the rose was so strong that the Christians made some adjustments and adopted the rose as a symbol of their own. In Christian and funerary art, the red rose became the symbol of martyrdom, while the white rose represented purity. In Victorian-era cemeteries, the rose frequently adorns the graves of women.

FRUIT, GRAINS, LEAVES AND VINES

It is common, especially in the Midwest and Great Plains cemeteries, to find images of the harvest or of plants and tree limbs that have been cut away from the body of the earth. The depiction of wheat or a sickle would show the reaping of the soul and the gathering of the harvest to the next world. But such depictions of death were not alone.

Apple: According to Christian lore, life here on earth would be much different if not for the apple. The crux of the story is found in Genesis 3, when Eve takes a bite of the forbidden fruit. Interestingly, however, no apple is ever mentioned, even though it's taken the blame for Eve's transgression. It has redeemed itself in funerary art. If you see an apple on a gravestone, it's meant to be an allusion to salvation.

Corn: It should come as no surprise that the most likely place to find corn on a tombstone is in America's heartland. Corn is one of the oldest harvested plants and has long been a symbol of fertility and rebirth.

Grape Clusters: Grapes and clusters of grapes represent the Eucharistic wine, which is the symbol of the blood of Christ. Grapes, of course, are made into wine. On tombstones, grape clusters are sometimes combined with wheat as a "wine and bread combination" to represent Holy Communion.

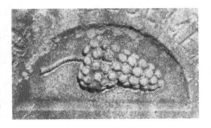

Ivy: Because ivy is eternally green, even under harsh conditions, it is associated with immortality and fidelity. Ivy clings to a support, which makes it a symbol of attachment, friendship, and undying affection.

Vine: The vine is one of the most powerful symbols of the relationship between God and man. It can commonly be found on late nineteenth century tombstones as a representation of this relationship.

Wheat: A sheaf of wheat on a tombstone is often used to denote someone who lived a long and fruitful life. It is one of the most basic foodstuffs and is thought to be a gift from God, particularly because its origins are unknown. It denotes immortality and resurrection because of its use as a harvested grain. When depicted with a sickle, it represents the harvesting of the spirit from this world.

Oak Tree – Acorns: The acorn represents prosperity and fruitfulness and for this reason, it's found gracing many coats of arms, column capitals, and tombstones. Two acorns paired together can represent male sexuality or, less graphically, truth and power

from two sources: the natural world and the world that waits to be revealed.

Oak Tree – Leaves: Oak tree leaves can symbolize many things, including strength, endurance, eternity, honor, liberty, hospitality, faith, and virtue. All these elements combined to make the oak a symbol of power of the Christian faith even in times of adversity. The oak is one of several trees that makes claim to being the tree that was made into the cross of Christ. But, long before the Christians adopted the oak, Celtic pagans used the oak in many of their rituals. It was considered a sacred tree to the Romans, Greeks, Norse, and Teutonic peoples.

Palm: Palm fronds have long been used as a symbol of victory. Christians adapted them to symbolize a martyr's triumph over death and by extension, any believer's triumph over death.

Thorns: Thorns are symbols of grief, difficulties, and sin. Roman soldiers put a crown of thorns on Christ's head as a satire of the Roman emperor's festal crown of roses. St. Thomas Aquinas taught that thorn bushes represented minor sins, while brambles represented major ones. Despite these associations and their prickly appearance, Christians have found a way to put thorns in a more positive light by depicting rays of sunshine coming out of Christ's thorny crown.

Trees and tree stumps: Trees, and most especially the famous "willow tree" motif, stood for human life and the fact that man, like a tree, must reach for the heavens. The willow itself often stood for mourning. Trees could also have other meanings, especially when the monuments were made to look like wood. They have become some of the most curious examples of funerary art and  were derived from the Victorian rusticity movement. In the late nineteenth century, just about any decorative art that was popular outside of the cemetery eventually made its way inside of the cemetery. Cemetery visitors can often find examples of chairs, centerpieces, and even entire monuments that are designed to look like the rough wood of a tree. These markers symbolize the fact that the tree has died, its life has been taken away, just like the life of the person the stone honors.

The heyday of treestone monuments was from the 1880s to about 1905. Where one treestone is seen, often many will be found, suggesting that their popularity may have been traced to a particularly aggressive monument dealer in the area or a ready supply of limestone, which was the carving material of choice.  Treestones could also be ordered from the Sears and Roebuck catalog, which may also explain why there seem to be more popular in the Midwest where more people read the catalog and became acquainted with the style.

ANIMALS, SYMBOLS, BODY PARTS, AND THE WEIRD AND WONDERFUL

There are other monuments where depictions of discarded clothing, opened books, or forgotten tools have been etched or carved. Such items are meant to symbolize the fact that the dead have left behind the burdens of life. Broken columns, inverted torches, spilled flower pots, and funeral urns were meant as simple images of lives that were ended too soon. Some graves were marked with the image of an hour glass with wings that represented the fleeting passage of time or with ferns and anchors that were meant to give hope to grieving loved ones. Much the same can be said of clasped hands, bibles, and pointing fingers. These symbols direct the mourners to look toward heaven and know that the worries of the world are now past. Suns, moons, planets, and stars have various meanings in the cemetery, from that of rising saints to that of glorified souls. They can also signify that heaven is the abode of the stars and the planets.

But there are also a number of symbols and markings – that you may have once overlooked – that are hidden in America's cemeteries. A close look might reveal some of the strange, weird, and wonderful images of the grave.

ANIMALS

Of all the varieties of symbols, it seems that animals have the most powerful connections with human beings. Like us, they are born, live, and die and most importantly, animals often have attributes that we wished we possessed. Who would not like to be as strong as a bull or as feared as a lion? Who has not gazed up into the sky and wondered what it would be like to fly like a bird? Or pondered how it would be to live life like a bear, fearing nothing except our own kind?

Whether it slithers, crawls, gallops, or flies, animals are an important part of the symbolism of the cemetery. Some animals are well-known religious symbols, like the lamb or fish. Others are symbols of immortality and rebirth, like the butterfly or the snake that eats its own tail.

These days, when one sees a carved dog in as cemetery, it's probably an homage to a beloved pet, but the virtues of fidelity, loyalty, vigilance, and watchfulness have long been attributed to man's best friend. The horse is one of the cemetery's most powerful symbols, representing stalwartness and strength. The stag, or deer, is used to symbolize piety, solitude, and contemplation because of the belief that the stag leads a solitary life. The stag's antlers are also said to represent the "tree of life." The butterfly is perhaps the most literal of funerary symbols. Its three stages of life – caterpillar, chrysalis, and butterfly – are easily recognizable as life, death, and the resurrection.

The dove is the most frequently seen animal symbol in the cemetery. It is portrayed in a number of poses, but most frequently is seen holding an olive branch, a reference to the dove sent out by Noah to search for land after the flood. The dove became a symbol of purity and peace and a living manifestation of the Holy Spirit. Many other birds appear in funerary art, including eagles (renewal); owls (wisdom); partridges (truth); peacock (immortality); pelicans (self-sacrifice); and roosters (vigilance).

The fish is one of the most common Christian symbols and can be found everywhere from tombstones to bumper stickers. The symbols of the fish developed as a Christian icon for several reasons. It was often used as part of a secret code during times of persecution by the Roman government and numerous drawings of fish can still be found in the catacombs beneath Rome. Other creatures connected to water can also be found on gravestones, including turtles (longevity) and even snakes, although their presence had largely vanished by the twentieth century. On nineteenth century tombstones, snakes are usually depicted biting their tails as a symbol of immortality. On earlier tombstones, they are often seen slithering on the corner or winding their way through a skull. In those days, the cold-blooded creatures were often used as symbols of mortality, like skeletons and death's heads.

Probably the creature to fare the worst in the cemetery is the cat. In Christian iconography, the cat is a symbol of laziness, lust, darkness, and the Devil. Although the cat is generally considered a negative creature, sometimes it is seen in paintings of the Nativity with a litter of kittens. Defenders of the cat point out that the animal is merely misunderstood, and its supposed attributes of trickery and laziness are actually remarkable powers of cunning and stealth. Even so, if you see an image of a cat on a tombstone today, you're probably standing over the grave of a cat lover. The cat as a symbol vanished from most cemeteries more than a century and a half ago.

In funerary art, lambs usually mark the graves of children and particularly infants, symbolizing innocence. The most heartbreaking, and often most eerie, monuments mark the graves of children. These images include the images of disembodied hands from heaven reaching down to pluck flowers from the earth and the previously mentioned lambs, lost and alone. Cribs and beds are sometimes seen, holding the images of sleeping children, or are often empty, symbolizing that these little ones are gone forever. Most disconcerting of all are the life-size images of the children themselves. They stare out at the cemetery visitor with lifeless, and occasionally frightening, eyes.

Which brings us to the "human condition" in cemeteries...

UNQUESTIONABLY HUMAN

The human body is most often portrayed in the cemetery in the form of strongly emotional sculptures. In addition to full-body likenesses of mourners and even the dead themselves, tombstones also contain images of the human body. The most commonly seen body parts are various configurations of hands, some with fingers pointing up, others with open palms coming down, and still others with hands clasped. Also common is the all-seeing eye on the gravestones of Freemasons and Odd Fellows.

There is nothing religious about the depictions of most graveyard statues. Many of them are representations of the family or the person who is buried at the site. The stone of the Di Salvo family in Mount Carmel Cemetery in Hillside, Illinois, is an elaborate and detailed marble statue that shows a family of five -- mother, father and three daughters. But the most amazing and unique aspect of this marker isn't its beauty or the intricate detail work of the sculptor. The entire statue is mounted on a

THE GRAVE OF JULIA BUCCOLA PETTA

platform and it rotates. It doesn't move on its own, but if you push it, the entire top half of the monument swivels 360 degrees. Considering the size and weight of the monument, it isn't too difficult to move, which means it must be close to perfectly balanced.

Mount Carmel Cemetery is also home to the grave of Julia Petta, whose life-sized form in a bridal dress stands on a marble block. Julia died in childbirth in 1921, at only 20 years of age. Shortly after her burial, her mother, Filomena Buccola, began having very strange dreams in which Julia told her that she was still alive and needed her help. The dreams continued for over six years, during which time Filomena tried without success to have her daughter's grave opened. Finally, she was able to get permission to have her exhumed and when the casket was opened, Julia's body was found to have not decayed at all. Funds were raised for the remarkable statue that appears on her burial site today. Two photographs are mounted to the stone – a portrait of Julia in her wedding dress and a second of Julia after her coffin was opened. Although the casket in the photograph has deteriorated badly, Julia herself appears to be only sleeping.

Mount Hope Cemetery in Hiawatha, Kansas, holds the elaborate resting place of John Milburn Davis, a very wealthy and very sad man. After the death of his wife of more than 50 years, Sarah, he decided to build a monument to

ONE OF THE STONE INCARNATIONS OF JOHN MILBURN DAVIS

his grief. He commissioned the construction of an elaborate grave monument, begun in 1932 and not completed until 1940. Ten life-size Italian marble statues depict John and Sarah as they aged. The eleventh statue is of John alone, missing his left hand (he'd lost it in a farm accident), sitting next to "The Vacant Chair" where Sarah would have sat. This last set of statues is made of granite, supposedly because Davis had exhausted his life savings on the project.

And the list of unusual sculptures goes on. There has been a long history of human mourners carved from marble, depicting the various stages of grief, placed on the resting places of the dead. Some are beautiful, others wistful, and some frightening. The most common gatherings of sculpted human forms in the cemetery are groupings of the virtues. There are seven virtues, usually divided into two groups. There are three religious virtues: Faith, Hope, and Charity; and four moral virtues: Temperance, Prudence, Fortitude, and Justice. They are always depicted as women. Faith is usually a woman holding a cross. Hope is often depicted with wings. Charity is almost always shown nursing an infant or in the process of revealing a breast. Temperance is rarely seen, but when she is, she holds a water pitcher or a sheathed sword. Prudence is rarely seen since, in art, she has two heads and doesn't fit well with the other virtues. Other times she is seen holding a mirror – not as a

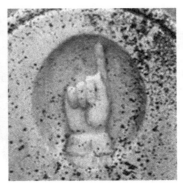

symbol of vanity, but wisdom in the quest for self-knowledge. Fortitude is a female warrior, and Justice is perhaps the easiest to identify since she's seen more often over the entrance to a courthouse than in a cemetery.

But, as mentioned, it's not just entire human forms that can be found in the cemetery. A determined visitor can find an array of body parts, including breasts. Breasts are a common symbol of love, nourishment, comfort, abundance, protection, and motherhood. In the context of motherhood, breasts symbolize rebirth and regeneration. In funereal symbolism, the word *breast* is discarded for the more chaste *bosom* (remember, this was popularized during the Victorian era) and the souls of the dead are often described as waiting in "God's bosom" for the resurrection. Female breasts are often displayed in cemetery art, however, regardless of the time period in which they were sculpted. Nudity is also used in cemetery art to refer to the condition in which we were all born – without worldly goods. It also represents innocence.

The human foot symbolizes humility and service and the eye – especially the all-seeing eye found on the back of the dollar bill – can be found on the graves of members of some of America's secret societies. The human heart is the symbol of man's deepest emotions, including love, courage, sorrow, and joy. In religious and cemetery symbolism, a flaming heart symbolizes religious fervor, a pierced heart indicates repentance and devotion, and a heart surrounded by thorns represents a promise made at the hour of one's death.

Hands are the most commonly found body parts in all cemeteries. The hand coming downward was used as a symbol of God. In early Christian art, it was forbidden to depict the countenance of God, but the Bible was packed with references to the hand or arm of God, which meant that the Almighty was usually shown as a hand coming down from the clouds. This interpretation continued on middle nineteenth century gravestones.

A hand with a finger pointing up indicated that a soul had risen to heaven. If the first two fingers are together and the deceased was a member of the clergy, the hand represented the hand of God. In this context, the remaining fingers (and thumb) represented the Holy Trinity.

Hands that appear to be shaking are usually a symbol of matrimony. Look carefully at the sleeves. One should appear feminine and the other masculine. If the sleeves appear to be gender neutral, the hands can represent a heavenly welcome or an earthly farewell.

RELIGIOUS DEVOTION

Most symbols in a cemetery have some connection to religion, but many are overwhelmingly religion specific, like crosses, which are associated with Christian ritual. There is a grouping of Christian symbols that are known collectively as the symbols of the Passion. They depict the events leading up to and immediately following Christ's crucifixion. Some of the most often used symbols include a cross and a chalice (Christ's agony at the garden); a lantern (betrayal); hammer and nails (crucifixion); cross and a sheet (descent from the cross); and an empty cross with nails (descent from the cross). In religious art, the events of the Passion are put together in a sort of timeline in the form of the Stations of the Cross, 14 scenes of Christ's journey from the time he was condemned to death until he is laid in the tomb. All these scenes are frequently found in churches and have translated over to funerary art.

The symbols of the Eucharist – wafers, grapes, and wheat – were mentioned earlier, as were doves to symbolize the Holy Ghost, but they stand out as outwardly religious symbols in cemeteries. Signs of the Passion, like crucifixion nails and a chalice can also be found. The chalice is also seen as the human heart's yearning to be filled with the true spirit of the Lord, symbolized by the wine. In Christian iconography, the key (which is often seen in a set of two) is held by St. Peter, who unlocks the gates of heaven. Scales in funerary art symbolize the scales in the hands of the archangel Michael, a reference to his task of weighing the souls of the departed.

Confusing to most non-religious cemetery visitors are what seem to be secret codes in letters that are often found emblazoned on crossed and overlaid on each other to resemble a dollar sign. Popular belief says that these letters HIS (Greek) or IHC (Roman) are an abbreviation for the Latin phrase *in hoc signo*, which is a shortened version of the banner with the words *in hoc signo vinces* ("in this sign you will conquer"), seen in a vision by the Emperor Constantine before he went into battle.

It's a good story, but it's not the origin of IHS.

The real story is not that exciting. Jesus' name in upper- and lowercase Greek lettering is IHSOYS or IHSUS; so HIS is derived from the first three letters of Jesus' name using the Greek alphabet: Iota, Eta, Sigma.

Another common lettering is INRI, but this one is more straightforward. It's the first letters of the Latin words for *Jesus Nazarenus Rex Judaeorum*, meaning "Jesus of Nazareth The King of the Jews." According to the Gospel of John, after Jesus was crucified, Pilate mockingly wrote these same words on the cross in Hebrew, Greek and Latin.

The letters RIP are much easier. They are seen on tombstones in cartoons and even schoolchildren are familiar with this abbreviation since cartoons are likely their first experience with cemeteries. RIP is an abbreviation for the Latin words *Requiesat In Pace*, which translates nicely to the English words "Rest in Peace."

ANGELS IN THE ARCHITECTURE

Besides tombstones, of course, the image that we think of most often associated with cemeteries is angels. Wander into a cemetery, particularly a Catholic burial ground or churchyard, and you're likely to see dozens of these heavenly messengers scattered across the landscape. Despite their winged similarities, they are tremendously different in posture and expression. While some are draped over tombstones in grief, others seem ready to take flight with joy. Tears stream down the face of one, another is filled with happiness, while another manages only a wistful smile. Skilled craftsmen have, indeed, brought cold stone to life.

It should come as no surprise that most angels in American cemeteries are rooted in Christian lore, but references to angels can be found in most religions, including Islam. The word *angel* comes from the Greek word *angelos*, which means "messenger," and in the Islamic faith, the chief duty of angels was to carry messages to Allah.

In the Christian faith, the Bible refers to angels in both the Old and New Testaments. Christian angels were inherited from the Hebrews of the Old Testament and frankly, carried out all of God's dirty work. In Genesis, God sent an angel with a flaming sword to guard the way of the tree of life. Angels were sent to warn Lot that Sodom and Gomorrah were going to be destroyed

and when he and his family were safe -- although we know what happened to his wife -- they wiped out every living person that remained in the two sinful towns. Countless people were slaughtered by angels – and they killed each other, too. Michael, the leader of the angels who remained faithful to God during the great war in heaven, overcame the fallen angels and cast Lucifer to earth. When God wanted something bloody to be done, he sent angels to do it.

But not all angels are so fierce and frightening. The Victorians invented the idea of "guardian angels," which were gentle and more comforting. The angel Gabriel, for instance, was the angel of the Annunciation. He is usually depicted with some sort of horn. It was Gabriel whom God sent to announce the birth of Jesus and he is the most depicted angel – aside from generic angels – in cemeteries. The angel with the horn is a natural device for signaling the departure of a soul from earth and its arrival in heaven.

Michael and Gabriel may be the best-known angels, but there are many more. At least seven angels are mentioned in the book of Revelation and the book of Enoch is full of angel names. Other angels make appearances as messengers, often in human form, in other chapters of the Bible. Most named angels actually come from secular writings – so many that scholars in the fourteenth century, employing some mysterious calculations used words as numbers and numbers as words, calculated the number of angels at 301, 655, 722. Albertus Magnus put the number at "6,666 legions with 6,666 angels per legion." Both calculations seem like weighty numbers – and while not enough for everyone to have their own personal angels, it is certainly enough to call on in times of need. Church sects may not agree on the exact numbers of angels, but most biblical scholars agree that it's a fixed number. Angels are not eternal like God, but they are immortal, a subtle but important difference. Aside from a few who fall from grace now and then, their numbers have been fixed since creation. But there's bad news: as our human population continues to increase, it spreads out the angel-to-human ratio. Even worse, the adversaries of angels – demons and devils – are able to reproduce.

According to one scholar, "they multiply like flies." But while demons multiply like men do, they also die like men do, which gives us a bit of hope – if you believe in that sort of thing, of course.

One of the most perplexing riddles about angels, though, is where they got their wings. Despite all the references to angels in the Bible, nowhere is their physical description offered in any detail. The earliest depictions of angels depict them as solemn young men. But, since angels have always been regarded as messengers between heaven and earth, it was inevitable that sooner or later they might sprout wings. The earliest depiction of an angel with wings is in a fifth century mosaic in the Church of St. Prudencia in Rome. Much of the way we perceive angels developed in the Middle Ages and was refined during the Renaissance. The vast amount of church and religious art during this period provided artists with a chance to refine the appearance of angels and separate them from their human counterparts. Halos, white garments, swords, horns, harps and, of course, wings, all provided material for angel-making by Renaissance artists.

The typical Renaissance angel was portrayed as heroic, beautiful, and glowing. At the same time, little child-like angels (little cherubs like Cupid) began making an appearance. These lighthearted angels opened the angel floodgates and we've been overwhelmed with them ever since. The Victorians took things ever further, introducing the idea that angels watched over lost children and good deeds, making them so benevolent that their blood-soaked past has been largely forgotten.

When it comes to viewing winged messengers, cemeteries are the place to go. Most angels in cemeteries are of the generic variety, but with a little searching, a visitor can usually find a horn or two, Michael with a sword and shield, or cherubs that adorn the graves of children. Often, a cemetery might have an angel that gets significantly more attention than others. They sometimes attract fresh-cut flowers, while others attract toys and teddy bears.

Unfortunately, some angels attract the wrong kind of people, too. Their fragile wings and sometimes lofty perches are frequent targets for vandals. Some have been toppled over, spirited away by thieves, or have had their wings or limbs amputated.

Some attract legends.

A strange black angel in Oakland Cemetery in Iowa City, Iowa, has long been connected to the supernatural. The angel is an eight-and-a-half-foot tall burial monument that was placed in the cemetery in 1912. The statue was erected by Teresa Dolezal Feldevert, a physician who had immigrated to America from Strmilov, Bohemia. Teresa and her son, Eddie, came to Iowa City, where she worked as a midwife. They lived in Iowa City until 1891, when

THE SO-CALLED "BLACK ANGEL" OF
OAKLAND CEMETERY IN IOWA

Eddie died of meningitis at the age of 18. He was buried in Oakland Cemetery and Teresa had a tree stump monument erected over his grave.

After Eddie's death, Teresa moved to Eugene, Oregon, where she married Nicholas Feldevert, who died tragically just a few years later in 1911. In the wake of this second loss, Teresa returned to Iowa City and she hired Mario Korbel, a Bohemian artist from Chicago, to design the angel that would hover over the body of her son and the ashes of her husband. The angel arrived on a railroad flatcar in Iowa City on November 21, 1912.

Soon after the angel was installed, Eddie's monument was moved from its original location to its present site alongside the angel. His remains, along with the ashes of Nicholas Feldevert, were placed in a repository under the angel's base. Teresa died of cancer on November 18, 1924, her ashes were also placed beneath the angel and before long, strange stories began.

Within a few years of its installation in Oakland Cemetery, the glorious bronze angel strangely began to turn black. Most have explained this as the natural oxidation of the metal but not surprisingly, other explanations have surfaced, blaming evil acts, freak storms, infidelity, and even murder.

One legend has it that Teresa Feldevert was a very mysterious woman and that her evil caused the angel to turn black. This strange shadowing was to serve as a constant reminder of the sins of her family – and as a warning for people to stay away from her grave. Some claimed that Teresa's wicked ways were evident in the design of the angel. Unlike most graveyard angels, which are usually positioned with their head and wings uplifted as a symbol of aiding in the ascent to heaven, the Feldevert angel is looking down to the ground and her wings are fallen. And strangely, there is no death date on the monument for Teresa Feldevert.

Others claimed the angel turned black after a freak thunderstorm on the night of Teresa's funeral. According to this, the angel was struck by lightning and this is what caused it to turn black. There are also stories that blame the black color of the angel on infidelity. In this version of the angel story, Teresa allegedly vowed over her husband's grave that she would remain faithful to him until the day that she died —swearing that his death angel would turn black if she ever cheated on his memory. The color of the angel, these stories claim, answer the question as to whether or not Teresa remained faithful.

Perhaps the harshest explanation for the angel's color claims that Teresa's son did not die from an illness, as the records stated, but rather because she murdered him. These stories claim that she fled to Oregon soon after and only her guilt brought her back to Iowa City. In shame, she moved his body to rest beneath the wings of the angel and soon after, it began to turn black as a reminder of her shame.

One legend created another, and a variety of stories sprang up, stating that any girl who was kissed at the angel's feet in the moonlight would die within six months. Others said that touching the angel on Halloween night would lead to death in seven years and, worse yet, kissing the angel itself would cause a person's heart to stop beating.

And while such stories may bear little resemblance to the truth, they do remain an essential part of the lore and legend of Iowa. For generations, local residents and University of Iowa students have come to Oakland Cemetery, often under the light of the moon, to ponder the mysteries of the angel. She is regarded as one of the region's most haunted sites, solely based on the odd stories, curses, and enigmas attached to her past and present.

THE ENIGMA OF THE CROSS

It's hard to think of a symbol more closely associated with religion than the cross is with Christianity. But the use of a cross as a symbol predates its association with the Christian faith by thousands of years. In fact, the cross may be mankind's oldest symbol. In its simplest form of two intersecting lines of the same length, it makes an X, as in "X marks the spot." The circle, the X-shaped cross, and the cross that looks like a plus (+) sign are used by all cultures. The ancient + cross took on many meanings among pagan cultures, most notably as a symbol that signified the division between heaven and

earth. This + cross was eventually adopted by Christians and is now known as the Greek cross.

But long before Christians adopted the cross as their symbol, other cultures were employing it and modifying it to fit their own uses. The ancient Druids were known to cut off all the branches of a giant oak tree except for two branches on either side of the trunk, forming a huge natural cross. Others took the basic cross and added to it. One of the earliest modifications to the simple cross was by Eastern cultures who added arms to the end of the cross to form a swastika, or fylfot cross. The original swastika was a symbol of good fortune and was used to decorate ancient pottery, jewelry and coins. It also became a power symbol for ancient fire-worshipping Aryan tribes because the arms of the swastika resembled the sticks with handles that tribe members rubbed together to make fire. Its various forms often represented the highest attainment possible, and it was used to represent both spiritual and worldly pursuits. Unfortunately, the swastika was also used by power-hungry madmen like Hitler and the Nazis and is now associated with evil.

Another type of cross that has its roots in ancient civilization is the Tau cross, which is shaped like a capital T. This cross has frequently been referred to as the Old Testament cross because it was so often used by Hebrew tribes. The Tau cross was probably derived from the cross of the Egyptian god Horus, known as an ankh, which looks like a Tau cross with an elongated O attached to the top. The ankh is most often seen in hieroglyphics, most often in the hand of a god or person of importance.

The Christian cross was eventually adopted by adherents of that religion, but it was not the faith's first symbol. Most scholars agree that, despite the popular mythology that claims early Christians scratched crosses everywhere they went, the first symbol they actually used was a fish. The use of the fish symbol likely came from Christ being portrayed as instructing his followers to be fishers of men, or some even say that the word for fish in Greek contains some of the first letters of the phrase, Jesus Christ, the Son of God, Savior. But, whatever the reason, within a few centuries, Christians tossed aside the fish as their prime symbol and adopted the cross.

In actuality, it's pretty strange that any form of the cross was adopted by Christians, since crosses had been used for centuries to punish and persecute Christians, as well as common criminals. In early Christian writings, the cross on which Jesus was crucified was referred to as the "accursed tree." Nevertheless, the story is that around the year 320 A.D., the Roman emperor Constantine couldn't decide if he should continue practicing paganism, which had served his predecessors well, or convert to Christianity, which many of the Roman citizenry (including his own mother) were either following or considering. The situation at hand for Constantine was a huge battle he was about to engage in with Maxentius, who was apparently enlisting the aid of supernatural and magical forces. So, Constantine decided to pray to the God of the Christians to help him defeat his enemy. During a midnight prayer, Constantine looked into the night sky and saw a group of stars that looked like a glowing cross. After he fell asleep, he had a dream in which he saw Christ holding the same symbol and he told Constantine to affix it to his flags and standards. In the battle that followed, Constantine defeated Maxentius. Needless to say, the emperor had the emblem of the cross applied to all of his banners and placed on the altars of the church. Thus, began the use of the cross as a Christian symbol.

Although there are dozens of types of crosses in cemeteries and thousands of types of religious crosses, there are basically three types that others evolved from: the Greek cross, which looks like a + sign; the Latin cross, which looks like the letter t; and the Celtic cross, which has a circle (nimbus) connecting the four arms of the cross.

Greek-style crosses, and other crosses with arms that are the same length, are more likely to appear as part of the decoration on a tomb or gravestone than as a freestanding cross. The St. Andrew's cross looks like an X. When St. Andrew was condemned to be crucified, the story goes that he asked to be nailed to a cross that was unlike the cross on which Jesus was crucified because St. Andrew thought he was unworthy to be put into the same category as Christ. Thanks to this, a St. Andrew's cross has come to signify suffering and humility.

The Maltese cross looks like a + sign with flared ends that are usually indented to form eight points. It is often associated with fraternal orders. Many of the Greek-style crosses are associated with heraldry and they were worn by a multitude of Christian warriors when they marched off to the Crusades. These crosses can often be seen in a cemetery as part of a family crest or again, as an emblem of a fraternal order. The best-known among these are the *flore* (floriated) cross, which has arms that end in three petal-like projections, and the *patte* (broadfooted) cross, where the arms like triangles with the tip of the four triangles pointed at the center. These rather broad arms represent the wings of a bird and symbolize the protective power of the cross.

The cross most commonly associated with Christianity is the Latin cross. There are many variations to this cross, including the Crucifix, which has an image of Christ nailed to it. In some areas, cemetery visitors will also see many Latin crosses with more than one cross arm. The most common of these is the Cross of Lorraine, which has a shorter arm above the long one. It was applied to the standards of Godfrey of Lorraine, one of the first Crusaders, after he was chosen ruler of Jerusalem. (This symbol is familiar as the cross that represents Easter Seals) A variation on the style of the Cross of Lorraine is the Russian Orthodox cross. This cross has an angled crossbar before the main crossbar. Where one is seen, there are many others nearby, since they generally appear in ethnic cemeteries, like in the coal-mining towns of Western Pennsylvania, where scores of immigrants labored underground.

Celtic crosses are, without a doubt, the most appealing of all crosses. Entire books have been devoted to their history. In American cemeteries that can be found as plain stone monuments, but more often they are embellished with intricate designs and symbolism. The basic form of a Celtic cross is of a cross enclosed in a circle. Of the dozens of varieties of crosses, the Celtic cross is most intensely associated with a person's roots. A vast array of sizes and styles of Celtic crosses adorn the graves of Irish and Scottish families. In fact, most Scots have a cross that is particular to their clan.

The Celtic cross is pagan in origin and predates Christianity by several centuries. In its early form, it was devoid of decorations and the top three arms of the cross (which represented the male reproductive organs) were totally enclosed within a circle (representing the female). As Christianity was adopted by the Celts, the circle began to get smaller, symbolizing either the triumph of

Christianity or the loss of the Goddess influence, depending on how you look at it.

The symbolism of the Irish cross is strongly tied to Mother Earth and national pride. The four arms represent the four elements – earth, air, fire, and water. In some Celtic crosses, the four arms correspond with four provinces of Ireland, with the circle used in creating a fifth province by incorporating pieces of the other four.

THE WEIRD AND WONDERFUL

It goes without saying that the cemetery is the best place to find symbols of mortality. In fact, many of these symbols can only be found in the cemetery. Most people don't want to be reminded that their time on earth is fleeting, especially in this modern age when professionals handle the business of death and most of us are totally disconnected from it.

Of course, it was not always this way.

A couple of hundred years ago, when infant mortality rates were high, and most folks died at home, the common person was very familiar with the process of dying and death. The dead were laid out in the parlor for all to see – and to remind us that death comes for us all. Once upon a time, people were more attuned to their mortality than they are today.

As a rule, the older the tombstone, the more literal is its mortality symbolism. It's unlikely that you'll find a skull and crossbones on a modern tombstone, but they were commonplace in the early days of America.

Perhaps the most tragically lost traditional symbol is the *Memento Mori*, an image (drawing, sculpture, or photograph) or an item (hair locket, vial of tears) that urged a person to "remember thy death." The tradition was started in the late Middle Ages, most particularly around the time of the Black Death. *Memento Mori* persisted through the nineteenth century. Its purpose, rather kept in the home or attached to the gravestone, is to remind the viewer that death is an unavoidable part of life; something that we should be prepared for at all times. *Memento Mori* images are graphic demonstrations that death was not only a more frequent occurrence in the past, but more of a part of family and community life than it is today. *Memento Mori* can also be in the form of an epitaph, like the one famous, "Remember me as you pass by, As you are now, so once was I. As I am now, so you must be, Prepare for death and follow me." This epitaph – and many variations of it – are commonly found in the graveyards of colonial New England.

Graphic mortality symbols can still be seen, but over time, their meaning has been lost for most people. But they are still visible as graphic reminders of the past – and as a promise of what awaits us in the future.

Skeletons

Skeletons can appear on grave markers in a number of ways, but ultimately, they are *memento mori* symbols. A reclining skeleton represents a passive figure of death, which sooner or later comes to us all. An upright skeleton usually has one or more "weapons of death": scythe, sword, arrows or a spear.

Skulls

It's hard to think of a death symbol that is as vivid as that of a skull. Other symbols may suggest death, but the skull literally is death and it reminds us that there is no escape from it.

Death's Heads

On early American gravestones, there is no more chilling a symbol to be found that the death's head. The evolution of this curious funerary symbol is a strange one. In Europe of the sixteenth century, there were few formal burial grounds for common people. The rich were buried inside church walls, floors and sometimes in specially constructed tombs. Eventually, the churches ran out of room and the dead were forced out of the church into the cemetery with everyone else. But with more money than the common folk, they had the chance of erecting a tombstone that gave them the chance to be remembered after they had gone.

And the death's head was born. At the time, the Puritans were in control of religious thought and practices and were known for being a pretty gloomy lot. They preached that only the elect had the chance of making it into heaven, while the rest of us were doomed to be born, live, die, and then rot. Nowhere is that attitude more aptly illustrated than in the graveyards. In the sixteenth century, those with the means to have a tombstone carved usually had their name, birth and death dates, and a skull, skull and crossbones, or a skull gnawing on a femur illustrating it. Usually the words *Here Lies the Body of* were placed before the name. The image of the skull, plus the word *body* pretty much summed up the attitude of the time. The religious beliefs of England were carried across the sea to the American colonies and similar gravestones found their way into the cemeteries of the New World.

But somewhere in the seventeenth century, the Puritans began to lose their grip on people's hearts and minds and slowly, religious attitudes began to change. With that change came the small hope that there was a possibility that when they died, they might actually make it into the next world. What that world might be (heaven, hell, or purgatory) was unknown, but at least there was hope.

Tombstone symbols began to change. The skulls and the crossbones were still there, but soon the skulls had wings, which gave the gravestone a lighter look and conveyed the message that life was a fleeting thing.

Over the next two centuries, the death's head and the inscription continued to change. The degree and speed at which it did so depending on the area, but it can be traced to the waning influence of the Puritan way of thought. The next major change in the death's head was the swapping of the skull for a human face (albeit one with a vacant stare) and subtle changes in the wording to phrases like *Here Lies the Mortal Remains of*, amplifying the idea of a person having a soul that was no longer connected to the body. It wasn't long before a face with human features and emotions replaced the vacant stare.

With the emergence of the garden cemeteries, the death's head was replaced by a winged cherub and any reference to the corruptible body had been essentially eliminated by inscribing the tombstone with such flowery phrases as *Sacred to the Memory of* and *Gone but not Forgotten.*

The horror had finally vanished from the graveyard.

Arrows, Spears and Swords

Projectiles such as arrows, spears, and swords, and bladed instruments like an ax or a scythe, can be grouped under the heading "weapons of death." They were normally used on the grave of someone associated with the military, but their symbolism is clear – death reaps all men, cutting their life short.

Empty Chairs

Vacant chairs are often used on the graves of young people or children. In many cases, these stone chairs are depicted with a small pair of shoes, with one shoe usually on its side, to symbolize the death of a child.

Broken Column

The broken column is a symbol for the end of life and more specifically, for a life cut short. It came into popularity around the middle nineteenth century and became one of the cemetery's most popular mortality symbols because of its visual impact.

Father Time

Father Time, the figure who drags his way to his inevitable demise on December 31, is usually depicted with a long robe and an hourglass on his head to remind us that our time is running out. Occasionally, he is seen seated with an elbow on an hourglass, but usually he can be found in a rather trudging-like pose, slowly going to his death.

Grim Reaper

The Grim Reaper, with his large scythe, is in the business of harvesting souls. This thin, often skeletal figure may have its roots in the ancient Greek myth of Charon, a rather sinister character who ferried the dead over the River Styx to the underworld. A coin, which was payment for the trip, is depicted in the mouth of the deceased.

Hourglass

The symbolism of an hourglass – especially those depicted with wings – is clear:

time is passing rapidly and with each passing day, one comes closer to the hour of death.

Sexton's Tools

These are the tools that the gravedigger uses to ply his trade. Depending on the stone carver and local tradition, various combinations of coffins and tools are depicted. Common tools are the spade and the pick. Sextons, as they were once called, cared not only for the maintenance of the church, but for digging the graves and the upkeep of the churchyard too.

Broken Wheel

The wheel is the universal symbol that represents eternity, continuation, and progress. A broken wheel can no longer turn, simply stating that the journey is now over.

The Inverted Torch

The inverted torch is purely a funerary symbol. It is unlikely that it would be found anywhere other than in a cemetery. The inverted torch comes in two forms. The most common is the inverted torch with the flame still burning, which while symbolizing death, suggests that the soul (fire) continues to exist in the next world. The other version is an upside-down torch without the flame, which simply means life extinguished.

Draped Urn

The draped cremation urn is probably the most common nineteenth century funerary symbol. There are cemeteries from this era that seem to be sea of such urns, topping gravestone after gravestone. The drape can be seen as a family in mourning or as a symbol of the veil between two worlds. Today, urns are used to contain the remains of the cremated dead, which seems to make the urn a very curious nineteenth century funerary device since cremation was seldom practiced. But in those days, urns seldom contained ashes. They were instead used as decorative devices, perched on top of columns, stones and mausoleums and carved into tombstones, walls and doors. The urn and the

willow tree were two of the first funerary motifs to replace death's heads when funerary symbolism started to take on a lighter feeling after the American Revolution.

There are still plenty of oddities to be found in the cemetery, although most are a less fearsome and intimidating variety than symbols of winged death and menacing skulls. Much of the world that we live in is composed of things that we have manufactured and built. In the world of cemetery symbolism, common items like doors, ladders, lamps, and anchors are now always what they seem.

When we see depictions of nature in funerary art, their meaning can be taken more literally: rocks call for permanence, water if more fleeting and temporary, stars tell of wonder and the moon hints at mystery.

Balls

Stone balls in cemeteries are almost always purely decorative. Cannonballs often appear on veteran's gravesites, but if they appear in a group of three, they may be in reference to gifts or money, like the three balls that symbolize a pawnbroker's shop.

These weird cemetery balls sometimes take on a life of their own, so to speak. In the town of Marion, Ohio, there stands just such a monument. A large sphere rests over the grave site of Charles Merchant and his family. The monument was built in 1887 and is a white stone column that is topped with

a granite ball. It is not an unusually unique monument, as there are many like it in cemeteries across America. It is simply a large marble ball that has been placed on top of a pedestal at the center of a family plot. It was so nondescript that it was a forgotten ornament in the cemetery for years.

In July 1905, workmen discovered that this sphere seemed to rotate on its own accord.

The stone ball, which weighs several hundred pounds, was set into a granite base and was not designed to rotate. Somehow, though, it managed to move and turned to expose the rough bottom of the sphere. It was at this spot where workmen had sealed the stone to the base – or so they thought. Caretakers were puzzled. It would take several men with pry bars and a block and tackle to move the granite ball and yet somehow, it happened. Perplexed, the officials at the cemetery poured concrete into the stone base and set the sphere back into position. Two months later, it was discovered to have moved again and the rough bottom patch was once again visible.

Curiosity seekers began traveling to the cemetery. One geologist theorized that the movement of the stone occurred because of unequal expansion caused by resting in the sun on one side and shade on the other. Others believed that weather might be the culprit. If moisture on the stone froze at night and then thawed in the daylight hours, the ball might shift slightly in its base as the dampness lubricated it. This theory seemed to hold up in the winter months, but what about in the summer, when the stone was also reported to move? The rotation was first noticed in July and has continued to turn ever since. And, how does the stone turn at all if it was designed and fixed to stay in place? The mystery remains unsolved to this day.

Anchors

Many cemetery visitors may spot an anchor on a tombstone and believe that the deceased was a ship's captain or somehow involved with boats or the sea, but this is not the case. The anchor is a symbol of hope and take its symbolism from a passage in the book of Hebrews, which describes hope as "an anchor of the soul."

Books

There are several variations to the book symbol that is found in funerary art. A closed book usually represents a completed life. It may also represent virginity, secrecy, and mystery. An open book is a favorite device for registering the name of the deceased. In its purest form, an open book can be compared to the human heart, its thoughts and feelings open to the world and God. The other variation usually features a crown resting atop a book, which symbolizes God and the Bible.

Curtain or Veil

The veil, which in funerary art just looks like a curtain, is the symbol of the passage from one type of existence to another. Veils are meant to protect as well as conceal. On a tombstone, the carving is indicative of passing from one life to the next. The veil, or curtain, is usually shown pulled aside.

Doors

The door is an obvious partition symbolizing transition from one world to the next. Unlike gates, with their porous nature, which provide us with an open view of what's on the other side of them, there is always a certain amount of mystery attached to a partially open door. Mysteries aside, though, doors are ultimately viewed as a sign of hope and opportunity in all cultures.

Ladders

When a ladder is seen ascending toward the clouds (heaven), it's known as Jacob's Ladder, a symbol of the pathway between heaven and earth. The most interesting aspect of the ladder as a method of reaching heaven is that its comprised of rungs, and each rung must be negotiated before another one is attempted.

Lamps

Lamps are also commonly seen cemetery symbols. Because of the light emitted by it, the lamp is a symbol of wisdom, faithfulness, and holiness.

Musical Instruments

Flutes are frequently mentioned in the Bible, usually in terms of entertainment rather than with any special spiritual attributes. Like the lyre, flutes are often seen as instruments of playfulness. Unlike the flute, the ethereal tones of the harp have long been associated with heavenly aspirations. Harps are mentioned often in the Bible as a source of musical entertainment and divine music. A lyre is usually depicted as a more playful instrument than a harp. In a funereal setting, a lyre is often show with a broken string, symbolizing a life that has been broken by death.

Feathers
Because of their lightness and their association with wings, feathers are used as symbols of the ascent to the heavens. A feather can also represent authority to administer justice because, even though a feather is very light, it is enough to tip the scales in one direction.

Flames
In the cemetery, flames usually represent eternal life or eternal vigilance. In Christian religious iconography, flames and fire represent religious fervor and, often, martyrdom because so many saints met their end by various methods of incineration.

Rock
In Christian lore, rocks are a powerful symbol. The Bible is filled with references to rocks being associated with the spiritual, from water flowing from the rock in Exodus to Christ referring to St. Peter as the rock and cornerstone of his church. In almost all cultures, rocks represent permanence, stability, reliability, and strength.

Stars
A star (or stars) lighting the heavens is a symbol of divine guidance. A single star is almost always a symbol of the Star of the East that guided the Magi to Bethlehem to see the Christ child. Twelve stars are a symbol of the Twelve Apostles or the Twelve Tribes of Israel. Other cultures, of course, abound with stars, which are often used to symbolize the highest attainment.

Sun and Moon
In the cemetery, the sun and moon together are likely to be fairly modern symbols, relating more to the heavens in general than to any specific religion. In Christian symbolism, the combination is meant to represent the attributes of the Virgin Mary and they are also part of the vast repertoire of Freemason symbols.

THE SENTIENT CORPSE

AMERICA'S OBSESSION WITH
PREMATURE BURIAL

"It may be asserted, without hesitation, that no event is so terribly well adapted to inspire the supremeness of mental and of bodily distress, as is burial before death. The unendurable oppression of the lungs—the stifling fumes of the damp earth—the clinging to the death garments—the rigid embrace of the narrow house—the blackness of the absolute Night—the silence like a sea that overwhelms—the unseen but palpable presence of the Conqueror Worm...We know of nothing so agonizing upon Earth—we can dream of nothingness half so hideous in the realms of the nethermost Hell."

-Edgar Allan Poe, The Premature Burial

Had it not been for popular literature such as Poe's, the panic that swept through America in the middle of the nineteenth century might have been nearly altogether avoided, leaving the fear of premature burial in Western Europe right where it had originated. Poe's fascination and fictional storytelling of individuals who met their hellish ends post internment helped to spark utter horror in the hearts of many, thus bridging the gap between Europe's paranoia and our own.

Taphephobia, or the irrational fear of being buried alive, had already long made its mark in Germany by the late eighteenth century. So widespread was this concern, it had inspired the invention and construction of "waiting mortuaries" or houses for the dead.

THE FAMOUS ANTOINE WIERTZ PAINTING OF A CHOLERA VICTIM WHO
WAS ACCIDENTALLY BURIED PREMATURELY – IT WAS A COMMON
NIGHTMARE OF THE TIME

German physician and philanthropist Christophe Wilhelm Hufeland designed and supervised the construction of the *Leichenhaus*, an "asylum for doubtful life' in his hometown of Weimar in 1792. It was designed to resemble a normal residential dwelling, but with an inner chamber to receive and supervise bodies. The attendant could care for as many as eight at a time, placed above a canal of heated water to ensure a warm environment, aiding decomposition. This was a rather unpleasant occupation, working amidst the overpowering stench of rotting flesh.

The second *Leichenhaus* was built in a cemetery in Berlin in 1795 but functioned in a much different way. Once a corpse was received, a series of strings were tied to it, attached to a large bell. Should one of the unlucky inhabitants stir, the attendant would be notified, and the individual, in theory, would be saved from an untimely burial.

With the popularity of such establishments, architects began designing and building more ornate and sacral structures throughout Germany. They were able to house a larger number of corpses, often surrounded by flowers to

CHRISTOPHE WILHELM
HUFELAND, PHYSICIAN WHO
DESIGNED AND BUILT THE FIRST
LEICHENHAUS, OR "WAITING
MORTUARY."

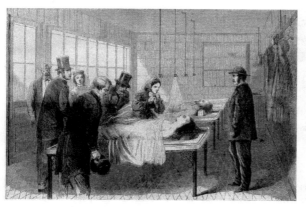

ILLUSTRATION OF A WAITING MORTUARY

both honor the dead and help mask the scent of decay. Various alarm systems were devised and implemented to alert attendants should a body suddenly reanimate during its 48-72 hour stay within the facility. This was problematic, however, as when natural decomposition occurred, the bodies would inevitably shift causing several false alarms.

In her book, *Buried Alive: The Terrifying History of Our Most Primal Fear*, author Jan Bondeson notes that, "It is clear that the ultimate decision, in the 1890s, to remove the alarm systems from many waiting mortuaries rested on the reality that for many years not a single case of apparent death had been detected in any German *Leichenhaus*."

Despite the many stories written and told of reanimations, there is no verifiable evidence that there had been even one resurrection among the over 46,000 corpses housed and observed.

While America had not adopted or implemented the idea of waiting mortuaries, it had certainly fallen victim to the fear that its citizens were at risk of being buried before their lives had fully expired.

The fear wasn't altogether without merit, however, as there had been isolated incidents of premature burial reported, but the number was highly suspect. Hurried burials due to epidemics of disease and the threat of contagion were to blame for a small number of premature internments, but it was largely through word of mouth and the sensationalized press of such events that created a new preoccupation among the Victorians, a people already consumed by and obsessed with the reality of death.

Dying was no longer the most haunting of thoughts; being left to die an isolated and agonizing death in an early grave was a fate far worse, and the fledgling medical community of the time began to develop more 'reliable' methods of diagnosing death. Physicians were directed by many of their patients to employ any means necessary, no matter how impractical or gruesome, to assure their deaths were genuine. Prior means of identifying death were as simple as detecting the lack of a pulse (long before the stethoscope was invented) or using a small flame or application of a mirror near the mouth or nose to determine whether the person in question was still breathing. These methods were initially thought sufficient, but new techniques were developed for further confirmation.

Salts and other materials considered 'foul-smelling' might be placed into the nostrils, or a live, crawling insect placed into the ear canal. Enemas of tobacco smoke or hot pokers inserted into the anus were also implemented. Decapitation was a sure-fire way to assure death had occurred (though had there been any question before the procedure, there certainly wouldn't remain any afterward.)

Brushes with harsh, stiff

ILLUSTRATION OF AN ELECTRICAL DEVICE CREATED BY DR. CHRISTIAN AUGUST STRUWE TO DETECT LIFE IN A CORPSE.

bristles would be applied to the most sensitive areas of the body, and sharp instruments were sometimes forced underneath the fingernails to arouse a reaction. Bizarre electrical devices were invented, and experiments were conducted on the eyes or on the internal structure of a body, which would most certainly reanimate anyone who had simply fallen victim to a cataleptic or trance-like state.

Despite the scores of strange inventions and invasive procedures, physicians actively cautioned that the sole indisputable sign of death was putrefaction, and that no body should be committed to the grave without first allowing it to rot. Families often kept the bodies of their loved ones close until obvious signs of decay set in, creating additional physical and emotional strain.

Undertakers of the era were all too willing to help alleviate fears of premature burial by offering peace of mind through the purchase of a "security coffin." These coffins were equipped with various alerting and life-sustaining systems. One model featured a breathing tube extending from the lid of the coffin to the surface above and a flag to signal that the individual below needed rescuing. Another featured a small belfry attached to the body

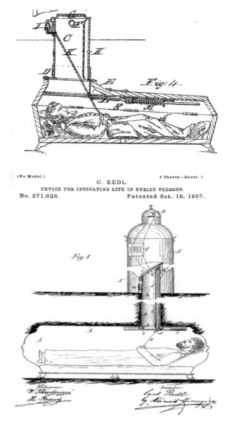

ABOVE: ADVERTISEMENT FOR
THE SALE OF SAFETY COFFINS

LEFT: TWO ILLUSTRATIONS
SHOWING HOW THE COFFINS
COULD BE USED TO PREVENT
THE CUSTOMER'S PREMATURE
BURIAL

by rope or string which could be
used to ring the bell above, drawing attention and signaling the need for help.
Many variations of these coffins were made available, yet there are no
documented cases of a living individual being rescued after having been
prematurely buried in a security coffin.

Over time, the need for elaborate security measures diminished as
advances in medicine allowed doctors to diagnose death more effectively, and
such inventions became largely obsolete.

In Europe, bodies *were* being brought back up to the surface, yet for an
entirely different—but no less harrowing—reason. Nineteenth century
"resurrectionists" were opening the graves of the recently deceased to pilfer
countless bodies from their intended final resting places to sell them to
anatomy schools for profit. Body snatching was a lucrative trade, as doctors

IMAGES OF SURVIVING MORTSAFES, OR
CAGED GRAVES

and medical students had few resources to legally obtain cadavers for dissection. In Edinburgh, Scotland, the law restricted the anatomical study of bodies belonging to deceased prison inmates, orphans, and sadly, suicide victims. The shortage in supply simply increased the demand, creating a nightmare for families who found the graves of their loved ones vacant and desecrated.

To combat the problem, strong cage-like structures called "mortsafes" were installed to ensure the recently interred remained where they were placed, safe from the ever-present threat of theft. A far greater number of still-surviving caged graves can be found in Europe, though a handful have been identified in early American cemeteries.

Over the years, these caged graves have steadily become the subject of great speculation. A creative, albeit incorrect theory is that mortsafes were used to keep the dead safe their graves, not to be kept out of the hands of body snatchers, but to spare the living from the possibility that their loved ones might rise again as vampires or the 'undead.' This is another example of fiction presented as fact online, in articles, books and various other publications. The truth may be far less interesting, but it is important in understanding how we have evolved in dealing with our dead.

A NATION OF SUFFERING

THE CIVIL WAR AND THE CHANGING RITUALS OF DEATH

Death came on swift wings for those who lived in early America. It came knocking on the doors of our ancestors in the form of disease, starvation, murder and every type of hardship that we can possibly imagine, and many more that we cannot.

But in the middle of the nineteenth century, America formed a new bond with death, entering into a civil war that proved bloodier than any other conflict in our history, a war that would come before the slaughter of World War I and the global carnage of the twentieth century. The number of soldiers who died between 1861 and 1865 -- an estimated 620,000 -- is approximately equal to the death toll of all of America's wars combined. The Civil War's death rate was catastrophic in the northern states, but even more chilling in the south. Confederate men died at a rate of three times that of their Yankee counterparts and in the end, one in five white southern men of military age did not survive the war.

But the military numbers only tell a part of the story.

The war killed civilians too, as battles raged across farms and in small towns, encampments of troops spread fatal diseases. Women and children were killed by guerilla violence and reprisals. Draft rioters killed innocent citizens in the big cities. Food shortages in parts of the south caused

DURING THE CIVIL WAR, AMERICANS EXPERIENCED DEATH IN WAYS
THEY NEVER IMAGINED – AND WERE CHANGED FOREVER

starvation. Historians have estimated that at least 50,000 civilians died
during the Civil War.

However, the impact and meaning of the war's death toll went beyond
the sheer numbers of those who died. Death's significance for those of the
Civil War generation came from a violation of the prevailing assumptions
about the proper end of life – about who should die, when and where, and
under what circumstances. Death was not unfamiliar to those of nineteenth
century America, but by 1860, the death rate in the country had started to
decline. Americans were well acquainted with death – it took a familiar
pattern. Americans of the early to middle nineteenth century endured a high
infant mortality rate but expected that most individuals who reached young
adulthood would at least live until middle age.

But the war changed all that.

It ripped away young, healthy men who should have lived a long time
and snuffed out their lives by bullet, by violence, and by disease. This marked
a sharp and alarming departure from existing ideas about who should die. A
soldier was five times more likely to die than he would have been if he had
not entered the army. Civil soldiers and civilians alike distinguished what
many referred to as "ordinary death," as it had occurred before the war, from
the manner and frequency of death in Civil War battlefields, hospitals,
prisons and camps, and from the war's disturbance of civilian lives.

During the Civil War, Americans reaped what many participants
described as a "harvest of death." By the midpoint of the conflict, it seemed

that in the south, "nearly every household mourns some loved one lost." Loss became commonplace. Death was no longer encountered individually – it had become the most widely shared of the war's experiences. As one Confederate soldier observed, death "reigned with universal sway," destroying homes and lives, demanding attention and response. The Civil War is an important point in our history because it ended slavery, but for those Americans who lived through the war, the texture of the experience was the presence of death. At war's end, this shared suffering overshadowed persisting differences about race, citizenship and state's rights, and memorializing death became the main thing that helped the north and south to reunite.

Death transformed America, as well as the hundreds of thousands directly affected by loss. The war created a nation of suffering when sacrifice and honor became inextricably intertwined. Citizen soldiers snatched from the midst of life generated obligations for a nation defining its purposes after a military struggle. A war about union, freedom, and human dignity required that the government attend to the needs of those who had died in service. The execution of these new responsibilities proved to be an important vehicle for the expansion of federal power that characterized post-Civil War America. The establishment of national cemeteries and the emergence of the Civil War pension system to care for both the dead and their survivors created programs of a scale and reach unimaginable before the war. Death created the modern American union, not just by ensuring national survival but by shaping enduring national structures and commitments.

Civil War Americans often wrote about what they called the "work of death" – the soldier's duty to fight, kill, and die. At the same time, their writings also invoked the battle's consequences: its slaughter, suffering, and devastation. "Work" in this usage incorporated both effort and impact and the important connection between the two. Death in war does not simply happen – it needs action and agents. It must, first, be inflicted, and several million soldiers dedicated themselves to that purpose during the war. But death also requires participation and response. It must be experienced and handled. It is work to die, to know how to approach and endure life's last moments. Of all living things, only humans consciously anticipate their death. The consequence of this is that we need to choose how to behave in its face – to worry about how we die. The need to manage death is the lot that has been cast upon us.

It is work to deal with the dead too – to remove them in the literal sense of disposing of their bodies, and it is work to remove them in a more figurative sense. The bereaved struggled to separate themselves from the dead through ritual and mourning. Families and communities had to repair the damage done to the domestic and social fabric, while the nation had to try and understand and explain the unfathomable loss.

There are rarely any passive victims of death. Those who die are part of a process – they prepare for death, imagine it, risk it, endure it, and seek to understand it. And if they are survivors of death, they have to assume new identities established by their persistence in the face of other's annihilation. The presence and fear of death touched the people of Civil War America by making them look closely at their most fundamental sense of who they were. Death inevitably inspired self-scrutiny and self-definition. They began to seek meaning and explanation for the war's destruction and in so doing, embraced the rituals and beliefs that helped them cope with loss.

BURYING THE DEAD

For the soldiers who traveled to fight and die on the nation's battlefields during the Civil War, their idea of burial after death took place in the local churchyard, family plot, or town cemetery. But the carnage created by the war's major engagements, and even the casualties of smaller skirmishes, presented a shocking challenge to those still reeling from the battle's physical and emotional impact. The soldiers had to disregard their own misery and attend to the wounded and the dead. The sheer number of bodies requiring disposal after battles at places like Antietam and Gettysburg defied both the imagination and the capabilities of the survivors. Every death that occurred posed a pressing and grimly pragmatic problem – what should be done with the bodies?

Nineteenth century Americans were forced to confront a horrific problem created by the scores of dead men that they suddenly had on their hands. There was, of course, the compelling need for disposal. But that was only the most tangible and immediate problem that the bodies posed. Redemption and resurrection of the body were understood as physical -- not just metaphysical -- realities, and therefore the body, even in death and decay, preserved a "surviving identity." Because of this, it was believed that the body required "sacred reverence and care." By not providing this, it signified a "demoralized and rapidly demoralizing community." The body was the repository of human identity in two senses – it represented the individuality of a particular person, and at the same time it incarnated the very humanness of that identity. Such understandings of the body, and its place in the universe, demanded attention even after life had fled. This meant that it required a "decent" burial, along with all the rituals of death that went along with it.

SOLDIERS OFTEN WORRIED ABOUT WHAT WOULD HAPPEN TO THEIR BODIES IF THEY DIED IN BATTLE. THEY WOULD HAVE BEEN SAD TO KNOW THAT THEY WERE OFTEN LEFT IN MASS GRAVES AND HASTILY DUG TRENCHES

Civil War soldiers worried deeply about their own remains, especially as they began to encounter circumstances that made customary reverence anything but possible. A South Carolina man, dying on the Virginia front, wrote that his greatest hope was to be transported home. Jeremiah Gage of the 11th Mississippi felt differently. As he was dying at Gettysburg, he wrote to urge his mother not to regret that she would be unable to retrieve his body. With his last words, he asked "to be buried like my comrades. But deep, boys, deep, so the beasts won't get me." Confederate Thomas J. Key had the same gruesome concern: "It is dreadful to contemplate being killed on the field of battle without a kind hand to hide one's remains from the eye of the world or the gnawing of animals and buzzards." Another Union soldier expressed a different worry with his final words – "don't let the rebels get me." To be returned home to one's family or, failing that, at least to be honorably buried with one's comrades and preserved from desecration by enemies, human and otherwise, were concerns shared by soldiers on both sides.

When the war began, military officials on both sides sought to establish some sort of burial procedures, in no small part because decaying corpses, and the "effluvia" that emanated from them, were believed to pose serious risks to public health. Many of the deaths in the initial months of the conflict came from epidemics of diseases like measles and mumps that broke out as men, often from isolated rural areas, crowded together in army camps and exposed one another to new illnesses. Both sides of the war ordered military hospitals to establish burial grounds. Each hospital of the Union army had to establish a mandatory "dead house," where post-mortem examinations could take place and where corpses would be stored until burial. When circumstances permitted, hospital staff members kept careful records of the men who were buried, provided them with respectful burials and, if the army remained stationary for a period of time, maintained graves.

But as the war escalated and the armies began to clash more frequently on the battlefield, the hospital cemeteries became entirely inadequate for those who were dying at the scene of the fighting, on scattered grounds, or in hastily established field hospitals. At the end of the war, a former Union hospital steward remembered with regret the failure to maintain careful records of the dead. Field hospitals, he wrote, were organized on an emergency basis: "Everything was therefore hurriedly arranged. You will therefore understand the seeming want of order in the burial of the dead... It was with the greatest difficulty and with terrible exertion on the part of my associates and myself that we were able to care for the sick and wounded – hence the little apparent care for those who were beyond help."

The first battle that took place at Bull Run in July 1861 yielded casualties that stunned military officials and forced them to reconsider their lack of preparation for so many fallen. In September, the Union army issued General Orders No. 75, making commanding officers responsible for the burial of soldiers who died within their jurisdiction and for the recording of those deaths with the office of the adjutant general. A little more than six month later, General Orders No. 33 detailed more elaborate instructions, requiring markers for graves, numbers and names "when practicable." Those final words marked the impossibility of such a measure. The structures and resources required to implement such policies were hardly even imagined, much less provided. The Union army had no regular burial details, no graves registration units and, until 1864, no comprehensive ambulance service. As late as the Second Battle of Bull Run in August 1862, a Union division took the field without a single ambulance for removing casualties.

The Confederate army passed several regulations specifying the commander's duty to bury the dead, dispose of their effects – and even pay their laundry bills. But they gave no more detailed directions as to how these orders were supposed to be followed then their northern counterparts did. Burying the dead after a Civil War battle always seemed to be an act of improvisation, one that called on the particular resources of the moment and circumstance, using available troops that could be detailed, prisoners of war deployed, or civilians that could be enlisted.

This lack of capacity and preparation was evident in the length of time it took to attend to the dead. The situation on the battlefield often delayed the care for the wounded, let alone the slain. If a military advantage seemed threatened, commanders might well reject flags of truce proposed for the removal of casualties from the field. Soldiers often lay dead or dying for hours – or even days – until an engagement was decided. After the first day of battle at Shiloh in April 1862, soldiers reported the disconcerting sounds of the wounded and dying as they moaned and cried out in the darkness of the night. No flag of truce for the removal of the wounded or dead was offered. Civilians and soldiers alike began to understand the meaning and urgency of the phrase they so often intoned: "Let the dead bury the dead."

More often the delay resulted from the failure to put the necessary manpower and resources toward the task. The battle that took place at Antietam on September 17, 1862 was the bloodiest single day of combat in American history and left both the Union and Confederate armies staggered by loss. When it was over, General Robert E. Lee slowly left the field – and the dead of both sides – to the Union army. George McClellan was paralyzed by the enormity of the engagement and failed to take advantage of his victory by pursuing the Confederates. A similar paralysis seemed to grip his troops as they confronted the devastation caused by the battle. Twenty-three thousand men and untold numbers of horses and mules lay killed and wounded. A Union surgeon reported that one week after the battle "the dead were almost wholly unburied, and the stench arising from it was such as to breed a pestilence." He described, "stretched along, in one straight line, ready for internment, at least a thousand blackened bloated corpses with blood and gas protruding from every orifice, and maggots holding high carnival over their heads."

Some commanders at Antietam had detailed squads to bury the dead soon after the fighting ceased. A New York soldier named Ephraim Brown, who had proudly captured a Confederate flag during the battle, found himself ordered two days later to bury rebel bodies at the same spot as his earlier triumph. His detail counted 264 bodies along a stretch of 55 yards. Brown may have resented having his bravery in battle rewarded with this grisly obligation, as units were often assigned to burial duty in response to some infraction or shortcoming.

Origen Bingham of the 137th Pennsylvania was comparatively rested after the battle at Antietam because his regiment had been held in reserve. But then he and his men found themselves faced with "the most disagreeable duty that could have been assigned to us; tongue cannot describe the horrible sight." The soldiers had been killed on Wednesday, September 17, and the 137th arrived on the field on Sunday. Although Union corpses had already been interred, likely by their own units and comrades, hundreds of Confederate dead remained on the field. Bingham secured permission from the provost marshal's office to buy liquor for his men because he believed they would be able to carry out their orders better if they were drunk. These were hardly conditions that encouraged the respectful treatment of the dead, and indeed, ribald jokes and inebriated revelry occurred on the bloody field.

Another burial party, overwhelmed by the number of bodies, tried a different method to make the task manageable – a squad of exhausted Union soldiers tossed the bodies of 58 Confederates down a local farmer's abandoned well.

The battle at Gettysburg the following summer presented an even greater challenge because the fighting extended over three days, delaying the attention to the dead for as long as the battle continued. By July 4, an estimated 6 million pounds of human and animal carcasses lay strewn across the field in the summer heat, while the small town desperately tried to deal with 22,000 men who were wounded and in desperate condition. One Union medical officer, who assumed responsibility for burying those he could not save, reported that he lacked even the basic tools to carry out his task: "I had not a shovel or a pick... I was compelled to send a foraging party to the farmhouses, who, after a day's labor, procured two shovels and an ax." So many bodies were unburied that a surgeon described the atmosphere as almost intolerable. Residents of the area complained of a "stench" that persisted from the time of the battle in early July until the coming of the frost in October. It was widely reported that the ladies of the town "went about with a bottle of pennyroyal or peppermint oil" to counteract the terrible smell.

Responsibility for the dead usually fell to the victor since it was his army that held the field. Early in the war, soldiers expressed outrage when the defeated abandoned their comrades without providing for their burial. After the first battle at Bull Run in July 1861, a Georgia soldier stated, "No set of heathens in the world was ever guilty of such acts. They never did come back to bury the first one of their dead." This was a scruple, though, that was abandoned as rapidly as the bodies themselves. "I cannot delay to pick up the debris of the battlefield," Union General George Meade boldly declared after the army's costly success at Gettysburg. The needs of the living increasingly began to outweigh the dignity of the departed.

Armies developed burial techniques intended to make the daunting task of disposing of bodies more manageable, but these procedures seemed horrifying even to those who executed them. Burial parties customarily collected the dead in a single location on the field by tying each soldier's legs together, passing the rope around the torso, and then dragging him to a row of assembled bodies. A bayonet, heated and bent into a hook, could keep the soldier from having to touch what was often a swollen and bloated corpse. The burial detail might then dig a grave, place a body in the hole, cover it with dirt from the next grave, and continue until the line of corpses was covered. But individual burials of this nature were usually reserved for one's comrades

SLAIN ENEMY SOLDIERS WERE OFTEN BURIED IN LONG TRENCHES. ONE SOLDIER DESCRIBED IT AS PILING THEM UP LIKE "DEAD CATTLE"

and for circumstances when time and resources allowed. The enemy dead were more likely to be buried in large pits.

Many buried the dead in trenches, about six feet wide and three to four feet deep. The dead were rolled on blankets and carried to the trench, where they were placed with their heads and feet alternating to save on space. Old blankets were usually placed over the pile of bodies and the earth was then thrown on top. One soldier worried that this process, which he had witnessed after Shiloh, reduced men to the status of animals or even vegetables. He wrote: "They dig holes and pile them in like dead cattle and have teams draw them together like picking up pumpkins."

Confederates at Gettysburg, buried in trenches containing 150 or more men, were often hurled into them rather than laid to rest. Sometimes the rotting bodies ruptured, forcing the burial parties to work elsewhere until the smell had dissipated. It was said that soldiers stomped "on top of the dead straightening out their legs and arms and tramping them down to make the hold contain as many as possible."

The press of the circumstances could, on occasion, require mass burial of even one's own men. A Connecticut chaplain remembered a skirmish that killed 23 men in his company during the last days of the war: "The best we could do in the brief interval of our stay was to bury the dead hurriedly in a common grave... in a long trench by the wayside, the officers by themselves, and the enlisted men near them." Of course, the names of the men buried in most of the mass graves were lost, even though the soldiers usually tried to bury them with their belongings so that a possibility of their identification might exist in the future. Trenches might also be marked, like one at Antietam, with a simple wooden sign that read, "80 rebels buried here." Customarily, Union and Confederate soldiers were buried separately. This is best represented by the outrage of a Union colonel who learned that some of the military hospitals were burying the dead indiscriminately, with no "distinction between the graves of our brave men who have died for the cause, and the grave of the worthless invaders of our soil. This is all wrong!" He could only think that this had been the fault of the undertaker "who cares only to get his money for covering their heads with earth." He believed that the hospitals should have separate sections of the cemetery for the Union and Confederate dead.

Rather than dig new ones, weary soldiers often took advantage of natural trenches and ditches on the battlefield. After the second battle at Bull Run, 85 dead men were laid beside a ridge created by a railroad excavation and then "covered by the leveling of the embankment over them as the most expeditious manner of burial." Virginia soldier James Eldred Phillips described burying the dead in the spring 1863 campaign by placing them "down in deep gullies on either side of the road and the dirt was dug from the side to cover them over." But spring storms followed, and Phillips later learned that "heavy rainfall had washed up all of the men that were buried in the gully and carried them down toward Fredericksburg."

The burial crews were often in a hurry and this caused the graves to be too shallow. Skeletons often emerged from the earth as wind and rain tore away the soil that had sheltered them. Worse, hogs often rooted around the battlefields in search of human remains. The remains were far too easy to find. For men buried on the field, coffins were out of the question. The best that a man could hope for was a blanket for his burial shroud. At the start of the war, Americans would have called the coffin a basic marker of the "decency" that distinguished a human burial and they would have agreed with John J. Hardin, an Indiana volunteer, that it was "dreadful to see the poor soldier just thrown in a ditch and covered over without any box."

Burials like these not only disrespected the dead but appalled many of the living. A Union chaplain wrote that in the pit burials, bodies were "covered over much the same as farmers cover potatoes and roots to preserve them from the frosts of winter; with this exception, however, the vegetables really get more tender care. Circumstances prevent such tenderness from being extended to the fallen hero." Frequently, corpses were quite literally naked, or clad only in their underwear, which still permitted a distinction between Yankee and Confederate corpses, for northerners customarily wore wool and southerners cotton. Soldiers desperate for clothing robbed the dead with little remorse. In addition, thieves and scavengers roamed the battlefields almost immediately after the last shots were fired.

Soldiers worried that the piles of the dead might include those still living, but unable to speak or let their presence be known or "extricate themselves from their former comrades." New York soldier William Gore related the frightening experience of a fellow soldier in Virginia who described a "narrow escape from a grave" already dug, when a nurse happened to intervene and indicate that she would arrange to have his body sent home to friends. While he lay awaiting shipment, he returned to consciousness – and eventually to duty. Since at least the late eighteenth century, Americans had displayed a deep anxiety about premature burial, devising caskets with bells and special protocols for resuscitation to prevent accidental burial of the living. Coming to term with the death toll of the Civil War began for many Americans with the difficulty of simply identifying and recognizing the end of life.

When bodies remained in the charge of their comrades and when troops were not hurried off to fight elsewhere, dead soldiers fared much better. Companies and regiments regularly preempted officially designated burial details by assuming responsibility for their own dead. Many close friends had sworn to provide one another with a "decent burial," and men searched the field in the nights and days after great battles to locate missing friends and family members. Soldiers did the best they could to bury their friends with respect and honor. They did all they could to compensate for the lack of coffins in the aftermath of battles, often using blankets, clothing, or knapsacks to shield their comrades from direct contact with the earth – the most basic demands of the "decent burial." They enacted the rituals of respect for the dead: brief prayers either with or without the participation of a chaplain. Confederate Thomas Key described the burial of two soldiers in 1864 accompanied by Bible readings, prayer, and a hymn "in the midst of heavy cannonading and singing of Minie balls." James Houghton of Michigan, "wishing to know that my tent mate was decently buried," returned to the field after Gettysburg and found that others had already performed the task while interring dozens of other fellow soldiers. He noted that all "pains possible was taken in their burial... in some cases their bloody garments were removed and washed and dried on the limbs of trees then replaced." Nurses in field hospitals performed services over the dead when time and circumstances permitted, but as the conflict wore on, these opportunities seemed to diminish. For months after assuming her duties, Confederate nurse Fannie Beers explained, "I insisted upon attending every dead soldier to the grave and reading over him a part of the burial service. But it had now [Fall of 1862] become impossible. The dead were past help; the living always needed succor."

In their efforts to find and honor their friends amidst the bodies of thousands, soldiers demonstrated their resistance to the war's casual destruction of individual human lives. As a Connecticut chaplain explained, "To say that 2,000 or 20,000 men are killed in a great battle, or that 1,000 of the dead are buried in one great trench, produces only a vague impression on the mind at the fullest. There is too much in this to be truly personal to you. But to know one man who is shot down by your side, and to aid in burying him, while his comrades stand with you above his open grave, is a more real matter to you than the large piece of astounding information."

Soldiers paid homage to their fallen comrades out of respect for the slain men, but they also did it for themselves – to reassert their own commitment to the sanctity of human life in the midst of so much carnage and death. They were reaffirming the larger purposes of their own existence and survival, and perhaps most of all, hoping that if they were killed, others would also honor them.

Inevitably, though, some individuals seemed to matter more than others. Officers received privileged treatment on the field, both at the hands of their own men and at the hands of the enemy, who customarily returned their bodies. In 1864, South Carolina soldier J.W. McClure described to his wife a practice common throughout the war when a flag of truce was used to provide for the exchange of "bodies of prominent officers" who had been killed and left in enemy hands.

Both Union and Confederate armies provided their dead officers with special treatment. In Richmond's Hollywood Cemetery, where men were brought from the surrounding battlefields throughout the war, the informal practice of burying officers together and separate from their men soon led to the establishment of a designated Officer's Section. After the battle at Cedar Mountain in 1862, most of the Federal dead lay unburied for days, although the bodies of officers were packed in charcoal and sent to Washington, where they were placed in metal coffins and shipped to their homes throughout the north. Confederate Charles Kerrison described a similar treatment according to rank when he attempted to retrieve the body of his brother, Edwin, a private killed in the spring of 1864. When one of four officers for whom metal coffins had been provided proved lost, Kerrison hoped that he might appropriate the surplus casket for Edwin. But he seemingly never questioned that a higher-ranking soldier should have been provided a coffin while his brother had none. A Texas soldier was less accepting. He wrote, "The officers get the honor, you get nothing." Oliver Wendell Holmes, searching for his son in the bloody aftermath of Antietam, took these contrasts for granted: "The slain of high condition, 'embalmed' and iron cased, were sliding off the railways to their far homes; the dead of the rank and file were being gathered up and committed hastily to the earth."

THE DEAD ON THE FIELD AT GETTYSBURG

It was not just soldiers who had to deal with the dead in the days after the fighting ceased. Combat respected no boundaries and spread across farms, fields, orchards, gardens, streets, and homes, leaving civilians with bodies in their front yards, in their wells, and among their corn and cotton fields. The capacities of cemeteries in towns like Richmond and Atlanta were strained, then exceeded, as communities struggled to provide graves for the growing numbers of the fallen.

After three days of battle, Gettysburg confronted the problems of thousands of slain men, far too many for the Union troops – who held the field when General Lee retreated southward – to bury with any sort of speed. Civilians joined in the burial of the dead out of both sympathy and necessity. Fifty dead Confederates lay on the Rose farm; 79 men from North Carolina had fallen in a perfect line on John Forney's farm; the widow Leister found 15 dead horses in her front yard; Joseph Shefry's barn, which had been used as a field hospital, was left a burned ruin with "crisped and blackened limbs, heads and other portions of bodies" clearly visible in the rubble.

No single battle in Virginia matched the death toll of Gettysburg, but the fighting in the corridor between Washington and Richmond went on for years, not just days. The local residents found themselves immersed in a permanent landscape of war. The Peninsula Campaign of 1862 compelled Richmond's Hollywood Cemetery to acquire additional acres to provide for the soldiers who died in battle and in the city's numerous military hospitals. Sometimes, the pressure of the burials at the cemetery became so great that as many as 200 bodies were left waiting to be buried. Chaplain Joseph Walker was often forced to conduct one service for several bodies in adjacent graves so that the interments could continue. Strangers visiting the cemetery often joined in the services, becoming replacement mourners for family members far away from where they loved ones had died in battle.

The emergence of this impersonal connection with the dead, one separate from any ties of family or friendship, was a critical part of the understanding of the war's carnage. The soldiers being buried did not belong to just their friends and relatives. Their loss was greater than just a loss to their own loved ones, which made them more than simply their individual selves. In rituals like those at Hollywood Cemetery, the fallen were transformed into an imagined community for the Confederacy, becoming a figure for which no name or identity was necessary. These men were now a part of the Confederate Dead, a shadow nation that would haunt the south for many years after the war had long ended. These soldiers no longer served the military effort of the south, but they became a part of the history and culture of the Confederacy in a way that attempting to provide meaning of the war and its great cost.

The mourners who came to Hollywood Cemetery were earnest in their need to pay tribute to the dead, but most civilians came out of desperation to locate and care for loved ones. The deaths of relatives far away from family was particularly disruptive to the fundamental nineteenth century belief in a "decent burial" and a "good death." Moreover, inadequacies in the means of reporting casualties in both the north and the south reinforced civilians' desire to find the bodies of their loved ones so they could be certain they were truly dead and had not just been misidentified.

At the beginning of the war -- when most believed it would be a short conflict and losses would be small in number -- several states in the north announced their intention to bring every slain soldier home. As late as 1863, Pennsylvania Governor Gregg Curtin declared that, at the

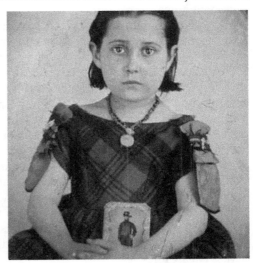

A YOUNG GIRL IN A MOURNING DRESS, HOLDING A PHOTOGRAPH OF HER SLAIN CAVALRYMAN FATHER

family's request, the state would pay the cost of removing a body from Gettysburg for reburial within the state. Several other northern states sent official agents to assist citizens in the removal of the bodies of their kin.

Mounting death tolls soon made those good intentions unrealistic. A number of both state-assisted and voluntary organizations – like the Pennsylvania State Agency, Louisiana Soldier's Relief Association, Central Association of South Carolina, and the New England Soldier's Relief Association -- nevertheless continued to try and help individual citizens bring their loved ones home. Late in 1863, as an example, the records of the Pennsylvania State Agency show that funds were advanced to Alice Watts to transport her husband, Thomas, who served in the 24th Pennsylvania Volunteers, to a grave near their home. Cities and towns sometimes offered desperate residents assistance, as well.

In the north, as the number of casualties increased as the war dragged on, the Sanitary Commission played an increasingly significant role in burials and handling the dead. This enormous philanthropic organization and its network of thousands of volunteers and hundreds of paid workers labored to provide needed supplies and assistance to soldiers – living and dead. Often, agents in the field assumed care of hospital burial grounds and death registries. Others worked to arrange for burials in the aftermath of battles and still others assisted families in locating lost loved ones and providing for their shipment home.

After the bloody battles in the west during the last year and a half of the war, agents for the Sanitary Commission in Chattanooga, for example, worked with counterparts in northern cities to arrange for the return of Union soldiers' remains. One agent, a man named M.C. Read, arranged for the disinterment of bodies, embalmer's services, metal cases, and shipping costs, telegraphing families when their loved ones were finally en route home. During a six-month period in 1864, the Chattanooga office handled 34 requests for disinterments, mostly, but not limited to, the bodies of officers. Families often made requests of the agents. The family of George Moore of Illinois made a personal request. The commission agent wrote of it to those who handled the body: "Have the undertaker secure a lock of his hair as a memento. Let his face be uncovered and inform us when the body is shipped." Often families deposited funds with a commission agent in the north to cover anticipated expenditures associated with locating and returning family members to avoid the difficulties of transferring money across enemy lines.

When armies moved, commission agents often made records of camp graveyards so that soldiers' bodies might be reclaimed at a later time. An

SOLDIERS KILLED IN BATTLE AND BURIED HAD TO BE DISINTERRED AT
A LATER DATE SO THAT THEIR BODIES COULD BE SHIPPED HOME OR
MOVED TO A CEMETERY

agent named Orange Judd gathered details of burials when the Union army moved from Belle Plain, Virginia, in May 1864 and he assembled them into an elaborate map. The graves had been marked with cracker boxes and inscribed with penciled names, but Judd rightfully feared that such markers could be destroyed by the enemy or the elements. His effort, he hoped, "would enable friends to find the bodies indicated." He outlined 26 graves, mostly with names and regiments attached. Six bodies remained unknown, but he offered descriptions of the men that he hoped would be useful, like "about 23; black hair; intelligent countenance; buried May 15." In nearby Port Royal, commission records of another cemetery mapped 23 graves, including three occupied by soldiers who had arrived in ambulances "with their pockets cut off and all records gone." They had been robbed of both their possessions and their identities on the battlefield. With the departure of the Union troops, the agent reported, "the graves were put under guard of George Smith, a colored man who lives just south of the ground and who will do all he allowed to keep them in order."

But the resources of the Sanitary Commission only stretched so far. For the most part, the bereaved were forced to rely on themselves and upon the emerging network of embalmers, undertakers, and private "agents" who followed the armies, finding work and profit by assisting grief-stricken families who had little idea how to bring home their lost husbands, brothers, and sons. W.R. Cornelius, an undertaker who worked frequently with the Sanitary Commission in Tennessee, also offered his services to families directly. He reported that he "shipped colonels, majors, captains, and privates by the carload some days," sending them both to the Union and Confederate states. Sometimes families procured friends to locate missing loved ones and arrange for the return of their bodies. Sometimes they set off by themselves, often arriving on the battlefield unsure of whether they had come to nurse an injured man or to transport his broken body home. For most from the impoverished south, or even simple farm people from the north, there was little hope that their fallen family members would be returned home if they did not go and retrieve them.

But even those of privilege and position faced challenges as they sought to find and honor their dead. In many situations, telegrams sent home notified family members that their loved ones had been wounded, but such notes did not reveal the severity of their wounds. When the searchers arrived at the field, they discovered their soldiers had since died and their bodies were usually only recovered after an intensive search. Shipping them home caused even more difficulty. Overburdened freight companies and railroads were often forced to put off the shipment of poorly preserved bodies for five days, a week, or even longer.

The Adams Express Company and its Confederate counterpart, the Southern Express, did a booming business during the war, establishing careful and elaborate regulations for the safe and sanitary transport of bodies. In the early days of the war, many bodies were shipped in wooden coffins, but weather and delays created situations that led to the shipping companies requiring metal caskets. Joseph Jeffries was one of the many entrepreneurs who flocked to Gettysburg after the battle to sell their services in retrieving and shipping bodies. He advertised "Metallic coffins... Warranted Air-Tight" that would not only meet shipping requirements but could "be placed in the parlor without fear of any odor escaping therefrom." A "zinc-lined box covered with cloth plated mounting" for expressing Captain R.G. Goodwin of Massachusetts cost $50 in 1862 -- no small sum, even for a person of some means. No wonder one shipping agent, at least, continued to be presented with wooden coffins. He responded by creating a small cemetery to hold bodies that he could not send and, in one particularly demanding week, buried more than 40 men. At the end of the war, these bodies were finally disinterred and returned to their families.

A New York man named Bowen Moon refused to be daunted by shipping regulations when he went in search of his brother-in-law William Salisbury after Antietam. A soldier from Salisbury's regiment described his dead comrade's gravesite and Moon managed to purchase a serviceable, if not elegant, wooden coffin from one of several local carpenters who now devoted themselves full-time to filling the sudden and almost overwhelming demand.

Moon hired a local farmer to help him exhume the body. Even though Salisbury shared his grave with two other men and two weeks had passed since the battle, Moon was able to identify him without any trouble. But he faced an unexpected setback when the railroad refused to accept the casket for shipping, insisting that it "did not carry dead bodies that had begun to decompose." Moon caulked the coffin,

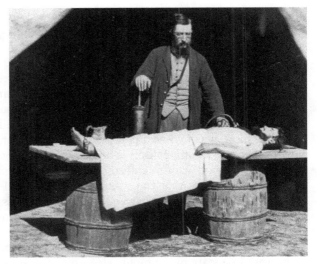

FOR FAMILIES THAT COULD AFFORD THE SERVICE, EMBALMING COULD BE DONE RIGHT AFTER THE BATTLE, SO THE BODIES OF THE DEAD COULD BE SHIPPED HOME

bribed the baggage manager, and succeeded in bringing his brother-in-law's body back home.

Some Americans had attempted before the war to preserve bodies using coffins that rested corpses on ice and such inventions grew more elaborate as families tried to retrieve growing numbers of war dead for burial at home. The Staunton Transportation Company, for example, distributed handbills to the civilians that came to Gettysburg in July and August 1863, promising that its new "Transportation Case preserves the body in a natural state and (as) perfect condition as when placed in it for any distance or length of time in any weather." The case was "so arranged as to readily expose the face of the dead for inspection," and the advertisement promised that it would "seem as though the subject had died on the day of arrival at home." The invention supposedly worked because "its construction makes it a portable refrigerator." The company offered a number of other services to the bereaved – regular coffins, "exhumers and guides who had surveyed the battlefield," as well as "deodorizers and army disinfectionists."

But even the elaborate refrigeration mechanism of the Staunton Transportation Case could not rival the advances in bodily preservation achieved by embalming, made more widespread by the war. New advances had come to America in the years just before the Civil War as the country adopted and patented chemical embalming procedures that had been used in Europe since the early 1800s. In the 1850s, embalming had been chiefly used not to prepare bodies for funerals, but to contribute to the study of anatomy and pathology by preserving cadavers for dissection. It was during the war, however, that embalming first began to be widely practiced, not just generating a transformation in the physical treatment of the dead but establishing a procedure that would serve as the foundation of the funeral industry and the role of the undertaker in American life.

But more was involved here than just purely practical concerns about how to stop the decomposition of bodies so that they could be shipped home. Americans did not want to endure the unprecedented separation from their deceased loved ones that the war had introduced. Families wanted to see their loved ones in a state that was as lifelike as possible. It was not just so that they could be certain of their identity – they wanted to bid them farewell. Embalming offered families a way to combat at least some of the threats the war posed to the idea of the "good death." To contemplate one's husband, son, or brother in a state of seemingly sleep-like repose was a means of resisting death's terror and even, to some degree, its reality. It offered a way of blurring the boundary between life and death. Corpses -- at least those that had not been dismembered in combat -- could be made to look lifelike and made to look as if they were on the verge of awakening in a new life to come.

Embalming attracted attention early in the war when the body of Union Colonel Elmer Ellsworth, killed in Alexandria, Virginia on May 24, 1861, by a Confederate sympathizer, was preserved. Ellsworth had been a friend of Abraham Lincoln and has escorted him east from Springfield when Lincoln came to Washington for his first inauguration amid rumors of plots to assassinate him before he could take office. He was killed during the opening days of the war -- and is regarded as the Civil War's first victim -- and the press detailed every aspect of his death, from his heroic demise to the honoring of his body in state at the White House, and finally his life-like corpse. His embalmer, Thomas Holmes, became the country's best-known practitioner during the war, setting up an establishment in Washington, D.C., where he embalmed more than 4,000 soldiers at a price of $100 each. Needless to say, the carnage of the war made him a wealthy man.

Neither the Union nor the Confederate military routinely provided embalming for deceased soldiers. Surgeons would sometimes offer this service to prominent individuals who died in army hospitals, and the undertakers contracted by the federal government to assist with the disposal of the dead might do embalming for a fee charged to the grieving families or comrades. In the spirit of benevolent paternalism, Union officers sometimes arranged for the special care of the bodies of their men. In one example, a captain left instructions with a nurse at a hospital of the Army of the Potomac, "To the embalmer at Falmouth Station: You will please embalm the body of Elijah Clifford, a private of my company. Do it properly and well, and as soon as it is done send me word, and I will pay your bill at once. I do not want this body expensively embalmed, but well done, as I shall send it to Philadelphia."

Embalming was much rarer in the south than in the north, largely because of the cost involved and because the invaded southern states were more compelled to focus on survival instead of elaborate treatments of the dead. But embalmers advertised throughout the war in the Richmond newspapers, announcing their readiness to perform "disinfections" and directing potential customers to newly opened field offices on the sites of recent battles. While

EMBALMING SERVICES WERE ESTABLISHED JUST ABOUT ANYWHERE IN THE WAKE OF THE BATTLES – FROM OLD BARNS TO TENTS AT THE EDGE OF THE BATTLEFIELD

the southern funeral industry remained far less developed and embalming less common than in the north well into the twentieth century, there were still many thousands of soldiers who were embalmed and sent home for burial in the Confederacy during the war.

The war marked the time when the American funeral industry truly came into its own. Such services had rarely been used before the war, but now they gained popularity. Embalming promised to transform death into slumber. Embalmers advertised both themselves and the process by exhibiting preserved bodies, which were often unknown dead men who had been collected from the field and embalmed.

FAY'S PATENT

SELF-SEALING, AIR-TIGHT, SHEET-METAL
BURIAL CASES AND CASKETS

The undersigned is now prepared to fill all orders for his Patent Air-Tight, Sheet-Metal BURIAL CASES AND CASKETS, which for Lightness, Durability and Style of Finish, combined with the price (which brings them within the reach of all) are unsurpassed by anything of the kind now in use. They are SELF-SEALING without the aid of cement, wax or putty. PLEASE CALL AND EXAMINE BEFORE PURCHASING ELSEWHERE.

L. FAY
Sole Proprietor and Manufacturer,

Despite its increase in popularity, though, embalming provoked suspicion. Embalmers were frequently accused of dubious practices and considered "disturbed," thanks to their "strange intimacy" with the dead. The stigma lingered for years. The role of the "undertaker" had come along well before the start of the Civil War, but the war years marked the beginning of the time when it began to be considered an important position. The word "undertaker" was actually in use as far back as 1698 and it originally meant the one who "undertook" arrangements for the dead and was charged with keeping the body safe. The duties of this person changed many times through the years and in fact, modern members of the industry dislike the word "undertaker." The term "funeral director" was first coined back in 1885, but it took nearly a century for it to catch on. In the early 1900s, the word "mortician" was also devised, but it was never popular.

But while undertakers and embalmers may have seemed distasteful in that era, this was not the main problem that families had with them. The U.S. Army was deluged with anguished protests from families of dead soldiers who believed they had been cheated by embalmers operating near the battlefront. Bodies arrived home in deplorable condition after families paid steep prices for the bodies to be preserved. During the war, military authorities permitted civilian embalmers to work within military controlled areas and not until the last year of the war did the Army require them to be examined to prove their qualifications. Finally, after scores of complaints,

General Ulysses S. Grant responded by withdrawing all embalmers' permits and ordering them behind the lines. But even so, the distances separating the dead from the loved ones continued to encourage embalming, despite the uneasiness about the practice and widespread hostility toward its practitioners.

Embalming was expensive, as were refrigerated cases and trips to the battlefield to recover lost family members. Wealthier Americans had resources to invest in managing and resisting death that their poorer brethren lacked. All but taken for granted through much of the war, this differential treatment began to be challenged as the federal government assumed a new responsibility for those killed in war. In 1862, in response to logistical problems caused by the growing number of the dead, the U.S. Congress passed a measure giving the president power to purchase grounds to be used as national cemeteries for the soldiers who died in service to their country. Without any appropriation or formal policy with which to implement this legislative action, the War Department established cemeteries as emergency circumstance required, mostly near concentrations of military hospitals where there were many dead that required burial.

Under the terms of this measure, five cemeteries were created in the course of the war. Each were burial grounds for the dead of a particular battle. Three of these cemeteries -- Chattanooga, Stones River, and Knoxville -- were created by Union Generals, and two -- Antietam and Gettysburg -- by joint actions of northern states whose citizens had participated in the battles. In each case, the purpose of the effort extended well beyond simply meeting the need for disposing of the dead. These cemeteries were intended to memorialize the slain and celebrate the nation's fallen heroes. Gettysburg represented a particularly important turning point. The large numbers of casualties in the massive battle were obviously the leading factor in creating the burial ground, but it is not insignificant that the bloody battle occurred in the north, in a town that had not had the opportunity to grow accustomed to the horrors of the constant fighting that had battered Virginia for two long years. Gettysburg made the dead starkly visible to northern citizens, so many of whom flocked to the small Pennsylvania town in the aftermath of the battle. The hard-pressed Confederacy could not afford the resources needed for a national cemetery, but the people of the north could – and they demanded it.

The impetus for the cemetery's creation came from a meeting of state agents in the weeks after the battle. With financial assistance from Union states that had lost men in the engagement, David Wills, a Gettysburg attorney, arranged to purchase 17 acres of land that adjoined an existing graveyard. In October, contracts were let for the reburial of Union soldiers in the new ground at a rate of $1.59 per body. In November, President Abraham Lincoln journeyed to help dedicate the new burial ground. The short, moving address that he gave "remade America," many historians have claimed, and signaled the beginning of a new significance for the dead in public life.

Among the dead, Lincoln spoke:

Four score and seven years ago our fathers brought forth on this continent, a new nation, conceived in Liberty, and dedicated to the proposition that all men are created equal.

Now we are engaged in a great civil war, testing whether that nation, or any nation so conceived and so dedicated, can long endure. We are met on a great battlefield of that war. We have come to dedicate a portion of that field, as a final resting place for those who here gave their lives that that nation might live. It is altogether fitting and proper that we should do this.

But, in a larger sense, we cannot dedicate -- we cannot consecrate -- we cannot hallow -- this ground. The brave men, living and dead, who struggled here, have consecrated it, far above our poor power to add or detract. The world will little note, nor long remember what we say here, but it can never forget what they did here. It is for us the living, rather, to be dedicated here to the unfinished work which they who fought here have thus far so nobly advanced. It is rather for us to be here dedicated to the great task remaining before us -- that from these honored dead we take increased devotion to that cause for which they gave the last full measure of devotion -- that we here highly resolve that these dead shall not have died in vain -- that this nation, under God, shall have a new birth of freedom -- and that government of the people, by the people, for the people, shall not perish from the earth.

The establishment of the great cemetery at Gettysburg marked the beginning of significant shifts in attitude and policy produced by the nation's confrontation with the slaughter of the war. Americans in the north and south learned new lessons imposed by the necessities of the war, forcing them to endure and practice new ways of handling the dead that would have previously seemed unthinkable. Not only did these actions dishonor the dead by treating them more like animals than men; they diminished the living, who found themselves abandoning commitments and principles that helped define their essential selves. Out of the horror of the Civil War burials, there grew, even in the midst of the bloodshed, a variety of efforts to resist these unwanted changes, to establish different sorts of lessons as the product of the nation's experience with the war. Civil War Americans worked to change death in ways that ranged from transforming the actual bodies of the dead through embalming to altering the circumstances and conditions of interment by establishing the national cemeteries and a massive postwar reburial program – the latter sponsored by the government in the north but also executed on a smaller scale by private voluntary actions in the south.

The participation of the Union government in these matters, first made highly visible in the Gettysburg dedication ceremonies, acknowledged a new public importance for the dead. No longer simply the responsibility of their families, the soldiers – and their loss – belonged to the entire country. These men had given their lives so that the nation might live and their bodies, repositories of their "surviving identity," as *Harper's Weekly* put it, deserved the nation's recognition and respect.

BELIEVING IN THE DEAD

On the eve of the Civil War, Americans found that their traditional systems of belief were both powerfully challenged and fervently reaffirmed. Although the United States had been established as a secular state by founders wary of religious influences on the government, religion defined the values of most mid-nineteenth century Americans. Nearly four times as many attended church every Sunday in 1860 as voted in that year's critical presidential election. Overwhelmingly Christian and Protestant, Americans were largely committed to the hope of salvation and eager to do what they needed to do so they could have a future beyond the grave. The Calvinist notions of predestination that had characterized much of American Christianity in the colonial era had yielded to waves of nineteenth-century revivals, culminating in widespread religious enthusiasm in the 1850s.

Still, reflective Christians in the nineteenth-century age of progress faced troubling questions about the foundations of their faith. New historical scholarship and new forms of textual criticism had raised doubts about the literal truth of the Bible. As southerners amassed evidence of scriptural support for slavery, northern abolitionists sought and found different meanings. These differences in interpretation revealed more than just a regional dispute – they represented a new uncertainty about the undisputed and indisputable power of the Bible itself, an unsettling fact that struck at the soul of every Christian.

Even more disturbing than issues of biblical interpretation were the questions that science posed for religious belief. Geological discoveries about the vast age of the Earth discredited scriptural accounts of creation, suggesting a much diminished and distanced role for any divine creator. Charles Lyell's *Principles of Geology*, published in the 1830s, challenged the veracity of Genesis by demonstrating that the Earth was millions of years old, not the six or seven thousand years claimed by scripture. Darwin's theories of evolution, shared and discussed by many American scientists before the publication of *The Origin of the Species* in 1859, further challenged the literal words of the Bible and replaced them with natural selection.

Nevertheless, most Americans clung to their religious traditions. They continued to regard science and religion as in alliance rather than in conflict well into the nineteenth century. They believed in God and they believed that he watched over them and had a hand in their daily lives.

And then along came the war, bringing carnage and mass death.

The suffering that came during the Civil War could not help but raise disturbing questions about God's benevolence and motivations. This was a frightening thing to the hundreds of thousands of Americans bereaved by the war. Loss demanded an explanation that satisfied both the hearts of the people and the lingering questions about whether God watched over them or not.

Religion remained the most readily available explanatory resource, even if it was being challenged by cultural and intellectual change. Of course, God watched over the soldiers who fought on the front lines and in fact, both sides believed that they were doing the will of God. And while the earthly fate of the soldiers was beyond their control, if they remained true to God, they were guaranteed a place in heaven.

Such convictions made both dying and mourning easier. Some historians have argued that, in fact, only the widespread existence of such beliefs made the acceptance of Civil War death tolls possible, and that religion thus, in some sense, enabled the slaughter. Confidence in immortality could encourage soldiers to risk annihilation. Firm conviction that God wanted a soldier to slay his enemy could yield confidence that bordered on heartlessness and, in some cases, behavior that approached recklessness. But the long tradition of Christian soldiery served almost as propaganda, emphasizing faith as a fundamental motivation to religious and patriotic duty. Evangelical tracts and preachers repeatedly used the word "efficiency" in their communications to the troops. The Christian soldiers, these preachers explained, would be an efficient soldier because he would execute his obligations "conscientiously" and would not be afraid to die.

For hundreds of thousands of soldiers – some of them believers before the war and others converted by revivals that swept through armies of both the north and south – death became a fixation. Often, sadly, it was not so much a fear but a promise, of relief, of salvation from war and suffering, and an escape into a better world. Death offered these devout men a "change" but not an ending. Heaven became preferable over the bloody fields of Georgia or Virginia. Spared the direct experience of combat, civilians were less likely to acknowledge an attraction to death, but they found in religious doctrines the means to diminish its horror and to manage the losses war inflicted on them.

There has been much discussion in our time about the denial of death. Such discussions began in the 1970s and continue even within the pages of this book. We have tried, in these modern times, to make death "invisible." Modern dying has been sanitized, mourning, some say, has become indecent and death has become as unmentionable as pornography. In the Civil War, though, death was hardly hidden, but it was nevertheless, seemingly paradoxically, denied – not through silence and invisibility but through an active and concerted effort to change it in such a way that it become a cultural preoccupation. Redefined as eternal life, death began to be celebrated in nineteenth-century America.

Religious leaders did all that they could to make death as attractive as possible to Americans of the era, assuring them that love and friendship

"THE TRIUMPH," AN 1862 ILLUSTRATION PREDICTING THE RELIGIOUS TRIUMPH OF THE UNION OVER THE CONFEDERACY. FREEDOM, HOLDING AN AMERICAN FLAG, IS FLANKED BY CHRISTIANITY AND JUSTICE. THEY ARE SURROUNDED BY HISTORIC FIGURES – INCLUDING LINCOLN – AND ARE FREEING THE SLAVE FROM THE MANACLES OF ALLIGATOR KING COTTON, THE RULER OF THE DARK UNDERWORLD OF THE CONFEDERACY. THE UNION – IT PORTRAYED – WAS FIGHTING ON THE SIDE OF GOD.

SOLDIERS FOR THE CONFEDERACY HAD THE SAME BELIEF

would continue on the other side. Such things would eventually become widely believed, but the transition remained incomplete when the Civil War began. Emily Dickinson was not alone in the concerns that she voiced about the forbidding nature of the afterlife in her wartime poetry and letters. "Heaven is so cold," she wrote, along with, "I don't like Paradise – because it's Sunday all the time." The transformation of heaven intensified as the war made questions about immortality more immediate and widely shared. Historians have numbered more than 50 books that were written about heaven in the United States between 1830 and 1875, but this total does not include fictional works, or the dozens of Civil War funeral sermons appearing as printed pamphlets that made heaven a central theme, or the many periodicals and newspaper stories with titles like "Heaven, the House of God," or popular poetry that addressed the nature of the afterlife in rhyme. The geography and society of the afterlife persisted as widespread concerns, for even when the slaughter had ceased, loss and grief remained.

An issue of particular focus in this type of literature -- and in the struggle to come to terms with death -- was the fate of human relationships in the afterlife. If death was no longer to be considered as an ending, then apparently it was also no longer a parting. Earlier versions of heaven only focused on the connection between God and man, even to the point of denying the persistence of earthly ties of family and friendship. But many religious thinkers of the nineteenth century began to espouse a more consoling portrait of paradise. The era of the Civil War could not tolerate the obliteration of the cherished ties of home and family. The widespread assumption that they would one day be reunited with lost kin was fundamental to the solace of religious faith. If soldiers needed to be assured that they would not really die, survivors yearned to know their loves ones were not – even if they were missing or unknown – forever lost. "They will not leave us for long," a South Carolina woman wrote. They were "only gone before." The Civil War made urgent the transformation of heaven into an eternal family reunion, encouraging notions of an afterlife that was familiar and close at hand, populated by loved ones who were just "beyond the veil."

Many bereaved Americans, though, weren't willing to wait until their own deaths reunited them with their loved ones and they turned eagerly to the immediate promises of Spiritualism. A decade or so before the war, in the late 1840s, a series of spirit rappings at the home of the Fox family in upstate New York created an intense interest in the idea of communication between the living and the dead. To an age increasingly caught up in the notion of science as the measure of truth, Spiritualism offered belief that seemed to rely on empirical evidence rather than revelation and faith. If the dead could cause tables to rise, tap out messages from the world beyond, and even communicate in lengthy statements through spirit mediums, then an afterlife must exist.

Men and women began to participate in regular spirit circles in hopes of communicating with the dead. The movement spread quickly across the country until there was an estimated two million Spiritualists in the early

SPIRITUALISM, WHICH WAS REGARDED AS A PASSING FAD 10 YEARS BEFORE THE WAR, TOOK ON NEW MEANING AS A WAY FOR THE LIVING TO COMMUNICATE WITH THE DEAD LOVED ONES THEY HAD LOST.

1850s, with the movement showing no signs of slowing down. It was astonishing to see the speed with which interest in Spiritualism spread across America. Much to the surprise of the critics, it was not just the so-called superstitious and uneducated who were drawn to the movement. Increasingly, many educated, wealthy, and prominent people could be found at séances. When the first large scale Spiritualist society was founded in 1854, its organizers included a former U.S. senator, four judges, two military officers, and several successful businessmen.

Spiritualism swept through the country but, as with most fads, interest began to wane. In fact, Spiritualism saw a period of decline between 1856 and 1860. In the years leading up to the war, the country had too much on its mind to pay much attention to talking with ghosts. In the post-war period, though, it would be the death and destruction of the fighting that made the movement stronger than ever. Thanks to the huge number of bereaved wives, parents, and loved ones, Spiritualism offered the hope of direct communication with those who had died. Soon, an even greater number of people from all economic levels began flocking to mediums and séances around the country. The idea of Spiritualism was attractive enough that even those who were not adherents to start with soon began to embrace the movement's possibilities. Mary Todd Lincoln sought regularly to communicate with her dead son,

Willie. She sponsored scores of séances at the White House, which according to records, the president himself also attended.

And Mary Lincoln was not alone. Henry Bowditch was no Spiritualist, but the teachings of the movement made his struggle with the loss of his son somewhat easier. He wrote later that he now believed that his slain son was only invisible and that he lived on in another, only temporarily inaccessible world. The ideology of Spiritualism even played a part in the young man's funeral sermon, which assured mourners that "he is just on the other side of the thin veil. He stands there, waiting for you to come."

In New Orleans, an officer of the Native Guard led an active Spiritualist circle called the Grandjean Séance. Within weeks of Andre Cailloux's death, the group made contact with this departed hero. Cailloux reported from the afterlife, "They thought they had killed me, but they made me live. It will be I who receive you into our world if you die in the struggle, so fight!"

Extensive marketing of the planchette, precursor to the Ouija board, during the 1860s, and especially in the years immediately after the war, offered everyone the chance to be a medium and turned Spiritualist exploration into a parlor game. A heart-shaped piece of wood on three legs, the planchette was believed to move in response to spirit forces that passed through the hands that rested on it. The device, usually equipped with a small pencil, could point to letters of the alphabet or actually write out messages from the dead. Especially popular in the northern states, planchettes were available in a variety of woods and decorative styles and transformed spirit communication into a fashionable and novel amusement.

Spiritualists held their first national convention in Chicago in 1864, marking a growing prominence that extended well beyond the realm of popular amusement. Amid a war that was claiming not only lives but identities, the promise, as one Spiritualist wrote, of the "imperishability of the individual and the continuation of the identical ego" after death was irresistible for many. As John Edmonds and George T. Dexter assured readers of *Spiritualism*, first published in 1853 and then reprinted throughout the rest of the century, "Physical death does not affect the identity of the individual."

Spiritualism responded to a question of pressing importance to the soldier and his family. As an 1861 article in the Spiritualist newspaper *Banner of Light* posed it, "he desires to know what will become of himself after he has lost his body. Shall he continue to exist? – and if so, in what condition?" Each issue of the paper provided many answers through the "Message Department" of "Voices from the Dead," transmitted through "Mrs. J.H. Conant, while in a condition called the Trance." Confederates and Yankees alike chimed in. Soldiers of all ranks reported that they had died well, that they had met relatives in heaven, and that, as one voice declared, "Death has taken nothing from me, except my body." General Thomas "Stonewall" Jackson weighed in to defend his actions ("I adopted the course I took because I felt it was right for me to do.") Willie Lincoln also sent regular communications from the other side.

Phillip Gregg, a Confederate killed three months before his appearance in print in April 1862, noted that "the emotions of the returning soldier, who has yielded up his life upon the battlefield, can be scarcely imagined." Those who indeed found the notion of posthumous emotions too much to imagine were presented with his vivid description, although Gregg cut the story short, concluding, "What I would say to my family the world has no right to hear."

Many messages contained the kind of information found in condolence letters written to inform relatives about the death of their loved ones in hospitals or in battle – trying to ease their pain by telling them that their men had died bravely and honorably. Whether or not Mrs. Conant was able to communicate with the dead, she certainly channeled the concerns of the living. She was often asked to pass along messages from her readers to those who had passed over, and vice versa. One of the spirits reportedly told her, "I lost my life in your Bull Run affair, and the folks want to know how I died and what became of me after death... I should like to inform them." Families were promised relief from the "dread void of uncertainty" about the earthly and spiritual fate of their sons and brothers.

Caleb Wilkins, private of the 11th Indiana, described from his own experience how bodies continue to live in the afterlife. At the same time, he offered an explanation of a puzzle that had tormented thousands of wounded men: why amputated limbs so often continued to hurt. He confirmed, "I can understand some things now that I couldn't before death." Wilkins reported that his leg had been amputated and that several days later, he bled to death. When Caleb met his brother in heaven and looked at himself, he declared, "that ain't my body... I lost a leg and this body is perfect." His brother, who had spent more time as a dead man, explained that Caleb was looking at his spiritual body. His "spirit foot and leg" were perfect and the pain that he had felt after his amputation in his missing foot had been a consequence of the separation of his material from his spiritual appendages. His amputation had been a kind of pre-death, a forerunner of the disjunction of material body and spirit yet to come. Wilkins and his brother helpfully provided readers with an explanation of body and soul, as well as the assurance that no man, and indeed not even any leg, was truly lost.

I'm sure the reader will not be shocked to learn that the story of Caleb Wilkins was not true. There was no Caleb Wilkins listed in the ranks of the

11th Indiana or in the database of soldiers compiled by the National Park Service. So, the *Banner of Light* did not present the story of any reader's actual kin. It did not provide accurate details of deaths and burials, the kind of information that families sought as they flocked to battlefields or inundated the Sanitary Commission's Hospital Directory with tens of thousands of desperate inquiries. The consolation of Spiritualism lay in its promise that there could and would be answers to these questions, even if it could not immediately provide them. There would be an ending to uncertainty – perhaps through contact with the spirit world, but certainly with the world beyond. The unfinished narratives of so many lives, Spiritualism said, would ultimately have a conclusion.

The *Banner of Light*, which continued to carry communications from dead soldiers for more than a decade after the war, affirmed for its community of readers that individual soldiers were neither dead nor lost. They were still themselves – still, as they described themselves, still young men, still the same height and looks, still northerners or southerners, each still possessing his own identity and name. And they were struggling to reach out to those they had left behind to console them with the reassurance at Spiritualism's core – "I still live."

There is no question that nearly every family in the nation, north and south, had been touched by the unwelcome presence of death and was paralyzed with grief. The scale of the carnage was almost unimaginable with more than 600,000 men and boys who were dead and another million who were wounded. Spiritualism offered relief and as a result, people flocked to spirit mediums in hope of hearing from their departed husbands, sons, brothers, and friends.

The Civil War gave birth to not only the "golden age" of Spiritualism, but ushered in a new era for religion, for embalming, burials, cemeteries, and a reverence for the dead. And at its end, came an event that would forever change how Americans mourned for the dead.

The country would never be the same.

TWENTY DAYS

The Lincoln "carnival of death" and how it changed the American traditions of death and mourning

On the night of April 14, 1865, President Abraham Lincoln was shot in the back of the head while seated in a private box at Ford's Theater in Washington, D.C. His assassin, popular American actor John Wilkes Booth, was a Confederate sympathizer who was enraged by the recent surrender of the southern military and the fall of Richmond, the Confederate capital. The Civil War was almost over, but Booth and a group of conspirators were determined to continue the hostilities.

After the shooting, Lincoln was rushed to a nearby boarding house and while everything possible was done to save his life, he died in the early morning hours of April 15. The nation was shattered by its loss. Although a controversial president who never even won the majority of the national vote when he first took office, Lincoln had managed to win the love and devotion of the American people through the horror of the war. He was a revered figure at the time of his second inauguration, but his death would make him a martyr – and would change the nature of mourning in America forever.

Two days after the death of the president, his coffin was ready, and soldiers carried it to the second-floor guest room in the White House where Lincoln's corpse had been resting since Saturday afternoon, when it had been moved there from the boarding house where he had died. The soldiers approached the president and lifted him from the table where he lay to the

THE DEATH OF PRESIDENT LINCOLN CHANGED MOURNING AND FUNERAL CUSTOMS IN AMERICA FOREVER

coffin – a coffin that now looked too small. He was deftly placed inside, but without his boots. Lincoln's lanky frame measured six feet, four inches, which was longer than most caskets of the day. As the soldiers lifted the coffin and carried it down the stairs, at least one of them must have considered the idea that the Lincoln funeral ritual was off to a rather inauspicious start.

Gaslight illuminated the silent, eerie journey to the famous East Room, where so many public receptions and events had been held. The coffin was taken to the center of the room and placed on the catafalque. It was a magnificent casket, more impressive than any Abraham Lincoln had ever seen. In life, Lincoln had dismissed his wife Mary's love of frills and finery. He never would have chosen such a stately and expensive coffin for himself. It had cost almost as much as he had paid for his house back in Illinois. He would have preferred a simple pine box, like the one he had helped build for his mother when he was a boy.

And then there were the decorations in the East Room. Lincoln had always laughed about Mary's obsession with decorating the White House. But no one who entered the East Room over the next two days mocked its lavish vestments of mourning. When the public and press saw it, they were so impressed that they named it the "Temple of Death." Lincoln, claimed his friend Ward Hill Lamon, had foreseen this stark tableau in one of his prophetic dreams.

Lamon recalled a small gathering at the White House a few days before the assassination where only he, the president, Mary Lincoln, and two or three other people were present. Lamon said that Lincoln was in a "melancholy, meditative mood and had been for some time." Mary commented on his demeanor and Lincoln replied with an odd little observation about how dreams were once considered to be messages from God to men but, "Nowadays dreams are regarded as very foolish, and are seldom told, except by old women and by young men and maidens in love."

Mary asked him if he believed in dreams. He replied, "I can't say I do, but I had one the other night which has haunted me ever since... somehow the thing has gotten possession of me, and, like Banquo's ghost, it will not go down." Lincoln then described his troublesome dream:

About ten days ago, I retired late. I soon began to dream. There seemed to be a death-like stillness about me. Then I heard subdued sobs, as if a number of people were weeping. I thought I left my bed and wandered downstairs. There the silence was broken by the same pitiful sobbing, but the mourners were invisible. I went from room to room; no living person was in sight, but the same mournful sounds of distress met me as I passed along.

It was light in all the rooms; every object was familiar to me, but where were all the people who were grieving as if their hearts would break? I was puzzled and alarmed. What could be the meaning of all this? Determined to find the cause of a state of things so mysterious and so shocking, I kept on until I arrived at the East Room, which I entered. Before me was a catafalque, on which rested a corpse wrapped in funeral vestments. Around it were stationed soldiers who were acting as guards; and there was a throng of people, some gazing mournfully upon the corpse, whose face was covered, others weeping pitifully.

"Who is dead in the White House?" I demanded of one of the soldiers.

"The President." was his answer, "He was killed by an assassin."

Then came a loud burst of grief from the crowd, which awoke me from my dream. I slept no more that night; and although it was only a dream, I have been strangely annoyed by it ever since.

Mary Lincoln recoiled from the account. "That is horrid! I wish you had not told it. I'm so glad that I don't believe in dreams, or I should be in terror from this time forth."

"Well," replied the president, "it is only a dream, Mary. Let us say no more about it and try to forget it."

Days later, Lincoln's body was on display in the East Room, just as he had dreamed it.

The funeral display in the East Room had been hastily arranged, just like everything else that took place in the wake of the president's death. Washington was a scene of chaos in mid-April 1865. As the search continued for Lincoln's killer, there was also the matter of swearing a new president into office, while others labored over the funeral for President Lincoln. The initial details of the proceedings were decided on and arranged by Secretary of War Edwin Stanton, who was embroiled in just about everything that was going on in Washington at the time. Unfortunately, there was little choice in the

matter. Mary Lincoln had locked herself in her room and young Robert Lincoln was still too stunned by his father's death to be of much assistance.

Stanton dealt with Lincoln's embalming and even supervised the dressing of the corpse. But once his corpse was ready for burial, it became unclear where that would occur. Mary had the right to choose the site, but given her mental state, she was in no condition to discuss the subject only hours after her husband's death. Stanton would confer with her and Robert Lincoln later. In the meantime, whatever the final destination of the president's remains, official funeral events would have to take place in the nation's capital within the next few days. Stanton did not have time to plan and supervise a major public funeral, the biggest, no doubt, that the District of Columbia had ever seen. He needed to delegate this responsibility and had to choose between several candidates, including Ward Hill Lamon, Lincoln's close friend and unofficial bodyguard. It had been Lamon who had organized Lincoln's trip to Gettysburg in November 1863, planning everything with less than one week's notice. There was also Benjamin Brown French, a Washington veteran with great experience with decades of historic events, including the deaths of other presidents. French was perfect but was needed for another role – decorator in chief of public buildings. He was needed to drape the city in mourning. Stanton also considered Major General Montgomery Meigs, the quartermaster general of the U.S. Army, an expert planner with superb organizational skills. But the war was not yet over and Meigs was still needed in the field. He also considered another military man, Brigadier General Edward D. Townsend, the assistant adjutant general of the army, but Stanton had Townsend in mind for a special duty of utmost importance, one even more critical than planning the president's funeral in Washington – getting the president home to Illinois, if that was where Mary wanted him to go.

In the end, Stanton chose George Harrington, assistant secretary of the Treasury. Harrington was experienced in the ways of Washington, was well-known and liked by both Lincoln and Stanton, and Stanton believed him to have the keen, quick, and organizational mind that was essential for the assignment. He was soon in charge of all the Washington events to honor the late president. Harrington accepted the appointment and quickly went to work.

Stanton was now free to focus on what should be done with Lincoln's corpse after the Washington ceremonies. Would he be interred at the U.S. Capitol, in the vault beneath the great dome that had once been intended as the final resting place of George Washington? Or would Mary Lincoln take the body back to Illinois, for burial in Chicago, the state's most important city, or in Springfield, the state capital and the Lincolns' home for 24 years?

The clock was ticking.

On April 17, Stanton requested an interview with Mary and Robert to ascertain the family's wishes for the final disposition of Lincoln's remains. Some federal officials argued in favor of the tomb at the capitol building. From Kentucky came an urgent telegram imploring consideration of Lincoln's birthplace as a suitable final resting place. Chicago, where Lincoln had practiced law in the federal courts and earned the nomination for the presidency, put in a bid. But the city of Springfield lobbied the hardest.

Within an hour after news of the president's death reached Springfield, the people began to stir, and the shocked city council met and began forming a plan to take to the citizens. A mass meeting was held at noon and it was decreed that Springfield was going to try and make sure that the assassinated president was laid to rest in the city that he had called home. Fortunately for Springfield's wishes, the newly elected Governor Oglesby and Richard Yates, the wartime governor and recent Senator, were both friends of Lincoln and were both in Washington. Through Robert Lincoln, they made an appeal to Mary, who was locked in her bedroom, asking that her late husband's body should be returned home to rest among his friends and neighbors.

MARY LINCOLN WAS BROKEN BY HER HUSBAND'S DEATH AND SPENT THE REST OF HER LIFE IN MOURNING

Mary, however, was torn between the fact that she had quarreled with just about all her old friends and her family in Springfield and never wanted to set foot there again, and the sincere desire to choose a burial place that would have been what her husband wanted.

On April 17, she insisted that Chicago was her first choice and her second was the crypt under capitol building. Her husband had promised her that after he left the Presidency, they would make a tour of Europe and then retire in Chicago and so she favored a quiet burial place near Lake Michigan. It appealed to her that he would be buried close to the resting place of his old adversary, Stephen Douglas. Of course, Mary had not been to Chicago since Douglas' death and did not know that his grave was desolate and after four years, had no monument to mark it.

And then she changed her mind again.

When Mary looked back at her last days with Lincoln, she realized that he had a foreshadowing of his own death. "You will see Europe, but I never shall," he told her. She also remembered her husband's dream to live once more in Springfield. She also recalled his saying, just a few weeks before his death, that he wanted to be buried in "some quiet place." He had once told her, back in 1860, that the new Springfield cemetery, Oak Ridge, was one of the most beautiful spots that he had ever seen. The day of the cemetery's consecration was a grand event in the city and just about everyone in Springfield walked the two miles to Oak Ridge in an informal procession. The new cemetery – made up from woods, hills, and unbroken forest – was a beautiful place. It made the overcrowded graveyard in downtown Springfield look shabby and old. Lincoln spoke of its beauty many times.

Mary agonized and then finally announced that Oak Ridge was the "quiet place" that Lincoln would have wanted and directed that his coffin be placed in the public receiving tomb until a proper site could be chosen for his monument. Her decision was telegraphed to Springfield and days and nights of frantic preparation were made. Mary wanted Lincoln to be buried at Oak Ridge --- but the city of Springfield had other plans.

As it happened, when the body of President Lincoln eventually arrived in Springfield, he actually had two different graves waiting for him. One of the graves was a temporary vault at remote and wooded Oak Ridge, which Springfield officials believed was no place to bury a fallen hero, and the other was a small hill located in the heart of the city. This spot was called Mather's Hill and it had been the site of the magnificent stone house that was owned by Thomas Mather. Builders were employed to work around the clock and convert the house into a tomb, complete with a handsome vault and stone urns on either side of the entrance.

Mary learned of the downtown tomb through "troublemakers" and sent a telegram stating that her husband absolutely was to be buried at Oak Ridge. Springfield officials remembered the Mrs. Lincoln of old and recalled her erratic nerves and fits of temper, so they tried to be very diplomatic with the widow. They telegraphed Edwin Stanton and told him that her wishes would be respected --- but continued the work at the Mather tomb. They simply could not believe that Mary would want her husband buried out in the woods and even if she did, they were sure that they could change her mind when she arrived in Springfield. Regardless of this, they did make the other preparations that she and Robert asked for – namely moving Eddie Lincoln's body to the vault at Oak Ridge. The boy had died many years before and had been buried in the cemetery downtown.

Even after Lincoln arrived in Springfield, the plan made by Springfield officials continued. They had placed Lincoln at Oak Ridge but still had no intention of leaving him there. They were so sure that he would be moved to the Mather Tomb that plans had already started to be made for a huge celebration. Mary once again refused to go along with it. In the summer of 1865, she moved to Chicago and a delegation from Springfield went to plead with her again. She refused to see them and at last, they surrendered to her wishes. A temporary vault was built for Lincoln at Oak Ridge and in seven months, on December 21, he was finally placed inside.

But in April, Stanton simply needed to find out where the body was supposed to go. If Lincoln's corpse was to travel to some distant place, it would be the War Department's and the U.S. Military Railroad's task to get him there. Such a journey would take time to plan and the Washington funeral was just two days away. Stanton did not want to be involved with Mary's dispute with Springfield, he only needed to know where to send the train. The Lincolns finally decided on Illinois. The president would return to Springfield.

Now the Secretary of War could plan the route and devise the timetables. The train could proceed directly to Illinois on the shortest and most direct route, stopping along the way only to replenish water for the steam engine and fuel for the fire. This was the most efficient route, but it was not the most desirable one. Lincoln had set a precedent four years earlier when he had traveled east as the president-elect. Instead of a hurried trip to Washington, he took a circuitous route through several of the major Northern states that had elected him so that he could meet the American people. Lincoln hoped to reassure the country, sustain support for the Union and avoid a civil war.

His train stopped many times. He offered impromptu, unscripted speeches, mingled with the people, accepted tributes and well wishes, and participated in public ceremonies. Lincoln presented himself to the people as a simple man who had been elevated temporarily to higher office. The inaugural train came to symbolize a living bond between Lincoln and the American people.

Now the beloved president was dead. In their grief, Americans had not forgotten the inaugural train of 1861. The nation now cried out to see the fallen president. Never had any nation so mourned a fallen leader. Lincoln's friends and admirers were heartbroken and even his numerous critics, who had mocked him in life, had ridiculed him as a baboon, and had damned him as an ignorant backwoodsman, now lamented his death and grieved for the country. It was the first time in the history of America that a president had been felled by an assassin's bullet and this was a tragic event in every corner of the Union.

Telegrams began to pour into the War Department from the cities and towns that had wished him goodwill on his journey four years before. Now they begged Stanton to send Lincoln back to them. Once the news spread that the president would make the long westward journey home to Illinois, a groundswell of public opinion clamored for his inaugural trip to be re-created in reverse. The assassination of the president was a national tragedy and yet the American people could not come from all over the country to see Lincoln's body and attend his funeral – so why couldn't Abraham Lincoln come to them?

It was possible to do what they wanted. It would require a special train fitted out properly to transport the body, a military escort to guard Lincoln's corpse around the clock to make sure that the remains were treated with utmost dignity, coordination between the military railroad and the major commercial lines, cooperation between the War Department and state and local governments, and the resources and will to do it. Stanton believed it could be done. There was only one obstacle – the president's grieving, tightly-wound, and unpredictable widow. The plan would be impossible without her explicit consent.

Stanton carefully broached the subject with the First Lady. He outlined the plan, asking her to try and assuage the people's profound sadness by allowing the president's body to take an extended route that would take him through Maryland, Pennsylvania, New Jersey, New York State, then turning west through Ohio, Indiana, Illinois, Chicago, and across the prairie to Springfield. The route would take many days to travel, longer than a quick run to Illinois. The exact duration of the extended trip would depend on the number of times the train stopped for water, fuel, and public ceremonies along the way. Stanton promised that if she agreed, he and his aides would handle all the details.

There was one more thing. The people wanted to see their president, not just his closed coffin. They wanted to look on his face, which meant an open casket. Mary had consented to this at the Washington ceremonies, but an open casket all the way to Springfield, a trip of more than 1,600 miles? In warm weather, without refrigeration, it would test the limits of the embalmer's art. Mary thought the idea seemed morbid and ghoulish, but a grand, national funeral pageant that affirmed her husband's greatness appealed to her. She consented to the trip.

Plans for the epic journey – unlike anything American had seen before – began immediately.

Lincoln's funeral services were planned for Wednesday, April 19, but the president's adoring public was allowed to view the body the day before. Many waited outside all night to make sure that they were in line when the gates opened. Upstairs, Mary Lincoln and Tad remained in seclusion in her room. Tad would have liked to see the people who came to honor his father. He would, perhaps, have found more comfort in the consoling company of strangers than in the dark, secluded bedchamber of his unstable mother, but Mary refused to allow him to leave her side.

The doors of the White House were opened on Tuesday morning and people crushed inside, inching past the body, weeping and speaking to the President, whose head lay on a white pillow with a faint smile frozen on his pale and distorted face. By the end of the day, an estimated 25,000 people had crowded past the mahogany coffin.

While the public viewing was taking place, George Harrington was becoming overwhelmed by the last-minute deluge of requests for funeral tickets, press passes to the White House, and permission to march in the procession. For every request that Harrington took care of, two more came in the door.

As final visitors filed past the coffin, carpenters anxiously loitered nearby, anxious to get started on their work. They impatiently watched the public file past, waiting for the last one to leave so that the doors could be closed and locked behind them. If the public had its way, the viewing would have continued through the night. Thousands of people were turned away so that crews could begin preparing the East Room for the funeral. Disappointed mourners would have one more chance to view the remains, after they were transferred to the capitol.

Harrington had been faced with a seating dilemma for the funeral. There was no way to fit enough chairs into the room for everyone that had to attend – so he would not seat the guests in chairs at all. He had calculated that, allowing for the space required for the catafalque and the aisles, it was impossible to squeeze 600 chairs into the room. He decided that only a few of the most important guests, including the Lincoln family, would have chairs.

EAST.

Admit the Bearer to the

EXECUTIVE MANSION,

On **WEDNESDAY,** *the*

19th of April, 1865.

A TICKET FOR ADMITTANCE TO THE LINCOLN
FUNERAL IN THE EAST WING OF THE WHITE
HOUSE. THE BLACK BORDER BECAME A
TRADITIONAL LOOK FOR MOURNING CARDS
AND CORRESPONDENCE

But if he built risers, or bleachers, for the rest, he could pack slightly more than 600 people into the East Room, the minimum number of important guests he needed to seat. The White House thrummed with activity after the viewing as men carried stacks of lumber into the East Room, where carpenters sawed, hammered, and nailed them into bleachers.

On Wednesday, Lincoln's body rested in the East Room, which was now hushed and dim and draped in hundreds of yards of black crepe. Upstairs, Mary was locked in her room, too deranged from grief and hysterical weeping to attend the services. Tad tried to console her. Though stricken himself, Tad would throw his arms about his mother's neck and plead with her, "Don't cry so, Momma! Don't cry, or you will make me cry, too! You will break my heart!" But it was no use, Mary was simply too crazed to be able to pull herself together.

Services began around 11:00 a.m. To thwart gate-crashers, funeral guests were not allowed direct entry into the Executive Mansion. Instead, guards directed the bearers of the 600 coveted tickets, printed on heavy card stock, next door, to the Treasury Department. From there, they crossed a narrow, elevated wooden footbridge, built just for the occasion, which led into the White House. As guests entered the building, none of them knew what to expect. The East Room overwhelmed them with its decorations, flowers, and the catafalque. It was an unprecedented scene. Two presidents had died in office, William Henry Harrison in 1841 and Zachary Taylor in 1850, but their funerals were not as grand or elaborate as this. No president had been so honored in death, not even George Washington, who, after modest services, rested in a simple tomb in Virginia.

The scene lives on today only in the written accounts of those who were there and a few artist's sketches and newspaper illustrations. No one took a photograph, before or during the funeral. It could have been done. Alexander Gardner had photographed more complex scenes, including the second inaugural, where he took close-ups of the East Front platform and one of his operators had managed to take a long view of the Capitol dome while Lincoln was reading his address. Edwin Stanton had failed to invite Gardner, or his rival Matthew Brady, to preserve the history of Lincoln's funeral.

The guests crowded into the East Room. Robert Lincoln, his face ashen and grave, was wearing his military uniform and he stood at the foot of the coffin. He tightly held the hand of his little brother and Tad trembled, his face swollen with tears. General Ulysses S. Grant, a black mourning band on one arm, sat alone at the other end, staring at a cross of lilies. He began to cry, unable to believe what had happened. He would always maintain that this was the saddest day of his life. By now, nearly all of Washington was there, including President Andrew Johnson and his Cabinet, Charles Sumner and his congressional colleagues, numerous military officials, Lincoln's personal cavalry escort, his secretaries and bodyguards, and mayors and government delegates from across the country.

Four different ministers spoke and prayed for Lincoln and after that, 12 reserve corps sergeants carried his casket out to the funeral car. As they stepped out into the bright, sunlit day, church bells all over the city began to toll. From the forts that still surrounded the city, cannons began to boom. Throngs of people lined Pennsylvania Avenue and thousands more peered from windows and roofs along the parade route. Many of these people had been there for hours, waiting for Lincoln's casket to appear. Federal troops moved into formation to accompany the hearse, which now waited outside the White House. The coffin was placed on a high platform, surrounded by glass and elevated so that everyone could see. Soon, the hearse moved forward, pulled by six white horses, all festooned with black cloth and decoration. The procession moved in a slow, measured cadence, a detachment of African-American troops in the lead. The hearse was followed by a riderless horse, befitting a fallen general, and all walked to the steady muffled beat of drums. The lines swelled with wounded soldiers, who left their hospital beds and marched along, ignoring their pain as they hobbled after their slain leader. There was a procession of black citizens, walking in lines that stretched from curb to curb, holding hands as they walked along.

Lincoln's body was carried to the Capitol building and placed in the rotunda. An honor guard took up position around it and remained in place until the next morning. Shortly after the sun appeared, wounded soldiers were allowed to file past the casket and pay their final respects. After this, the viewing was opened to the public once more. The crowds were so large that the soldiers outside had to remove wooden barricades around the building so that no one would be injured. It was said that more than 3,000 people per hour filed past the coffin before the doors were finally closed at midnight.

Noah Brooks, a Washington correspondent for a California newspaper and frequent visitor at the White House, described the scene: "Directly beneath me lay the casket in which the dead President lay at full length, far, far below; and like black atoms moving over a sheet of gray paper, the slow-moving mourners, seen from a perpendicular above

CROWDS LINED THE STREETS IN WASHINGTON, D.C. TO ACCOMPANY LINCOLN'S BODY TO THE CAPITOL BUILDING

them, crept silently in two dark lines across the pavement of the rotunda, forming an ellipse around the coffin and joining as they advanced toward the eastern portal and disappeared."

While Lincoln lay in state in the Capitol rotunda, Stanton received a telegram from Governor Andrew Curtin of Pennsylvania, asking if Mary Lincoln would accompany her husband's remains on their journey. He wanted to offer his home to her while the train was passing through his state.

But Governor Curtin did not know Mary Lincoln's condition. Overwrought, she still had not left her room, or viewed the President's remains and did not attend the funeral. She had refused almost all visitors, even close friends of the president from Illinois and high officials in her husband's administration. She had already started her first descent into instability, a journey she would make without the President to save her from drifting away.

Stanton promised to relay the governor's kindness to the first lady, but he suspected it would be met with silence and indifference. Mary did not accompany the President on the train. He would make the journey home without her.

On Friday, April 21, one week after the assassination, Edwin Stanton, Ulysses S. Grant, Gideon Welles, Attorney General James Speed, Postmaster General William Dennison, several senators, members of a delegation from Illinois, and various army officers arrived at the Capitol at 6:00 a.m. to escort

THE LINCOLN FUNERAL TRAIN

Lincoln's coffin to the funeral train. Soldiers removed the coffin from the catafalque in the rotunda and carried it down the stairs of the East Front. Four companies of the Twelfth Veteran Reserve Corps stood by to escort the hearse to the train. This was not meant to be a grand procession. There were no drums, no band, and no cavalcade of thousands of marchers. It was a short trip from the Capitol to the Baltimore & Ohio Railroad station, just a few blocks away, but this did not deter the crowds. Several thousand onlookers lined the route and crowded the station's entrance. Although this last, short journey in the capital was not part of the official public funeral events, Stanton supervised it himself to be sure that the final movement of Lincoln's body in the nation's capital was conducted with simplicity, dignity, and honor.

Earlier that morning, another hearse had arrived at the station. It had come from Oak Hill Cemetery in Georgetown and carried the body of Willie Lincoln, the president's son, who had died a few years before. When the soldiers carried Abraham Lincoln aboard the private railroad car at 7:30, Willie was already there, waiting for him. Lincoln had planned to collect the boy himself and take his coffin home when his term in office ended, but now two coffins shared the presidential car.

The railroad car that would transport Lincoln's body across the country was never meant to be a funeral car. Constructed over a period of two years at the U.S. Military Railroad car shops in Alexandria, Virginia, the car was built to be a luxurious vehicle intended for the living president's use. However, even though it was completed in February prior to Lincoln's second inauguration in 1865, he never rode in it or even saw it. The elegant interior, finished with walnut and oak, and upholstered with crimson silk, contained three rooms – a stateroom, a drawing room, and a parlor or dining room. A

THE SPECIAL TRAIN CAR THAT WAS REDESIGNED TO CARRY THE
BODIES OF PRESIDENT LINCOLN AND HIS SON ACROSS THE COUNTRY

corridor ran the length of the car and offered access to each room. The exterior was painted a dark brown, hand-rubbed to a high sheen, and on both sides of the car hung identical oval paintings of an eagle and the coat of arms of the United States. As soon as Stanton knew that Lincoln's body would be carried home to Illinois by railroad, he authorized the military to modify the car, decorate it with symbols of mourning, and build two catafalques so that it could accommodate the coffins of the president and his son.

Before the train could leave the station, members of the honor guard took their places beside Lincoln's coffin. Under protocols established by Stanton and General Edward Townsend, the president was never to be left alone. Townsend later recalled, "There was never a moment throughout the whole journey when at least two of this guard were not by the side of the coffin."

ROBERT LINCOLN
IN 1865

The hearse and the horses that had carried Lincoln's body to the train were not boarded. Instead, in every city where the train was stopping for funeral services, local officials were required to provide a suitable hearse to transport the coffin from the train to the site of the ceremonies.

At 7:50, Robert Lincoln boarded the train, but he planned to leave it after a short while and return to Washington and wrap up his father's affairs. Mary Lincoln did not come to the station to see her husband off – nor did she permit Tad to go. He should have been allowed to come to the station and then ridden with his father and brother to Illinois. After Willie's death, Tad and his father had been inseparable. Sometimes, Tad would fall asleep in the president's office and Lincoln would carry the boy over his shoulder and take him to bed. Tad loved to go on trips with the President and relished their recent visit to Richmond after it had fallen to Union troops. He loved to see the soldiers and he enjoyed wearing a sort-of junior-sized army officer's uniform, complete with a short sword, that his father had given him. Tad would have marveled at the sights of the 1,600-mile journey to Illinois and he would have been proud of, and taken comfort in, the tributes paid to Lincoln. But it was not meant to be.

A pilot engine departed the station ten minutes ahead of the funeral train to inspect the tracks ahead and then, with five minutes to spare, Lincoln's secretaries, John Nicolay and John Hay, arrived from the White House and boarded the train to be sure that all was in order. In all, about 150 men were on the train that morning, including 29 men from the Veteran Reserve Corps who would serve as the guard of honor. There were also a number of military officers, senators, congressmen, delegates from Illinois, four governors, seven newspaper reporters, and David Davis, an old friend of Lincoln's and a justice on the U.S. Supreme Court.

With so many dignitaries arriving at the station, two of the train's most important passengers went unnoticed. In the days to come, the success of the funeral train would depend on their work. To make sure that all ran smoothly, they had to have unfettered access to the president's corpse at any time day or night. Those two men were embalmer Dr. Charles Brown and undertaker Frank Sands. For the next 13 days, they had to try and control the decomposing flesh of Abraham Lincoln.

The train left the station in Washington at exactly 8:00 a.m. Over the course of the next two weeks, the train steamed north and then westward, passing through the greatest crowds ever assembled in America at that time. Reporters followed its passage, telegraphing details to their newspapers back home of the strange, circus-like atmosphere surrounding the funeral train. It is believed that seven million northerners looked upon Lincoln's hearse or coffin and that at least one million actually looked upon his silent face. Ninety different funeral songs were composed in his honor while thousands (or even millions) cried, fainted, took to their beds, and even committed suicide in the frenzy of Lincoln's passing.

Lincoln's train would first stop in Baltimore and in the days ahead, it was scheduled to stop many times for official honors, processions, ceremonies, and viewings, but, for the most part, those plans were merely words and timetables printed on paper. The official documents said nothing about the things to come – the spontaneous bonfires, torches, floral arches, hand-painted signs, banners, and masses of people who haunted the tracks at all hours of the day and night. No official in Washington had ordered these strange public manifestations. Edwin Stanton never expected the train to literally take on a life of its own and to become a venerated symbol in its own right.

The progress of the train was moved along not just on fire and water, but on human passion, which animated it and moved it down the tracks. At each stop, it took on the tone and temper of the town and its people. The train was almost like a battery, soaking up the energy of the place. The more time that it spent on the road, and the greater distance it traveled, the more it absorbed the emotions of the nation's pride and grief. It became more than the funeral train of just one man and evolved into a symbol of American sorrow – about the death of a president and the cost of the great Civil War. It came to represent a mournful homecoming for all the lost men. In the hearts of the grief-stricken American people, an army of the dead -- and not just its commander in chief – came home aboard that train.

In every city where the train stopped – or even just passed through – the people knew it was coming and had read newspaper accounts of the events that had occurred in other cities that preceded it up the line. This created a fever pitch of excitement and created a desire to outdo the honors already offered in other cities.

This would create an American "carnival of death" like nothing the country had ever seen before.

The train arrived first in Baltimore, where a hard rain had started to fall, four hours after leaving Washington. Baltimore was a strange but necessary destination. Maryland had remained in the Union during the war, but it was anti-Lincoln and pro-Confederate. Four years earlier, when president-elect Lincoln passed through the city, he had to do so secretly in order to avoid being killed. The threats from a Baltimore conspiracy, uncovered by Pinkerton agents, were real. A gang of dozens of men had sworn to kill Lincoln. Disloyal, rioting mobs attacked and killed Union soldiers in the street. Lincoln arrived in the city in the middle of the night and had to change trains, which involved uncoupling his car from one train, using horses to pull it one mile along tracks to another station, and then coupling it to a second train. This was the moment of greatest danger, but his enemies did not know that he had passed through Baltimore until after he was gone and had arrived safely in Washington.

Lincoln's escape in Baltimore led to public ridicule and false charges that he had adopted a disguise or that he was a coward who abandoned his wife and children to pass through the city on another train. Cartoonists caricatured Lincoln sneaking through the city in a plaid Scotch cap and even kilts. Later, he regretted slipping into Washington, believing that it was not an auspicious way to begin his presidency.

Baltimore was the home of John Wilkes Booth and he had recruited some of his conspirators there. This alone made it seem to some that it was wrong to stop Lincoln's train in Baltimore. Who in the city would mourn the president when they had wished him ill and might be reveling in his assassination?

Lincoln's men feared the worst, but they could not have been more wrong. Lincoln was mourning in Baltimore. As the train arrived, guns boomed, and church and firehouse bells tolled. The schedule only allowed Lincoln to remain in the city for four hours, so thousands jammed the train tracks, hoping for a glimpse of the President's coffin. The casket was removed from the train and the pallbearers had to elbow their way through streets jammed with people, many of whom were selling funeral crepe and photographs of Lincoln. The coffin was placed in what Baltimore newspapers called "the most beautiful hearse ever constructed," made from genuine rosewood, gilded and fitted with a back and two sides of French plate glass. The procession of military and civic representatives was so large that it took three hours to get to the Merchant's Exchange, where the coffin was opened for viewing. The coffin was displayed next to flowers -- heaps of flowers, a mountain of striking and fragrant fresh-cut flowers -- which would set the standard for the journey. Soon, the lilac, above all other flowers, would come to represent the death carnival for Lincoln's corpse. It went on to become the "death flower" for generations of American funerals.

In Baltimore, there were no official ceremonies, sermons or speeches; there was no time for anything. Instead, as soon as Lincoln's coffin was in position, and after military officers and dignitaries saw him first, they threw open the doors and allowed the public mourners inside. Over the next four hours, it was believed that nearly 10,000 people looked on Lincoln but thousands more were turned away, disappointed that the funeral train had to be on its way. There was no argument and no one to intercede for those turned back or for the long lines of schoolchildren who stood patiently in the rain for a last look at the president.

Those few hours changed the way that officials looked at Baltimore. It was a city in grief. Lincoln's enemies could have masqueraded as mourners and come to gloat over his murder, but the crowd would have torn them to pieces.

While in Baltimore, General Townsend established two rules that became the standard for every stop during the 13-day journey to come. No bearers, except the veteran guard, were allowed to handle the president's coffin. Whenever Lincoln's body needed to be removed from the train, loaded or unloaded from a hearse, or placed upon or removed from a ceremonial platform or catafalque, his personal military guard would handle the coffin.

Each city would furnish a local honor guard to accompany the hearse and to keep order while the public viewed the body, but these men did not lay hands upon the coffin. Townsend also forbade mourners from getting too close to the coffin, touching the president's body, kissing him, or placing anything, including flowers, relics or other tokens, in the coffin. Any person who violated these standards would be seized at once and removed.

But nothing untoward occurred in Baltimore. The viewing ended at 2:30 p.m. and Lincoln's bearers closed the coffin and carried it back to the hearse. The orderly scene in Baltimore was a good omen for the long journey ahead.

As the train passed through Pennsylvania, people began to line the tracks and watch it pass. Little towns were filled with people waiting to honor of the president and local bands played funeral dirges as the train went by. The old and sick were carried to the stations to see the train pass by and babies were held up high to get a glimpse of it.

Only at the station in York did the train make a stop. The women of the city made an urgent request to lay a wreath of flowers on Lincoln's casket. General Townsend could not allow dozens of emotional mourners to wander around inside the train and hover around the coffin. He offered a compromise: He would permit a delegation of six women to come aboard and bring the wreath. While a band played a dirge and bells tolled, they approached the funeral car with great ceremony, stepped inside, and laid their large wreath consisting of a circle of roses and, at the center, alternating parallel lines of red and white flowers. The women wept bitterly as they left the train. Soon, at the next stop, their wonderful flowers would be moved aside in favor of new ones.

In Harrisburg, thousands waited all night in the rain for a glimpse of Lincoln the following morning. Unfortunately, violent thunderstorms had descended on the city but despite the rain, the massive crowds still came. Jagged streaks of lightning crossed the sky as church bells rang and cannons thundered. The crowds followed the hearse and its military escort to the House of Representatives at the State Capitol, where a black-draped catafalque was waiting. The procession took so long that the casket was not opened for viewing until late that evening. Thousands passed in a double line until the next morning when the funeral train once again prepared to leave.

Before the casket was closed, though, the undertaker was forced to re-chalk Lincoln's face to hide the growing discoloration. Lincoln had become America's first public embalming and it would be some time before the methods of preservation would be perfected. In addition, the body also had to be dusted. The coffin had been opened and closed so many times that the President's face and beard had started to attract dust particles from the air.

It was still raining the next morning, but more than 40,000 people still jammed the streets to watch the procession as the casket was returned to the funeral train. At a few minutes after eleven, the train steamed out of Harrisburg toward

THE LINCOLN FUNERAL TRAIN IN
HARRISBURG, PENNSYLVANIA

Philadelphia, passing through Middletown, Elizabethtown, Mount Joy, Landisville, and Dillersville. As it steamed through the countryside and moved slowly through Lancaster, the men on board saw a huge sign that had been erected by the crowd. It read, "Abraham Lincoln, the Illustrious Martyr of Liberty, The Nation Mourns His Loss. Though Dead, He Still Lives". While in the city, 20,000 people, including Congressman Thaddeus Stevens and Lincoln's predecessor, former president James Buchanan, paid tribute. The train pushed north through Penningtonville, Parkesburg, Coatesville, Gallagherville, Downington, Oakland, and West Chester. At every depot, and along the railroad tracks between them, people gathered to watch the train pass by.

In Philadelphia, more than 500,000 people were already waiting at Independence Hall when the train arrived on Saturday, April 22. It was in Philadelphia that a new aspect was added to the viewing of Lincoln --- violence. For the first time, people were actually hurt in the frantic crush to get into Independence Hall and see the president's body. The trip into the city had been orderly. Thousands had come out beside the tracks to stand in silence, or kneel, while the train passed. All the shops had closed, and farms stood silent and deserted in Lincoln's honor. For miles before the Philadelphia station, there were no gaps in the crowd, just solid lines. The train arrived at Broad Street station in late afternoon, more than two hours ahead of schedule, but then the careful organization of the city officials began to go to pieces.

It took nearly two hours to get the procession under way and afterward, the city would claim that it offered the most gigantic display of all. Eleven military divisions marched to the inevitable booming of cannons, tolling of bells, firing of guns, roll of muffled drums, and eerie funeral dirges. At the square, when the Old State House was passed, a large transparency was uncovered --- a picture of Lincoln with a background of a huge coffin, spectacularly lighted by gas jets that formed letters that spelled out "He Still Lives." The coffin was carried to the East Wing of Independence Hall, where the Declaration of Independence had been signed. The hall was filled with flowers, emitting what the newspapers called a "delicious perfume." Those accounts failed to describe the practical purpose of the sweet-smelling flowers, but they were there for a reason. Lincoln had been dead for a week and the embalmers were fighting against a ticking clock. They had slowed but they could not stop the decaying flesh – and fragrant flowers masked the odor.

LINCOLN'S FUNERAL PROCESSION MAKING ITS WAY THROUGH THE STREETS OF PHILADELPHIA. THE MASSIVE NUMBERS OF PEOPLE LED TO THE FIRST CROWD CONTROL ISSUES OF THE JOURNEY

The viewing that night was by invitation only and handpicked people had been given cards by the mayor. As these special guests departed during the early morning hours, they passed long lines of the general public, which were already forming to be admitted hours later. The exhausted throngs waited all night and by Sunday morning, the entire city was on edge. When pickpockets began to terrorize a portion of the line, it surged into a mob, pressing against the guide ropes. Then the ropes were cut --- by "villains" the newspapers later said --- and bedlam broke out. People who had been almost to the doors were sent back by the police to the end of the nearly three-mile-long double lines to wait for another six or seven hours. The crowd surged out of control and the police fought to keep order. Bonnets were pulled from women's heads and their hair turned loose, dresses were torn away and ripped, all to a chorus of women's screams. As many of the young women fainted, they had to be extricated from the lines and passed over the people's heads. One woman had her arm broken and word got out that two little boys were dead but were finally revived. The closer people got to Lincoln, the more impassioned they became. The police refused to let people stop for even a second to view the body, insisting that they keep moving at all times. Even with these precautions, a number of women tried to climb over the wooden barricade to touch the president or to kiss his face.

It was all finally over early on Monday morning and the casket was returned to the train. It steamed on toward New York, where ceremonies had begun the day before. The entire city, it seemed, had been draped in black and in the hours before the train's arrival, the streets of the city became impassable. The police and military fought to keep them open, but it was no use.

Thousands of people line the tracks on the journey to New York City. In the early morning darkness of Monday, April 24, the train stopped in Trenton, New Jersey for about half an hour. Trenton was wounded because it was the only state capital on the route where Lincoln was not taken from the train and funeral services held. The people stood and stared as the train pulled into the station and one observer noted that "it did not occur to the male part of the throng that a general lifting of the hat would have been a silent but becoming mark of respect to the dead." Far different, he noted, was the scene at Newark, where every man removed his hat and feelings were so deep that women also removed their bonnets out of respect.

The train arrived in Jersey City at a few hours later. Crowds had been gathering there since early morning. Only ladies and their escorts were allowed into the gallery at the depot, where the large clock had been stopped at the precise moment of Lincoln's death. When the train arrived, a German singing group thundered forth with a funeral dirge. New York had been building a magnificent hearse, but it would have been risky to ferry it across the Hudson, so the coffin was sensibly transferred to a small hearse and carried across the river. A second ferry took the train's funeral car, with Willie's casket in it, and a third took the big car that carried the official escort that journeyed through to Springfield. In New York, a new engine, a new pilot engine and seven cars would be supplied by the Hudson River Railroad.

New York would be the biggest test of the funeral procession since it had left Washington. New York had the biggest population, the greatest crowds, and the most volatile citizens in the north. New Yorkers had proven that they loved a good riot, most notably during the recent Civil War draft riots. Given the strong Copperhead presence, still loyal to the Confederacy, in the city many believed that Manhattan cried false tears for the fallen president. But mourning Unionists outnumbered Lincoln's enemies on the streets of the city in April 1865.

Lincoln's body was taken to City Hall and more than 600,000 spectators accompanied it while more than 150,000 stood in line for a glimpse

THE LINCOLN FUNERAL ARRIVED IN NEW YORK. AS IT PASSED THROUGH THE STREETS, IT WAS WATCHED BY A YOUNG BOY NAMED THEODORE ROOSEVELT

of the president. The honor guard had a full-time job on their hands trying to keep people from touching Lincoln and trying to keep women from kissing his face and hands. Although no rioting broke out, as it did in Philadelphia, the police had their hands full with surging crowds, most of whom were beaten back with clubs, and with pickpockets, who freely roamed the area, stealing at will. Only one thing happened to break the boredom of the wait – someone threw a lighted cigar at the black festoon just under a huge banner proclaiming "The Nation Mourns." It burst into flames, but a brave officer climbed up and tore down the mass of burning material and others stamped out the fire on the stone steps.

During the viewing at City Hall, some people tried to do more than touch Lincoln. Some of them wanted to place mementoes in the coffin. Captain Parker Snow, a commander of polar expeditions, presented some relics to the honor guard from Sir John Franklin's ill-fated expedition. They consisted of a tattered leaf from a prayer book, on which the first legible word was "martyr," a piece of fringe, and some portions of a uniform. These relics were found in a boat lying under the head of a human skeleton. What possible connection did these relics have to Abraham Lincoln? They did not belong in the coffin and the officials refused to place them there. Such practices, if tolerated, would have turned Lincoln's coffin into a traveling cabinet of curiosities that would have weighed more than the president's corpse.

That night, after the doors were closed, the embalmer brushed a heavy coating of dust from Lincoln's face, beard and clothing. He also rearranged his facial features, which had become twisted from exposure.

The coffin was closed at 11:00 a.m. on Tuesday. The final procession back to the train became New York's moment of glory. Peter Relyea, the official undertaker for the city of New York, had been issued a special permit to accompany Lincoln's body to Springfield. For three days, he had been building an elaborate funeral car before marveling crowds on the city streets. He had been living and sleeping in the car, trying to get it finished before the procession. Now, just in the nick of time, he led the hearse into the park enclosure in front of City Hall. The hearse, pulled by 16 gray horses, was said to have nearly paralyzed all who saw it. Its platform was huge --- 14-feet-long and almost

NEW YORK'S CITY HALL, WHERE LINCOLN'S BODY WAS DISPLAYED TO HUNDREDS OF THOUSANDS OF MOURNERS

seven-feet-wide --- and on the roof of the canopy was a gold and white Temple of Liberty with a half-masted flag on its crown. Inside of the canopy was white fluted satin that matched the inside trimmings of the coffin and hanging down from it, so that it would hang directly above the casket, was a glittering gilt eagle with its wings spread. It was an amazing work of art and would remain the most elaborate creation on the funeral route.

An hour later, Lincoln was placed aboard the Relyea creation and the procession began to move. Led by a squad of mounted police, who made sure the route was clear, it started off with 100 dragoons with black and white plumes and red, yellow, and blue facings on their uniforms. They were followed by military officers and their staffs and then the magnificent hearse. Behind that were more than 1,100 soldiers, Irishmen in bright green with black rosettes in their lapels, Zouaves with baggy red trousers and black ribbons on their chests, military and government representatives from foreign countries, and eight divisions of civilians. One of them was made up from the trades --- cigar-makers, waiters, cooks clerks, carpenters, and others --- and there were divisions of medical men, lawyers, members of the press, the Century Club, the Union League, Freemasons, Civic Societies, and finally, nearly 300 African-Americans.

The procession took nearly four hours to pass each point on its route. The streets were jammed with spectators and it was said that window seats could be rented for $50 from those who lived in the apartment buildings along the path. At Chamber Street, a shaggy St. Bernard dog trotted out from the crowd and walked alongside the hearse for a block or so. A whisper spread that the dog and his master had recently paid a visit to Lincoln at the White House and the President had kindly patted the dog on the head. A spurious legend -- or could the dog have known who he trotted next to in the amazing hearse?

All through the afternoon, church bells and fire bells tolled, bands wailed, guns boomed, and people wept for the great and fallen leader. Eventually, the train moved on to Albany, leaving thousands disappointed. Many who did not get a chance to see the president boarded trains and planned to try again in Chicago or in Springfield. The Springfield delegates, who were accompanying the train, realized in horror just how many people could be descending on the small city. One of the delegates hurried to Springfield to prepare for the worst.

After leaving the city, the train steamed across the countryside toward Albany. It passed scores of small towns along the way, where people gathered to watch it pass. Each of the towns had gone to enormous trouble to build a display, an arch, or to inscribe a huge motto for the train as it passed. At towns where there was no station, there was often a minister and his parishioners, kneeling or singing a hymn. At Yonkers, the people lined up and the men all raised their hats. At Tarryton, a gathering of young women appeared, all dressed in white, save for black sashes, creating an effect both chaste and mournful. At Peekskill, the train stopped as a band played a dirge and guns fired. At Poughkeepsie, the train made another stop. The hilltop there was black with people, guns were fired, and church bells and fire bells clanged with a fury. The train also stopped at Garrison's Landing, opposite the U.S. Military Academy at West Point. The corps of cadets assembled to honor their fallen commander in chief. They passed through the funeral car and saluted. It was now growing dark and as the train continued on toward Albany, torches and bonfires illuminated the tracks.

At Hudson, thousands of people gathered to see the train. General Townsend described the scenes as "one of the most weird ever witnessed." Along the Hudson River, people assembled with torches, illuminating the bizarre tableau they had created. Beneath an arch hung with black and white drapery and evergreen wreaths was a scene that represented a coffin resting on a dais. A female figure in white, mourning over the coffin, stood on one side while a soldier and a sailor stood at the other end. While a band of young women dressed in white sang a dirge, two others entered the funeral car, placed flowers on the president's coffin, knelt for a moment of silence, and then quietly withdrew. Townsend noted that the solemnity of the scene was "intensified by the somber lights of the torches, at that dead hour of night."

It was approaching midnight when the train entered Albany. The coffin was carried to the State House and all through the night, the residents of the capital and the neighboring countryside passed by it.

The next day, there was another procession but this time, the 300 people now accompanying the train, except for a portion of the military, went straight to two hotels where the city had arranged them to be lodged. They were worn out both physically and emotionally from the never-ending mourning ceremony and there were still six more funerals ahead of them. Albany had been there first chance to really rest on the route so far.

At noon on Wednesday, April 26, Albany's grand parade got under way with a specially built catafalque, marchers, bands, tolling bells, and huge crowds of people. It was a grand event but was not the type of "circus" that Albany crowds had been expecting. Van Amburgh's traveling menagerie was in town and had been planning to offer a parade and celebratory show to entertain the crowds when the assassination occurred. The circus owner, Van Amburgh, quickly proclaimed, "There will be no exhibition given until the president's remains have left the city and the grand parade scheduled for this morning will be postponed until tomorrow." Albany was probably the only one of the funeral cities that had the chance to pick up its spirits so rapidly after being drenched in sorrow.

It was while the funeral train was in Albany that a disquieting incident that had occurred in New York reached the ears of Edwin Stanton. As was the usual, General Townsend had telegraphed Stanton when leaving the city to let him know that all was well. But his telegram did not mention what had taken place while Lincoln's remains were on view at City Hall. When Stanton learned of the incident by reading newspapers later that night, he became enraged and dispatched an angry telegram that threatened to ruin the reputation and military career of the man he had personally chosen to command the funeral train.

Stanton wrote: "I see by the New York papers this evening that a photograph of the corpse of President Lincoln was allowed taken yesterday at New York. I cannot sufficiently express my surprise and disapproval of such an act while the body was in your charge. You will report what officers of the funeral escort were or ought to have been on duty at the time this was done, and immediately relieve them and order them to Washington. You will also direct the provost-marshal to go to the photographer, seize and destroy the plates and any pictures and engravings that may have been made, and consider yourself responsible if the offense is repeated." Stanton ordered

THE CONTROVERSIAL POSTMORTEM PHOTOGRAPH OF PRESIDENT
LINCOLN THAT GENERAL TOWNSEND ALLOWED TO BE TAKEN IN NEW
YORK. EDWIN STANTON WAS ENRAGED WHEN HE HEARD ABOUT IT

Major Eckert at the War Department to make sure that it was sent and hand-delivered to Townsend that very night.

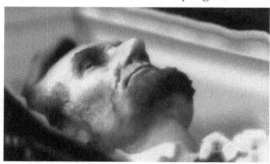

MODERN TECHNIQUES HAVE ALLOWED A
CLOSER VIEW OF THE PRESIDENT'S FACE,
WHICH WAS NOT AVAILABLE TO VIEWERS
OF THE PHOTOGRAPH IN 1865

Stanton had assumed, no doubt, that close-up images had been made of Lincoln's face. That was not an unusual custom in the nineteenth century. It was common for mourners, especially the bereaved parents of deceased infants and children, to commission photographers to preserve for eternity the faces of the loved and lost. Many photographers would pose the children in their arms of their parents, as though sleeping and not dead. But Stanton was likely thinking about the condition of Lincoln's body. By the time he was photographed in New York, he had been dead for nine days. Mortuary science of the era could not preserve his body indefinitely. The undertakers attended to the body aboard the train, but there were limits as to what they could do. Stanton undoubtedly feared that horrific images depicting Lincoln's face in a state of gruesome decay would be distributed to the public.

Stanton's telegram did not reach Townsend until the morning of April 26 and he was stunned by its contents. He knew Stanton well, including his propensity for angry tirades. If Stanton sounded this upset on paper, Townsend could only imagine how furiously he was raging back in Washington. And once Stanton knew the whole story, Townsend feared, the man that Lincoln referred to as his "god of war" would become apoplectic.

It was Townsend himself who had allowed Lincoln's corpse to be photographed. He decided, before others could report the details of what he had done, to confess and accept the consequences. He immediately telegraphed Stanton: "Your dispatch of this date is received. The photograph was taken while I was present, Admiral Davis being the officer immediately in charge, but it would have been my part to stop the proceedings. I regret your disapproval, but it did not strike me as objectionable under the circumstances as it was done. I have telegraphed General Dix your orders about seizing the plates. To whom shall I turn over the special charge given me in order to execute your instructions to relieve the officers responsible, and shall Admiral Davis be relieved? He was not accountable."

When Stanton learned that Townsend had permitted the photograph, he decided not to relieve him of command. The train was on the move, in the middle of a complicated cross-country journey, and no one on the train possessed greater organizational skills than Townsend. He sent him a tempered reply, excusing Admiral Davis from fault and laying the blame with Townsend. He told him that he could not relieve him of command because there was no one to take his place but filled the man with guilt by stating that the taking of photographs had been expressly forbidden by Mrs. Lincoln. Stanton added, "I am apprehensive that her feelings and the feelings of her family will be greatly wounded."

Townsend, offended by the suggestion that he had disobeyed an order from the martyred president's widow, tried to defend himself. He replied, "I was not aware of Mrs. Lincoln's wishes, or the picture would not have been taken with the knowledge of any officers of the escort. It seemed to me the picture would be gratifying, a gratifying view of what thousands saw and thousands could not see."

But Townsend had not admitted to everything. It was bad enough that he had allowed the photographs. It was even worse that he had posed in the pictures while standing next to President Lincoln's body. Stanton might have considered this perceived attempt at personal publicity unforgivable. But Townsend did not see it that way. The remains had been arranged at City Hall at the head of a stairway, where the people could ascend on one side and descend on the other. The body was in an alcove, draped in black, and just at the edge of a rotunda formed of American flags and mourning drapery. The photographer was in a gallery that was 20 feet higher than the body and 40 feet away from it. There was no equipment to make the camera seem closer than it was in those days. It offered a distant view. Townsend stood at one end of the coffin and Admiral Davis stood at the other. No one else was in view. The effect of the picture was taking in the scene as a whole, not offering the features of the corpse.

General Townsend was not the only one worried about the situation. The man who had photographed Lincoln, Thomas Gurney, proprietor of one of Manhattan's most prominent studios, T. Gurney & Son, was also concerned. He had taken unprecedented, newsworthy, and commercially viable photographs. No other American president had been photographed in death and no one – not the famous Mathew Brady nor Alexander Gardner, not any of the photographers along the funeral train route – had succeeded in photographing the president in his coffin.

Gurney hoped to gain publicity by distributing prints of the photograph to the press as newspaper woodcuts and to reproduce the photo for sale to the public. On April 26, Gurney sent an urgent telegram, not to Stanton, but to a man he thought might be more sympathetic, assistant secretary of war, Charles A. Dana. Gurney also reached out to Henry Ward Beecher, the widely-known clergyman, abolitionist, and author, as well as Henry Raymond, the famous editor of the *New York Times*. He asked them to lobby Stanton and prevent the seizure and destruction of the glass-plate negatives. They agreed and Beecher and Raymond both telegraphed the War Department. It earned Gurney a temporary reprieve, of sorts. A telegram from the War Department arrived at Gurney's studio, saving the negatives from destruction for the time being, but only if Gurney surrendered all the glass plates and agreed to abide by Stanton's decision once he determined whether or not to smash them.

Gurney surrendered the glass-plate negatives, plus all the photographs that he had already printed from them. He had no choice. In the aftermath of Lincoln's assassination, emotions in the country were running high. More than 200 people had been shot, stabbed, lynched, or beaten to death for making anti-Lincoln statements or for defending his killer. Stanton had ordered the indiscriminate arrest of more than 100 people, including the owners of Ford's Theater, as suspects in the crime. In Baltimore, a mob stormed into a photography studio based on rumors that the proprietor was selling images of the infamous John Wilkes Booth.

During this turbulent time, Gurney had no legal avenue to pursue. If Gurney had attempted to sue to protect his photographs, no court would have recognized his First Amendment right to protect and publish the images. If he failed to surrender them voluntarily, the War Department would have raided his studio and seized them. He complied. The next day, an army general notified Stanton from New York that the offending images were in government custody.

Stanton's suppression of the photographs did not succeed entirely. He had wanted to prevent Gurney's images from surfacing in any form, but the photographer had already gotten the prints into the hands of a few artists. At least two newspapers printed front-page interpretations of the scene and Currier & Ives published a fine engraving based partly on Gurney's work. But Gurney's negatives were never seen again. Perhaps Edwin Stanton had them brought to his office in Washington and, after viewing them, smashed them into pieces. Perhaps he put them away in some secret place, where, to this day, they languish in some dusty and forgotten War Department file box, never to be seen again.

However, Stanton could not resist preserving one image of Lincoln's corpse for himself. Almost a century after the president's death and burial, a sole surviving photographic print made from one of Gurney's negatives was discovered by a student in an old archive. It was traced back to Stanton's personal files. Perhaps he saved it for history. Or perhaps he never intended for it to be seen and to remain his private memento – a vivid reminder of the spring of 1865.

On Wednesday afternoon, the train left Albany and steamed east through Amsterdam, Fonda, Palatine Bridge, Rome, Green Corners, Verona, Oneida, and Kirksville. Late in the evening, the train made a short stop at Syracuse, where veteran soldiers paid honors, a choir sang hymns, and a little girl handed a small bouquet to a congressman on the train. A note attached to the flowers read: "The last tribute from Mary Virginia Raynor, a little girl of three years of age."

In Rochester, at 3:20 a.m. on Thursday, a collection of military units stood in a line on the north side of the station, and on the south side stood the mayor, 25 members of the common council of Rochester, and former

MASSIVE CROWDS GREETED THE FUNERAL TRAIN IN BUFFALO, BUT THE EVENT WAS A BIT OF A LETDOWN AFTER THE FUNERAL SERVICES THAT HAD ALREADY BEEN HELD IN THE CITY

president Milliard Fillmore, who got on board and rode to the next stop, which was Buffalo.

The city of Buffalo holds an unusual place in the history of the funeral train. It was the only city on the list that was likely disappointed by the arrival of the President's body. A short time earlier, on the day of the Washington funeral, Buffalo's citizens, grieving at the news of the assassination, were not content to simply hold church services. Instead, the people put on their own mock funeral, just as though the coffin and body had been there. They had built a magnificent catafalque, had a huge procession, offered prayers and eulogies and had gone through the motions as if the real thing was taking place. Then when they got the news that their city had been chosen to hold a funeral on the procession route, there was, along with a feeling of pride, a bit of a letdown, as well. Buffalo had exhausted its first frenzied extravagance during the mock ceremony, although citizens assured themselves that having the real thing would be many times better. Somehow, though, when the time came, it wasn't.

They used the same magnificent hearse car with its six white horses, draped in black and the well-attended viewing was held in St. James Hall, with the coffin up-tilted and brilliantly lit. Thousands filed past the coffin, but between the dirges, the silence was oppressive and the "utter decorum" and "remarkable order" were somehow not as much of a tribute as the wild straining to get near the coffin or to touch the President's hand, as had occurred in other cities.

Under a simple canopy of drooping black crepe, the coffin was placed on a dais while the Buffalo St. Cecelia Society, a musical group, sang "Rest, Spirit, Rest." Women from the Unitarian Church placed an anchor of white camellias at the foot of the coffin. For more than 10 hours, thousands of people, including many from Canada who crossed the border for the occasion, viewed the remains.

At some point, while crowds were passing by the coffin, news reached Buffalo by telegraph that electrified General Townsend and the mourners in line: John Wilkes Booth had been killed in Virginia.

The coffin was closed that evening and Lincoln's body was returned to the train. It steamed on through New York and into the darkness of the night. Townsend knew that the train had begun to leave behind waves of emotion that swelled by the hour. He later wrote, "As the president's remains went farther westward, where the people more especially claimed him as their own, the intensity of feeling seemed if possible to grow deeper. The night journey of the 27th and 28th was all through torches, bonfires, mourning drapery, mottoes, and solemn music."

The train pushed on through North Hamburg, Lakeview, Angola, and Silver Creek. Just after midnight, the train passed through Dunkirk on Lake Erie. There, 36 young women, representing the states of the Union, appeared on the railway platform. They were dressed in white, and each wore a broad, black scarf on her shoulder and held an American flag in her right hand. The tableau was so irresistible that when officials in other cities read about it in the newspapers, they copied the idea for their local tributes.

The train later passed through Brocton and then stopped in Westfield, where, during Lincoln's inaugural journey, he visited with Grace Bedell, a little girl who had during the 1860 campaign written him a letter that encouraged him to grow a beard. She told him that it would make him more appealing to women, who would then, Grace promised, make their husbands and brothers vote for him. Lincoln grew the beard and won the election. Now, four years later, a delegation of five women, led by a woman whose husband had been killed the previous year during Grant's futile assault at Cold Harbor, came aboard bearing a wreath of flowers and a cross. Sobbing, they approached Lincoln's closed casket and were allowed to touch it. They "considered it a rare privilege to kiss the coffin." They knelt and each in turn kissed the coffin. Kissing the coffin, with its solid barrier of wood and lead, was a desperately futile gesture but it never failed to move those who watched the action to tears.

The train crossed the Ohio state line and passed through Kingsville, Ashtabula, Geneva, Madison, Perry, Painesville, and Wickcliffe, where Governor John Brough received the funeral party.

General Joseph Hooker, now commanding the Northern Department of Ohio, also boarded the train there. Although Lincoln had once given command of the Army of the Potomac to the boastful general, Hooker failed him several times. After the disaster at Chancellorsville in May 1863, Lincoln fired him, but Hooker never lost his personal affection for the president. When the funeral train crossed the Ohio line into Indiana, Hooker did not disembark. He stayed with Lincoln all the way to Springfield.

THE LINCOLN FUNERAL IN CLEVELAND

Vast crowds stood on the hills outside of Cleveland as the train passed beneath prepared arches that bore sad inscriptions. Of all the funerals held, Cleveland's was the strangest so far. The funeral was both a solemn wake and a theatrical pageant of flowers, with the city showing its appreciation for the president by introducing an Oriental note to the proceedings. In the city park, a huge Chinese pagoda was erected for Lincoln's coffin to be displayed on for what turned out to be more than 100,000 mourners.

Thirty-six cannons fired a national salute to the president. At that moment, noted the reporters who looked out of the window of the car, a bizarre scene was taking place – perhaps the strangest of the journey so far. A woman, identified in the press only as "Miss Fields of Wilson Street," had erected an arch of evergreens near the tracks. As the train passed, Miss Fields, wearing a costume, stood under the arch and struck poses and attitudes of the Goddess of Liberty in mourning.

The train arrived on the outskirts of Cleveland in the early hours of Friday, just one week after leaving Washington. As it moved slowly into the city, officials on board the train saw crowds of people on the hillsides and high up, a young girl draped in a flag under an archway that read "Abraham Lincoln." People had flocked to the city from all over northern Ohio, western Pennsylvania, and eastern Michigan and boatloads of them had arrived by water from Detroit. All the ladies in attendance had been warned to leave the hoops for their skirts at home --- the breakage of such attire by the throng, officials said, would be swift and total. With the thousands in attendance however, standing in the pouring rain, there was not a hint of disorder.

Legions of marchers and mourners descended on the city park, with its Chinese Pagoda, built for the president. The wooden structure was eccentric, to say the

A NEWSPAPER ILLUSTRATION OF THE PAGODA THAT WAS USED FOR THE CLEVELAND FUNERAL

least. It was an amazing confection of wood, canvas, silk, cloth, festoons, rosettes, golden eagles bearing the national shield at each end, and "immense plumes of black crepe." As with all the other venues along the journey, the interior was stuffed with flowers. Evergreens covered the walls, and thick matting carpeted the floor to deaden into silence the sound of all footsteps. Over the roof, stretched between two flagpoles, was a motto from Horace: "Extinctus amabitur idem" (Dead he will be loved all the same).

The embalmer opened the coffin and judged the body ready for viewing. The journey was taking its toll on the corpse. Lincoln's face turned darker by the day and the embalmer tried to conceal this with a flesh application of chalk-white potions.

All through the day and night, people came, thousands upon thousands of them, before the gates to the park were closed at 10:00 p.m. An hour later, the coffin was carried by hearse back to the train.

The rain continued to fall as the train traveled from Cleveland to the Ohio state capital of Columbus. But the foul weather did not keep people from coming to watch the train pass along the route. Bonfires and torches were lit, buildings were draped in mourning, bells tolled, flags flew at half-mast, and the sorrowful inhabitants stood in groups, rain and tears streaming down their faces, as the cortege moved slowly by.

The city of Columbus also offered a funeral of flowers. People had roses in their hands, which they tossed under the wheels of the hearse as it passed and invalid soldiers from the Soldier's Hospital had literally covered the street near the hospital for several hundred yards with lilac blossoms.

THE LINCOLN FUNERAL PROCESSION IN COLUMBUS, OHIO

The Columbus hearse was a somber vehicle, drawn by six white horses, but it did have one aspect to it that would have amused Lincoln himself. On one side of the dais, in silver block letters, was the name "Lincoln." The President tried, whenever possible, to avoid the obvious. When, in the spring of 1864, he had been asked to sign a letter presenting a sword to General Dix, Lincoln signed his name and then was asked to add "President of the United States." His answer, putting down his pen, was, "Well, I don't think I'll say, 'this is a horse'." When the coffin was placed on a dais at the State Capitol building, the platform was noticed to have been also fitted with the same helpful identification. Lincoln would have gotten a chuckle out of this bit of tragic absurdity.

The Columbus procession moved through drapes and flowers and mottos from the city to the sounds of guns firing, bells ringing, and the muffled beat of drums. The hook and ladder car of the fire department carried 42 young ladies on it, all singing hymns. The coffin was placed on the dais, which had no canopy and no flags. However, instead of black velvet, the surface of it was a carpet of moss and tender green leaves, which let off a fragrant aroma as the casket sank into it. The people gathered in the rotunda watched in awe as the undertaker unscrewed the coffin lid, made a slight adjustment to the position of the body and then made a motion that the viewing could begin. People began to stream by and their passing was in complete silence. A carpet had been laid in the hall so that the shuffling of feet and the click of shoe leather would not be heard. For the eighth time, thousands of Americans said goodbye to their fallen president.

In the press accounts of the funeral train, little mention was made of Willie Lincoln. His coffin was never unloaded from the train. He did not ride in the hearse with his father in any of the funeral processions. His closed casket – he had been dead for three years – did not lie next to his father's casket at the public viewings. But in Columbus, Willie was not forgotten. General Townsend was the recipient of the gesture: "While at Columbus, I received a note from a lady, wife of one of the principal citizens, accompanying a little cross made of wild violets. The note said that the writer's little girls had gone to the woods in the early morning and gathered the flowers with which they had wrought the cross. They desired that it might be laid on little Willie's coffin, 'they felt so sorry for him.'"

From Columbus, the train steamed on toward Indiana, crossing the state line in the middle of the night. More scenes appeared along the line while in Ohio. At Woodstock, there were 500 citizens waiting beside the tracks and a contingent of young women was allowed to board the train and lay flowers in the funeral car. At Urbana, more than 3,000 people surrounded a huge, floral cross as the train steamed on toward Indiana. At Richmond, Indiana, the first town across the border, the church bells of the town rang for an hour as the train arrived and over 15,000 people greeted the funeral with pantomimes, scenes, and stage effects that must have looked ghastly and somewhat horrifying to the party looking out from the railroad car windows. One such display featured a beautiful young woman who was illuminated by red, white, and blue lights over a mock coffin, creating one of the most eerie displays on the funeral train's journey.

The train reached Indianapolis near midnight, arriving during a torrential rainstorm. At first, it was hoped that if the rain stopped, the procession could go on during the afternoon. However, the rain continued to fall, increasing in power from minute to minute, until the black decorations on every house hung soggy and the black dye formed dark streaks on the front of stone buildings. Reluctantly, the huge Indianapolis procession had to be canceled and the time devoted to it was set aside for viewing instead. All the way from the train depot to the State House, soldiers were lined up at attention, forming two long lines of blue uniforms and drawn swords. The hearse was pulled by eight white horses, six of which had pulled Lincoln as the president-elect a few years before. They took the coffin into State House square and under a large arch to which portraits of Lincoln, Indiana Governor Oliver Perry Morton, General Grant, General Sherman, and Admiral Farragut had been affixed. On the points of it were busts of George Washington, Daniel Webster, Henry Clay, and Lincoln. The busts were all crowned with laurel wreaths.

The first to view Lincoln were 500 Sunday School scholars and the last were the Colored Masons and hundreds of African-American citizens who each carried a copy of the Emancipation Proclamation. The casket lay under a black velvet canopy, which was sprinkled with golden stars. The mourners all saw a coffin that was heaped with flowered crosses and wreaths.

It had been during this epic cross-country journey that an American tradition was created. Prior to Lincoln's funeral, it was not customary to send flowers to funerals. With the death of a beloved President, many people searched their hearts about the best way to express their sympathy and thousands of them decided upon flowers. Although with the best of intentions, the sheer numbers of flowers sent to Lincoln were greatly overdone, emptying the contents of each city's hothouses. The colors ran heavily to red, white, and blue, which would have pleased a President who stated that he felt emotional each time he looked at the flag. In Springfield, there would be a tremendous red heart, covered with thousands of red roses, that would travel with the coffin all the way to the tomb.

When the viewing was completed, the coffin was escorted back to the train with Governor Morton and most of the population of Indianapolis following behind. The governor had greeted and entertained Lincoln when he was traveling to Washington as the president-elect and he watched his casket leave the state with great sorrow.

AN IMPROMPTU SERVICE WAS HELD AT MICHIGAN CITY BEFORE THE TRAIN CONTINUED ON TO CHICAGO

With Indianapolis behind, the train steamed on toward Illinois. There was a massive funeral planned in Chicago and then, it would go on to Lincoln's home town in Springfield. But due to an unexpected delay, there was to be one more funeral, an impromptu service at the depot in Michigan City, Indiana. The funeral train was supposed to travel straight through and arrive in Chicago during the late morning hours of Monday, May 1. But it was forced to wait for one hour in Michigan City for a committee of more than 100 important Chicagoans who were coming out to escort the train into the city.

The residents of Michigan City made the most of the unexpected stop, especially since the rain of the past few days had cleared to brilliant sunshine. The occupants of the train were greeted by the depot arch of evergreens and roses, decorated with black ribbons and "tasteful" portraits of Lincoln.

The 300 weary mourners that traveled with the funeral were taken off the train for a large breakfast in the station. After that, the rule was broken about not opening the coffin except in the cities that were putting on funerals. The townspeople were allowed to pass through the car and view Lincoln and then a small funeral service was held with young women singing hymns.

Abraham Lincoln had always been among the first to alter procedures and break rules on the spur of the moment for something better. His office hours were always flexible, and he often received people at all hours of the day and night. He was the bane of all who tried to protect his time from the people. The people wanted so little, he often said, and there was so little that he could give – he must see them. Because of this, the Michigan City meeting with the people would have gladdened Lincoln's heart.

A short time later, Lincoln was almost home. As the train steamed into Chicago, he was finally entering the greatest city of his home state, which had been a prairie mudhole when he first settled in Illinois and now was a rich and crowded city of more than 300,000 souls. Although a few years away from the Great Fire that would change the city forever, Chicago was already claiming its place as one of the greatest cities in America. Lincoln had many ties with the city. He had spent a lot of time there pleading cases as a lawyer and it was in Chicago that his presidential nomination was garnered. And it was in Chicago that, just before the famed Lincoln-Douglas debates began in 1858, Lincoln and Stephen Douglas spoke to large audiences on successive July nights, gaining the attention of newspapers and readers across the country.

It was to this magnificent city that Lincoln's body came on Monday, May 1, 1865. It had traveled more than 1,500 miles to reach this point and the hearts of the people who awaited him in Chicago were heavy.

The funeral train did not go the entire distance on the Illinois Central tracks to the Union Depot but stopped on a trestle that carried the line out in the lake some distance from the shore. The train arrived in silence, save for the ringing of its bell. A temporary platform had been built, with steps leading down to the ground, and from there, a Veteran Guard carried the coffin the short distance up the street to where a platform was waiting beneath a dramatic Gothic, three-section arch. The city had employed three distinguished architects and had spent more than $15,000 to create the arch, design the hearse, and build the decorations for the Court House. Thirty-six

LINCOLN'S FUNERAL CAR IN CHICAGO

young women walked beside the platform that carried the president and they showered flower petals in all directions. The streets were packed with over 100,000 people as excursion trains had been coming into the city for more than 24 hours, carrying curiosity-seekers from the east. Thousands lined up at the courthouse in the rain and mud to see Lincoln. Exhausted soldiers and police officers recalled that the lines moved less than one foot per hour on Monday and Tuesday. More trains arrived, bringing more people to add to the chaos as at least 125,000 lined up to view the casket. Ambulances came and went, carrying injured onlookers and women who fainted from grief and exhaustion. At one point, a section of wooden sidewalk gave away and plunged hundreds into the mud and water below.

The route of the funeral procession ran through what was the most elegant section of town. It passed down Michigan Avenue first, then along Lake Street, then along Clark to Court House Square, avoiding the world's largest stockyards, the McCormick Reaper Works, and the flour mills. On each side of the hearse walked six pallbearers, each of them old friends of Lincoln. Marching second on the left-hand side was "Long John" Wentworth, the mayor of the city. Standing six feet, six inches in height, he had started off in Congress as a Democrat but later became a Republican and a staunch supporter of Lincoln. When Wentworth was elected the mayor of Chicago in 1857, he made cleaning out crime and corruption his top priority. The story went that the rough and tumble candidate once made a one-sentence campaign speech from the front steps of the Court House --- "You damn fools, you can either vote for me or go to hell."

The procession in Chicago was much as it had been in other cities. There was a legion of clergy with white crosses adorning their black armbands and a division of Zouaves in baggy red pants.

THE PRESIDENT'S FUNERAL SERVICES IN CHICAGO

There was also a group of captured Confederate soldiers who had taken the oath and now belonged to the Union Army. They were followed by a troop of more than 10,000 schoolchildren, walking with saddened faces and wearing black ribbons in their hair, along with sashes, armbands, and badges. In the procession were also immigrants from Germany, France, Ireland, and Eastern Europe. They were butchers, bricklayers, tailors, and carpenters, all carrying banners with clumsily worded but unmistakably heartfelt messages about the President. The parade was followed up with a humble, yet unwanted, procession of "colored citizens."

When the hearse finally arrived at the city's Court House, the great bell in the tower began to ring so loudly that it could be heard in the farthest reaches of Chicago. It was not until early evening that the doors were opened to the public and the viewing went on all night long and all through the following day. It was believed that more than 7,000 people per hour passed by the coffin for a quick viewing of the President.

The light in the Court House was kept purposely dim but there was a general feeling that the discoloration that had been present under Lincoln's eye from the bullet wound was starting to spread over his entire face. The continual application of white chalk was no longer able to hide the dark stains. It had been in New York that the blackness had really started to distress the mourners but now, the body was starting to look even worse. Lincoln had started to shrivel, making it appear as though his coffin – once considered too small -- was many sizes too big for him. To many, his cheeks

ONE OF THE NUMEROUS PIECES OF
SHEET MUSIC THAT WAS
PRODUCED AFTER THE DEATH OF
PRESIDENT LINCOLN

seemed hollow and his face much more gaunt than it had been in life. The reporters had been positive that after New York, there would be no more open casket viewings, but constant care and powdering had managed to keep the body in a decent condition. Even so, the undertaker was glad that Chicago was nearly the last stop on the route.

Late Tuesday evening, the great procession re-formed and by the light of 10,000 torches, the eight black horses drew the hearse with Lincoln's coffin on it back to the railroad depot. The train finally began the last leg of its journey on that night, leaving Chicago and passing under arches which were illuminated with bonfires and decorated with sentiments like "Coming Home," "Bear Him Home Tenderly," and "Home is the Martyr."

As the train passed out of Chicago, the excitement on board increased. This was the last night of travel. In the morning, the funeral train would reach its destination and the journey would come to an end. Lincoln was in his home state now and the grief of the people huddled around fires along the tracks reached a fever pitch. The passengers on the train saw more signs that they passed in the darkness. "Illinois clasps to her bosom her slain but glorified son, Come home," read a sign posted on a house in Lockport. "Go to thy rest," said a sign atop a large arch in Bloomington.

The sun came up on the funeral train as it reached Atlanta, Illinois, and then steamed on towards the south. Emotions ran high aboard the train as it steamed into Lincoln, a town that had actually been named for the president when he was still a young lawyer. In 1853, Lincoln had been called upon to draft the town's incorporation papers and the founders decided to name the place in his honor. Lincoln responded to the suggestion with his usual humility. "I think you are making a mistake," he said. "I never knew of anything named Lincoln that ever amounted to much." Lincoln then presided over the town's dedication and on April 27, the official story has it that he poured out juice from a watermelon to christen the ground, but other stories say that he spit out a mouthful of seeds as a christening instead. Knowing Lincoln's sense of humor, the latter is probably correct.

During the night of May 2 and during the early morning hours of May 3, the residents of Springfield were restless. They had anticipated Lincoln's homecoming since they had heard the news of his death. After the initial battles with Mary Lincoln about her husband's burial site, it was not clear that Lincoln would return to Springfield at all. But once the citizens knew that Springfield would be his final resting place, they began frenzied preparations.

They had finished hanging the decorations and painting the signs. Crepe and bunting blackened the town. The townspeople had waited 20 days since Lincoln's death and 13 days since the train had left Washington. Beginning on May 3, Springfield would show the nation that no town loved Abraham Lincoln as much as they did. Springfield would be the final stop in the "carnival of death."

The train steamed into Springfield at mid-morning and was greeted by a mass of people at the station and on the surrounding rooftops. They met the train in silence. Only the sound of weeping could be heard. It seemed the entire city of Springfield had been draped in black but two of the most important buildings to be decorated with mourning weeds were the old State House in the center of the town square, where the body

THE ONLY HOME THAT LINCOLN EVER OWNED WAS IN SPRINGFIELD AND IT WAS DRAPED IN BLACK FOR THE ARRIVAL OF THE SLAIN PRESIDENT'S BODY IN THE CITY

would be placed for public viewing, and the home that Lincoln had owned and lived in for nearly sixteen years. The house now belonged to the Tilton family. Lucien A. Tilton was the president of the Great Western Railway and over the four years of their occupancy, had been kept busy by an estimated 65,000 people who had visited the home and had asked to tour it. Mrs. Tilton was rather apprehensive about what might happen during the Lincoln

THE ILLINOIS STATE CAPITOL BUILDING IN
SPRINGFIELD, WHERE LINCOLN'S BODY
LAY IN STATE BEFORE THE FUNERAL

funeral, but she was a kind-hearted person and had already resolved herself to the fact that she was going to allow people to take grass from the yard, flowers from her garden, or leaves from the trees. She had no idea what was coming --- by the end of the funeral services, her lawn and gardens had been stripped, paint had been scraped from her house, and bricks had been carried away from her retaining wall as souvenirs.

The rotunda of the State House had been draped in black cloth and the second floor House of Representatives, where Lincoln was to lie in state, had been renovated with the speaker's podium being removed to allow more people to pass through it. The columns inside had been draped with black and banners and signs decorated the interior. At the center of the room, a catafalque had been built to hold Lincoln's coffin. The catafalque was one of the most amazing of the entire funeral route. Its canopy was "Egyptian" in design with columns and "half-Egyptian" suns depicted between the columns. It was 24-feet-high and more than 10-feet-long. The top was made from black broadcloth and at the tops of the columns were black plumes with white centers, hiding large eagles. The inside roof of the canopy was blue, spangled with silver stars.

It was at the State House where Lincoln had served as a legislator, given his famous "House Divided" speech and, in another part of the building, set up an office after his election as president. Springfield was not a great American city and its officials knew that they could not hope to rival the pageantry displayed in Washington, Philadelphia, New York, or Chicago. Springfield couldn't match the impressive crowds or financial resources marshaled by the major cities. Indeed, the president's hometown had to borrow a hearse from St. Louis. However, what the Illinois state capital could not offer in splendor, it vowed to outdo every other city in the nation when it came to their emotion over the loss of their native son.

Few in Springfield were disappointed that Mary Lincoln was not on the train, even if it meant no Lincolns had made the trip from Washington. This morning, for the first time since the funeral train left Washington, the honor guard also removed Willie's coffin from the presidential car.

On the morning of May 3, the public viewing was scheduled to begin, and thousands of people began to gather outside of the State House. Long before the imposing procession arrived from the station, huge, motionless lines began to form at the north gate. Time ticked by and soon, people began to grow restless --- but there was an unavoidable delay inside. When the undertakers had opened the coffin upstairs, even these hardened professionals were shocked. Thomas Lynch was a courtesy undertaker for the occasion and he had been invited to assist Dr. Charles D. Brown, Lincoln's embalmer. The doors of the room were locked and Dr. Brown, in great distress, informed the other man that he had no idea how to remedy the condition of Lincoln's face – it had turned totally black.

Lynch later wrote, "I asked to have the body turned over to me and the other undertaker readily consented. Making my way with difficulty through the crowds which thronged the corridors of the State House, I called at a neighboring drugstore and procured a rouge chalk and amber, with such brushes as I needed, and returned to the room. I at once set about coloring the President's features, placing the materials on very thick so as to completely hide the discoloration of his skin. In half an hour, I had finished my task and the doors were thrown open to the public."

The crowds were admitted, and they walked upstairs to the House of Representatives, where they were sorted out by guards and were sent in groups past Lincoln's casket. Everyone was afforded a few moments to look inside and then they were ushered out through the exit and down the stairs. Before they left, they were asked to make a donation to the Lincoln Monument fund. Very few of those who filed past the coffin shed any tears. They were too shocked by what they saw. But outside on the street, they broke down and wept. Over the next 24 hours, thousands streamed past the coffin, but these were not the hysterical crowds of New York and Chicago, these were the folks that Lincoln had known and loved in life. They were the people he talked to in the street, laughed with, ate with, and the people he had missed while living in Washington. They were now the people who wept in the streets of the city that he had called home.

On the morning of May 4, the last service was held in Springfield. Robert Lincoln had arrived. His mother and Tad remained behind in Washington. She was still refusing to leave her room – and the White House. Andrew Johnson, Lincoln's successor, was unable to take up residence there.

GENERAL HOOKER LED LINCOLN'S RIDERLESS HORSE, "OLD BOB," IN THE SPRINGFIELD FUNERAL PROCESSION.

Shortly before the service, Dr. Charles Brown worked to make Lincoln presentable for one last occasion, dressing him in a clean collar and shirt and applying more powder to his face. He finished just before the procession formed outside. The procession included Robert Lincoln, who rode in a buggy with members of the Todd family; John Hanks, one of Lincoln's only remaining blood relatives; elderly Sarah Lincoln; Thomas Pendel, Lincoln's door man from the White House, and a representative of the household servants; and Billy, Lincoln's black barber and friend.

The final parade was presided over by General Joseph Hooker and he led "Old Bob," the tired and rider-less old horse that Lincoln had ridden the law circuit on. The parade, like the others before it, was long and marked with music, banners, and signs. The journey was to end two miles away at quiet Oak Ridge Cemetery, traveling over what were then rough, country roads. From time to time, bands broke out in dirges, including four newly composed "Lincoln Funeral Marches." When the music was silent, all that could be heard was the unbroken and ominous roll of drums. Finally, the procession wound under the evergreen arch at the cemetery's entrance, down through the little valley between two ridges, along the small stream and to the receiving tomb that was half-embedded in the hillside. It stood with its iron gates and heavy new vault doors open to receive the President. With no delay, the coffin was carried from the hearse and placed on the marble slab inside of the vault. As soon as the hearse and horses moved away and let the people come close, it could be seen that there were two coffins on the slab. The small casket of Willie Lincoln had been brought to the vault first and was waiting for his father's casket to arrive.

People were standing and sitting behind the tomb on the hillside and along the valley in front of it, with the brook, swollen by the spring rains,

THE SCENE AT OAK RIDGE CEMETERY WHEN LINCOLN WAS
TEMPORARILY LAID TO REST IN THE RECEIVING VAULT

dividing the audience. Robert Lincoln stood grimly on one side of the tomb and Ward Hill Lamon, stood nearby. Lamon had stayed close to the President's body all the way west, skipping meals and acting as if he were still protecting his old friend from danger. He alternated between helpless weeping and helpless rage over the fact that he had not been present that night at Ford's Theater. On this day in May 1865, Lamon cried unashamedly at the fate of Abraham Lincoln.

As the service began, Reverend A.C. Hubbard began to read Lincoln's words from his second inaugural address. As it drew to a close, Bishop Matthew Simpson of the Methodist Church rose to give his funeral oration. The Bishop's voice was shrill and harsh, and people found it unpleasant, but the sound was forgotten when they listened to the words that he spoke of their friend and fallen leader. He spoke so eloquently that people applauded parts of the sermon. When he was finished, a hymn was sung and then Dr. Gurley, who had officiated at the funeral in Washington, delivered the benediction. A final hymn was sung, the words printed on black-edged cards that were distributed throughout the audience, and then the gates to the tomb were closed and locked. The key to the tomb was handed to Robert

Lincoln, who passed it to his cousin, John Todd Stuart, who would become the guardian of the President's body for many years to come.

When the lock turned in the door of the President's tomb, the seemingly endless days of travel and the grand spectacles were finally over. Lincoln was laid to rest in Oak Ridge Cemetery in the holding crypt while his tomb and monument were constructed.

Carl Sandburg wrote about those last moments at the crypt better than any witness who was present that day. He wrote:

Evergreen carpeted the stone floor of the vault. On the coffin set in a receptacle of black walnut they arranged flowers carefully and precisely, they poured flowers as symbols, the lavished heaps of fresh flowers as though there could never be enough to tell either their hearts or his.

And the night came with great quiet.

And there was rest.

The prairie years, the war years, were over.

The 20-day "carnival of death" transformed Abraham Lincoln from a man to a legend. On the day he was assassinated, he was not universally loved – even in the north. His traveling corpse became a touchstone that offered relief from the pain that the American people had been suffering from during the four bloody years of the war. They mourned for the president and yet, the outpouring of sorrow was greater than for just one man. They mourned for every husband, father, son, and brother who died during the war. It as though, on that train, all of them were coming home. The frenzied death carnival for Abraham Lincoln was a glorious farewell to the president and to the hundreds of thousands of men of the Union who, like Lincoln, had perished for cause and country.

It was also the start of a great change about how Americans felt about death. It introduced mourning customs that had never been considered in this country before. Soon, combined with the popularity of mourning customs introduced by Queen Victorian in England, these new ideas would become a part of the fabric of American death.

The Civil War had changed the way that America looked at death but Lincoln's "carnival of death" that followed would create a funeral industry that endures to this day.

THE ART OF MOURNING

THE VICTORIAN TRADITIONS AND RITUALS OF DEATH

In Colonial America, death was often a man's closest neighbor. It came knocking on the doors of our ancestors, bringing disease, starvation, murder, poor medical treatment, and every kind of hardship that can be imagined. This was the reason that people had so many children -- because so few of them would live to be adults.

In those days, death was an ordinary part of life. It was accepted. And while feared, every American had a close relationship with it. People died at home in those days, not in a sterile hospital room. Lives were short in those days and death was accepted as a matter of fact. Funerals were stark, though social, affairs. Burials generally took place on family land with friends and neighbors present. Local women prepared the corpse in the family kitchen, washing the body, and dressing it in the deceased's finest clothes. Embalming did not exist at the time, so burials took place quickly in plain, pine boxes that were made by family or friends. It was more important to get the dead into the ground than to spend a lot of time honoring them. That was usually done after the burial was completed, over food and a batch of corn liquor.

There were few changes to the American way of death prior to the Civil War. Perhaps the greatest was when cabinet and furniture makers began to

IN THE PAST, DEATH OCCURRED AT HOME – AND SO DID THE FUNERAL. BODIES WERE LAID OUT IN THE PARLOR AND FRIENDS AND LOVED ONES CAME TO PAY THEIR RESPECTS

realize there was another market for their craft and they took the first steps toward creating a funeral industry by building coffins and offering burial services.

As recounted in an earlier chapter, it was the Civil War that forever changed the face of death in America. Over 600,000 soldiers died during the conflict, as well as over 50,000 civilians. Never before had Americans seen death on such a scale. Overwhelmed, grieving, and suffering from tremendous loss, they were forced to learn to deal with death. National cemeteries were created, the fledging funeral industry was forced to grow, and people were taught to accept that fact that men were dying every day from an "unnatural death."

The Civil War also created the custom of embalming. While most ordinary soldiers were buried on the battlefield – sometimes exactly where they fell -- and were later removed to national cemeteries, the families of wealthy officers often demanded that the bodies of their fallen dead be shipped home. In order to make the lengthy train trip, enterprising inventors created fluids to preserve the bodies. The techniques they used in the 1860s are basically what are still being used today.

And while the war changed the way Americans looked at death, it was an event that occurred after the war that created the way that we mourn for the dead -- the assassination of President Abraham Lincoln. The outpouring of American grief over the president's death was not only the feeling of loss for a beloved leader, but it was also a public representation of American grief over all the men who perished during the war.

The American traditions created to mourn the fallen president were greatly influenced by the mourning rituals introduced by England's Queen Victoria after the death of her husband, Prince Albert, who died of typhoid in 1861. For the next 40 years, she mourned his death and maintained a domestic routine that bordered on the bizarre. D. Lyn Hunter wrote, "Each morning, servants set out Albert's clothes, brought hot water for his shaving cup, scoured his chamber pot, and changed his bed linens. The glass from which he took his last dose of medicine stayed by his bedside for nearly four decades."

Taking their cue from the beloved monarch, Victorians on both sides of the Atlantic, made a fetish of mourning, giving themselves over to elaborate, highly formal death rituals. Lincoln's death was the first public event to occur in what came to be known as the "Victorian Celebration of Death."

Middle- and upper-class funerals reached dizzying heights of ostentation, with opulent hearses, luxuriously upholstered coffins, and extravagant processions. Etiquette manuals appeared to spell out the complex dress codes for widows and entire industries emerged to sell mourning dresses, appropriate jewelry, black-edged stationary, and embossed "memorial cards" that were handed out as souvenirs.

AFTER THE DEATH OF HER HUSBAND, PRINCE ALBERT, QUEEN VICTORIA SPENT THE REST OF HER LIFE IN MOURNING. THE TRADITIONS SHE ESTABLISHED WERE IMITATED BY THE BEREAVED ON BOTH SIDES OF THE ATLANTIC

Inside the home, parlor walls were adorned with somber lithographs of grieving women weeping over tombstones or around funeral urns. Shelves displayed little glass domes that covered the dried remains of old funeral flowers. Fireplace mantels were filled with photographic portraits of dead children laid out in their cribs. Beautifully landscaped "garden cemeteries" because a favorite spot for Sunday outings. Tearful ballads with titles like "Little Sister Has Gone to Sleep" became sheet music bestsellers, while poets composed ballads about the tragic demise of innocent victims.

Death had become an industry – and an obsession.

AT THE HOUR OF DEATH

Death was still a common occurrence in the last half of the nineteenth century. Three out of every 20 babies died before their first birthdays and

WHEN A DEATH OCCURRED, MIRRORS WERE COVERED, CLOCKS WERE STOPPED, AND FAMILY PHOTOS WERE TURNED TO FACE THE WALL.

those who survived could not expect to live more than for 42 years. Death would take place most often in the home.

When a death occurred, the entire house stopped and went into mourning. An elaborate ritual then went into motion, all of it part of the detailed mourning traditions of the era. Children in the home were not sheltered from the deaths around them. They were instructed at all ages on the meaning of death and its rituals. Rules and regulations about what was proper were established for just about every aspect of life at that time, including that of proper death procedures and funeral rites. It was considered quite a scandal if any of the rituals were broken.

First, the windows of the house were closed so that the spirit of the deceased would not fly out the window and become lost. Clocks were stopped at the time of death to honor the moment when the soul left the mortal coil. Mirrors were covered throughout the house because it was believed that a mirror, or any reflective surface, could cause the spirit to be trapped in it. Some also suggested this helped prevent vanity among the bereaved living in the house. Often, family photos and paintings would also be turned upside down or turned to face the wall. A wreath made from laurel, yew, or boxwood – tied with black ribbons – was hung on the front door to alert passersby that a death had occurred. If a wreath was not used, then black crêpe would be tied to the door knobs to let people know that someone had died in the home. This was also done to prevent a visitor from knocking or ringing the doorbell, which would serve as a jarring reminder of life. Many times, the front door would be left ajar so that mourners could enter quietly.

When news spread of the death, friends called to offer their services, but family members were not expected to visit with anyone except for their closest friends, whose duty it was to make all arrangements for the burial. They consulted with the family about details, received those who called to pay their respects, and fulfilled any and every requirement that arose. Visits of condolence were not made until after the funeral was over.

The deceased was watched over every minute until the burial, hence the custom of the "wake." It served several purposes, including watching over the body to make sure that the spirit did not leave it. A common superstition that surrounded this suggested that those

WHEN VISITS OF CONDOLENCE WERE PAID, ALL GUESTS WERE REQUIRED TO ENTER SILENTLY, AND MEN ALWAYS REMOVED THEIR HATS

who sat with the body should always cover their mouth if they yawned so that the spirit of the deceased couldn't enter them.

A wake also served as a safeguard from burying someone who was not dead, merely in a coma. The Victorians were just as obsessed by the horrific possibility of premature burial as their ancestors had been.

Most wakes lasted for 3-4 days to allow relatives to arrive from far away. The use of flowers and candles helped to mask the room's unpleasant odors, which were common in the days when embalming was still a relatively new science.

When the day of the funeral arrived, more rituals and traditions were in place, beginning with how the deceased was to be removed from the home. The dead were always carried out of the house feet first. This prevented the spirit from looking back into the house and beckoning another member of the family to follow him or her to the grave.

Previously, funerals were arranged between the family and the church and were small, private affairs. In the Victorian age, however, a funeral was expected to be a long, elaborate, and public process, requiring a funeral director, hired black horses for the hearse, elaborate floral displays, invitations, crêpe, pallbearers, professional mourners, photographs, and a huge feast for the mourners.

Families who were not wealthy often set aside funds for an impending death and the subsequent pageantry that was required. Some families refused to dip into the "funeral fund" even for basic daily necessities, which, ironically, occasionally caused the death of a family member. As one commenter of the era wrote: "The stigma of a pauper's burial was so great that families would go without food and heating in order to put by a penny a week

FUNERAL PROCESSION AND HEARSE

for each child, two for the mother and three for the father towards funeral expenses."

The cost of a "proper" funeral could be outrageous, but in the society of the era, it was seen as a necessity. One tradition that seems nearly unbelievable to us today was the hiring of professional mourners to appear at the funeral services. Having the most austere and elaborate funeral was not only regarded as a duty, but it was also an unspoken competition among prominent families. They wanted everyone to know that their grief was greater than everyone else's, so they hired professional mourners – often dubbed "mutes" – who were hired to follow behind the coffin or stand nearby, looking forlorn. It was said that they brought a great sense of solemnity to the affair, while allowing the grieving family to keep up the stiff appearance that the funeral required. Even though great emphasis was placed on grief in the Victorian culture, it was considered unseemly to publicly weep at a funeral.

Between six and eight pallbearers were chosen from the immediate friends of the deceased, all near to him in age. A very young girl might be carried to the hearse by girls of her own age – all wearing white, which was the proper color for children in mourning. The duty of the pallbearers was to carry the coffin from the house to the hearse and from the hearse to the grave. They rode in a carriage that preceded the hearse and each wore gloves and a black crêpe armband. Those were furnished by the family through the undertaker. Each would have received a handwritten note, requesting their services.

Those who attended the funeral also received an invitation. In cities and towns where death notices were inserted in the newspaper, the heading "Friends Invited" was regarded as sufficient invitation to the event. But in smaller places – and among the more elite – it was necessary to issue invitations to those whose presences was desired. The invitations were engraved on small note paper with a black border.

When funerals were held at the house, the family did not view the remains after people started to assemble. Just before the clergyman started the service the mourners were seated near the casket – the nearest one at the head and the others following in order of kinship. If possible, they were placed in an adjoining room, where the words of the service could be heard but they were not seen. That way, they were spared the pain of giving way to their grief before onlookers.

Invited guests were expected to look at the deceased before taking their seats for the service. It was customary for the master of ceremonies – usually the undertaker – before the casket lid was closed, to invite all who desired, to take a last look before parting forever.

The casket was never opened at the church, unless it was the funeral of a prominent man. In that case, the assembled group was likely too large to accommodate at home, so the church was necessary.

When the funeral procession departed for the cemetery, the carriages containing the clergyman and the pallbearers always went first. The hearse followed and behind it were the carriages of the immediate mourners, in their proper order. At the cemetery, the minister preceded the casket.

Of course, the family never had to worry about any of those details during the Victorian era. By then, the role of the undertaker had been thoroughly established and he directed all of the details so that the family had no part in any such painful duties.

A TIME OF GRIEF

The mourning period began immediately after death, according to Victorian ritual and tradition. Mourning clothing was readily available in every woman's wardrobe. Men had it relatively easy -- they simply wore their usual dark suits along with black gloves, hatbands and cravats. Children were not expected to wear mourning clothes, though girls sometimes wore white dresses. Anyone who entered a home where someone had died was required to wear at least a black ribbon – even household pets and chickens.

The length of mourning depended on your relationship to the deceased. The different periods of mourning dictated by society were expected to reflect your natural period of grief. Widows went into deep mourning immediately following a death and, except to attend the funeral and church, did not leave the house for at least a month. She might remain in deep mourning for as long as two years. Everyone else presumably suffered less – for children mourning parents, or vice versa, the period of time was one year; for grandparents and siblings, six months; for aunts and uncles, two months; for great uncles and aunts, six weeks; for first cousins, four weeks.

Mourning clothes represented a family's outward displays of their inner feelings. The rules for who wore what and for how long were complicated. The rules were outlined in

A BOOK ON SOCIAL ETIQUETTE – LIKE THIS ONE PUBLISHED IN 1896 – WOULD PROVIDE A WOMAN WITH ALL OF THE RULES IN REGARDS TO MOURNING DRESS AND BEHAVIOR

popular journals or household manuals, like *The Queen* or *Cassell's*, both of which were very popular among Victorian housewives. They gave detailed instructions about appropriate mourning etiquette. For instance, if your second cousin died and you wanted to know what sort of mourning clothes you should wear and for how long, you consulted one of the many manuals – all the answers were there.

Black – symbolic of spiritual darkness – was the customary color for a widow's mourning weeds during the first year. Dresses for deepest mourning were usually made of serge, non-reflective paramatta silk, or the cheaper bombazine. Dresses were trimmed with crêpe, that hard, scratchy silk with a peculiar crimped appearance that was produced by heat. Crêpe was always associated with mourning because it doesn't combine will with any other clothing – ladies couldn't wear velvet, satin, lace, or embroidery with it. She also replaced her usual hat with a black bonnet and was expected to wear a veil over her face during the first three months, then trail it down the back of her bonnet for another nine months.

A VICTORIAN WOMAN DRESSED FOR MOURNING

After a specified time period, the crêpe could be removed from the trim. This was called "slighting the mourning." In the second year, the color of cloth lightened as the mourning went on – to gray, shades of purple, mauve, and white. She could also begin wearing glossier silks and other fabrics This was referred to as "half mourning."

Besides not leaving the home for the first month of mourning, there were several other restrictions placed on widows – and often on their friends and family, as well. The first calls of condolence were usually made by friends within 10 days of the death. However, acquaintances were not expected to call until the family made its first appearance in church. When those in mourning felt able to receive visits, they announced the fact by sending out black-edged cards in envelopes to those who they wish to have call upon them. When visiting, it was best not to allude to the sorrow unless it was seen that they were expected to do so.

Ladies in mourning – as well as gentlemen – were expected to use black-bordered cards and stationary for all their correspondence, until the period of mourning expired. If they wrote any letters about business, they were expected to use plain white stationary.

As noted, widows did not go out into society during their period of deep mourning and did not pay visits to friends or family. They did not attend the theater or public places of amusement until their period of "half mourning" began.

LOVE AFTER DEATH

Ornaments of any kind were out of the question during a widow's deep mourning, but some objects – made only from certain materials – were deemed appropriate after a certain amount of time had passed. Some acceptable ornaments were photographs that were mounted as a pin or necklace. These would contain the likeness of the deceased. Rings, bracelets, necklaces, and earrings were limited to onyx or jet, a hard, black fossilized coal.

In addition to these dark stones, another material became quite common in jewelry-making of the time – the dead loved one's hair. While these seems macabre to modern readers, it was perfectly acceptable for the second stage of mourning. The hair would be woven into jewelry or encased in another form of ornament, like a locket, pendant, or brooch.

Hairwork jewelry was already popular in Victorian society. Artisans made everything from bracelets to necklaces, rings, and stickpins, all fashioned from intricately woven hair. Some of these items were love tokens, others were made to commemorate important events, while others were purely decorative. This kind of jewelry became even more popular when people started using them for memorial purposes, usually to accessorize the elaborate bereavement costumes that widows were required to wear.

Wearing such jewelry allowed mourners to keep a piece of their loved ones close to their hearts, but there was a more practical reason for its popularity too – not everyone had easy access to photography. A locket of someone's hair – woven into jewelry – gave a person a touchstone to remember the deceased every day. These items weren't limited to women, either; men could have memorial cufflinks or pocket watch fobs that were braided from the dead person's hair.

Hairwork jewelry came in various shapes and styles. One of the most popular was the oval pendant or pin with a glazed compartment that contained a lock of the loved one's hair. Even more common was the rectangular brooch or medallion depicting a gravestone inscribed with a memorial motto like "Not Lost, Just Gone Before," "Sacred to the Memory," "I Weep, Heaven Rejoices," or some other maudlin phrase. Rising behind the tombstone would be a weeping willow tree whose branches were composed of actual pieces of the deceased's hair.

SOME HAIR JEWELRY CONTAINED STRANDS OF THE DECEASED'S HAIR
THAT WAS ENCLOSED IN A LOCKET OR BROOCH. OTHERS (RIGHT) WERE
WOVEN FROM THE HAIR OF THE LOVED ONE WHO HAD DIED

Many mourners made their own hairwork jewelry. It was an affordable, middle-class activity – like knitting or crocheting. Since the material needed to make the jewelry was nearly unlimited, the custom spread across the country, first becoming popular during the Civil War, when women made jewelry from the hair of their husbands, brothers, and sons who went off to fight. The artwork became so popular that hairwork templates began to be published in ladies' newspapers. The "Victorian Celebration of Death" turned what was once a sentimental craft into a way to pay tribute to the dead.

Another form of mourning art was the hair wreath. It followed the same process as the weaving that was done for jewelry, but in this case, the hair was turned into a mourning wreath that could be made up of one person's hair or as a composite of an entire family. As family members died, hair was saved in a "hair receiver." When enough was accumulated, the hair was fashioned into flowers and leaves by twisting and sewing it around shaped wire forms.

Patterns and advice on creating hair wreaths could be found in catalogs and manuals, including the popular *Godey's Lady's Book*. Shapes were then combined into a U-shaped wreath with the most recently deceased's hair having a place of honor in the center of the wreath. This is why – when you do find a wreath that has survived over time – there may be a different in hair colors and textures.

A family hair wreath was a way of preserving a family's history. The open end at the top of the wreath symbolized the deceased's ascent to heaven. Wreaths were framed and displayed with the open end up, like a horseshoe.

Hair wreaths never achieved the same kind of popularity that hair jewelry did – you could even find hair jewelry in the Sears and Roebuck Catalog in the early 1900s – but they can still sometimes be found today, serving as a time capsule of another era.

Like any trend, the popularity of hairwork eventually faded away. As ready-made goods took center stage in the twentieth century, a customer could not guarantee that the hair sent out for work would be the same hair they received in the finished product. Also, as the Victorian mourning culture began to decline at the end of the nineteenth century, the hair jewelry fad followed suit. Hair jewelry began to be seen as old-fashioned and backward in a new, faster-moving society, and the intricate pieces were put away in drawers, shoved into the back of jewelry boxes, or tossed in the trash – sadly, too often lost for all time.

CATCHING YOUR FEELINGS:
The Myth of Victorian Tear Catchers

As we have already established the Victorians were experts in the art of mourning – they wore black for extended periods, created spectacular grave monuments, turned the hair of the dead into jewelry, and wept – so the story goes – into delicate glass bottles called "tear catchers."

But did they really? History says – probably not.

With death antiques such a hot market today, it's easy to find high-priced pieces in online auctions and markets. You can buy jewelry made from hair and postmortem photographs in every price range. Another item that commonly turns up is the vintage tear catcher – also called a "lachrymatory bottle" – that sellers claim was used in America after the Civil War as a way to measure the time of grieving. A widow would collect her tears in the bottle and once the tears that were cried into it had evaporated, the mourning period was over.

It's a good story – too good, in fact. Both science and history agree that there's no such thing as a tear catcher.

The blown, usually clear glass bottles, decorated with patterns, gilding, and colorful enamel, that so many people have heard about and are searching

for, are nothing more than throwaway perfume bottles. They became "tear catchers" through a combination of historical accident and deceptive – yet effective – marketing.

The myth probably began with archaeologists and an oddly chosen term. Small glass bottles were often found in Greek and Roman tombs, and early scholars dubbed them "lachrymatories" or "tear bottles," for lack of a better term. But those bottles held perfumes, not tears. Scientists later performed chemical tests on the bottles and disproved the romantic theory. But, as we all know, society rarely lets the truth get in the way of a good story.

If there was a practice of tear collecting during the Victorian period, it is certainly not very well documented. No first-hand accounts have been found. No books or scholarly works have been written. The lack of information – even misinformation – is suspicious. There have been no discussions of lachrymatory custom in etiquette manuals, nor do they appear in product catalogs of the Victorian era.

BOTTLES LIKE THIS ONE HAVE BEEN SOLD FOR YEARS AS "TEAR CATCHERS" – THEY'RE NOT. IT'S A PERFUME BOTTLE

There are no descriptions of real or fictional characters making actual use of a tear bottle as a normal part of Victorian mourning practice.

"Tear catchers," it seems, became popular with the rise of the internet. The idea seemed legitimate, especially when considering the Victorian fascination with death and mourning accoutrements. It's possible that the bottles were misidentified because of the theories that surrounded the bottles found in ancient tombs – and just as likely that someone simply made it up. The bottles that were turning up in antique stores were perfume bottles but once a seller attached the words "Victorian" and "mourning" to them, buyers got excited.

"People ask to buy them all of the time. At least a few people a week," writes Christian Harding, owner of an oddities and collectibles store in Seattle. "It's a beautiful idea but no one really cried into the bottles. Through the years, after reading many different articles and speaking with other collectors, I realized that the stories were, in fact, just myth." When asked about "tear catchers" by folks eager to add to their mourning collection, Harding explains the true uses of the decorative bottles, but many customers don't want to believe it—and some just don't care.

"I have probably sold dozens at this point," writes Katie Kierstead, owner of an online Victorian antique shop. She did her research and regularly stocks them—in the perfume section. "They are worth the same amount to a perfume bottle collector as to someone interested in mourning."

But not every seller is so transparent, which helps the tale of the "tear catcher" persist. Most online information continues the myth and so many sellers just go along with it, hoping to make money off misidentified antiques. The internet, as we know, is a folklore-creating machine. Even if people know better, when they see a story enough times, they consider it to be true.

It's easy to see how it happened. Those who have been fascinated by the culture of the "Celebration of Death" have placed their own sorrows on the Victorians, endowing their trinkets with romantic symbolism. It was a culture that celebrated death, and, in a way, those of the modern era envy them their ceremonies, customs, and rituals. In their need to glorify every aspect of the culture, they search for anything – truth or fiction – that might make the era even more romantic than it already was.

Any cosmetic historian or Victorian glass expert could tell a customer in 30 seconds that the bottles are not "tear catchers" and the colorful internet descriptions of Civil War widows are silly, at best – but would that customer listen? Or are they too enamored with the idea of a "tear catcher" that the truth no longer matters?

THE "CELEBRATION" COMES TO AN END

By the end of the nineteenth century, the Victorian's "Celebration of Death" was coming to an end. It hung on for a few more years but with the arrival of the Great War, the world was faced with the wholesale slaughter of its young men. Death no longer seemed like something that should be celebrated.

It was now something to be feared.

The war -- followed by the Great Depression a decade later -- largely brought about an end to the kind of excess that celebrated death in homes and cemeteries across America. By the middle part of the twentieth century, hospitals, funeral homes, and traditional cemeteries began following uniform procedures to distance the dead from the living. The mourning customs and garden cemeteries of yesterday had become relics of the past.

The living had moved on and the dead became the easily forgotten reminders of the past.

SUFFER THE CHILD

CHILDREN AND DEATH IN THE NINETEENTH CENTURY

"In the midst of life, we are in death."

Once upon a time, death was an everyday part of life in America – not just for adults, but for children as well. The birth rate was high, but only slightly higher than the number of children who never lived to see adulthood.

Today, death rightfully belongs to the elderly. The death of a child —even the death of a young adult—is called a tragedy. Such a death, we believe, reverses the natural order of things. Yet in the nineteenth century, the death of a child was an event that was suffered by almost every family. Deaths occurred at birth, or if they cleared that hurdle, they came about thanks to accidents, hunger, and disease. America could be a cruel place for adults and children alike. By the time of the Civil War, the average American might live into his mid-forties.

A child was often lucky to become an adult at all.

When photographs became common, postmortem photographs (detailed in the next chapter) gained popularity. Deceased adults were frequently the subject of such photographs, but they were far outnumbered by children. Since photography was expensive, a postmortem photo might be the only photo the family had of their deceased child. Such images were treasured. Children were posed with family members, sometimes with a toy or sitting with a sibling, and often they looked as though they were sleeping. It seems morbid to many people today but only because we are so far removed from death.

CHILDREN WERE ALWAYS PART OF THE MOURNING PROCESS AND
WERE TAUGHT THE PROPER WAYS TO TAKE PART IN IT. (LEFT)
"DEATH KITS" WERE SOLD FOR LITTLE GIRLS SO THEY COULD LEARN
TO PARTICIPATE IN DEATH TRADITIONS. (RIGHT) LITTLE GIRLS OFTEN
PRACTICED MOURNING – OR POSED FOR THEIR VERSIONS OF
POSTMORTEM PHOTOGRAPHS

At times, the grieving for the loss of a child went beyond mere photographs. Following the deaths of babies and young children, families sometimes commissioned mourning or "grave dolls." These were usually realistic wax figures that were dressed in the deceased child's clothing and sometimes even incorporated the deceased child's own hair. The dolls had soft cloth bodies filled with sand that had a lifelike weight and feel, and flat backs so that they would like neatly in their toy coffins. Many families kept them in their homes as a memento, usually in a glass case or a crib.

If a child did survive to adulthood, by then he had seen his fair share of death. Unlike today's children, they were surrounded by it. They saw their loved ones die at home, saw corpses laid out in the parlor, and witnessed – and likely participated in – the butchering of farm animals. Compared to how things used to be, American life now shields children for the harsh realities of death. As this book has explored, we have all become "disconnected from death." It's been sanitized, glossed over, and beautified and children will never know what its was like to have death as a next-door neighbor.

That will never be said about the children of the nineteenth century.

They actively took part in the death rituals of home. Children helped to wash the corpse of the deceased. They "sat up" with mothers and aunts during wakes. The girls helped to make the food for the dinners that followed the funerals, while the boys helped their fathers and uncles dig the graves. During the Victorian era, they dressed in white mourning clothes and followed all the traditions of the time.

Since women were tasked with the complicated business of mourning, it's not surprising that their daughters were trained to follow in their footsteps. In the same way that little girls were given versions of cooking utensils, pots and pans, and cleaning tools, they were also taught about death rituals. By the 1870s, "death kits" were available for dolls, complete with coffins and mourning clothes, as a means of training girls for participating in, even guiding, death traditions and the grief that accompanied it.

Books were published geared toward children that emphasized the duties of families in times of grief. Death was used a children's entertainment, too. Kids gobbled up picture books like *Who Killed Cock Robin?* that featured lavishly illustrated funeral scenes and recited poems and sang songs about little children who died.

They knew all the superstitions about death – if the deceased lived a good life, flowers would bloom on his grave. If he was evil, only weeds would grow. Never wear new shoes to a funeral. If you lock the door of your home after a funeral procession has left the house, you'll have bad luck. If rain falls on a funeral procession, the deceased will go to heaven. If you hear a clap of thunder following a burial it indicates that the soul of the departed has reached heaven. If you don't hold your breath while going by a graveyard you will not be buried. If you see an owl in the daytime, there will be a death. If a sparrow lands on a piano, someone in the home will die. Two deaths in the family means that a third is sure to follow. And the list went on and on.

"FROZEN CHARLOTTE"

Death was, without question, part of daily life in bygone America. Our ancestors were so connected to death that even children's toys had undertones that most would consider unnerving today. One such toy was a "Frozen Charlotte" doll. Intended for use by children in the bathtub, these porcelain figures took from a macabre poem that was published during a frigid January in 1840.

The poet, Seba Smith, wrote "Young Charlotte" after reading a tragic story in the *New York Observer* about a young woman who froze to death while riding to a New Year's Eve ball in an open sleigh with her sweetheart. The first stanzas tell about the vain young woman, who refused to take her mother's advice and wrap a blanket around herself during the long ride.

*"O, daughter dear," her mother
cried,
"This blanket 'round you fold;
It is a dreadful night tonight,
You'll catch your death of cold."*

*"O, nay! O, nay!" young Charlotte
cried,
And she laughed like a gypsy queen;
"To ride in blankets muffled up,
I never would be seen."*

FROZEN CHARLOTTE

The poem later inspired a folk song by William Carter called "Fair Charlotte," which became very popular. This tale is perfect for a tragic folk ballad and it's still popular today. Near the end, the sad story unfolds:

*"He took her hand in his — O, God!
'Twas cold and hard as stone;
He tore the mantle from her face,
Cold stars upon it shone.
Then quickly to the glowing hall,
Her lifeless form he bore;
Fair Charlotte's eyes were closed in death,
Her voice was heard no more.*

In a culture where death was commonplace, the popular tune inspired a doll that Americans dubbed a "Frozen Charlotte." Originally manufactured in Germany during the 1850s as bath time dolls, they also caught on in England as fun surprises that could be baked into a pudding or a cake for children to discover at Christmastime.

The dolls were very small and since they only cost a penny, they were affordable for children from even the poorest families. This added to their popularity in American homes during the Victorian era.

For modern readers, the dolls can still be found today in antique stores and collectible shops, although few know what they actually are. For those aware of the customs of the past, they are grim reminders of a time when death was all around us and even our children confronted it every day.

THE "HEARSE SONG"

Rhymes and folk songs have been used for many years as a way to soothe and entertain children. They were supposed to either put them to sleep or help them have fun. On the surface, these rhymes were supposed to educate and to provide a moral lesson, but if you scratch the surface of just about any old lullaby, you'll find a more complex – and much darker – history.

From the Great Fire of London that is chronicled in "London Bridge" to the devastation of the plague in the eerie "Ring Around the Rosie," many of these simple tunes can trace their roots back to a past that is dark and macabre. And while the meanings of these songs have largely been lost in modern times, there is one childhood song for which the content of the song cannot be mistaken for anything else.

Officially it's known as the "Hearse Song," but a lot of us know it as "The Worms Crawl In" when we were younger. It's a favorite folk song of American children – either learned from family members or on playgrounds – and frankly, it's about the gruesome subject of decomposition. There are reports that the song has its origins in the nineteenth century, when it was sung by British soldiers during the Crimean War, but it certainly dates to at least World War I, when it caught on with British and American soldiers. It was first collected in World War I songbooks in the 1920s but, by then, it was being hummed, whistled, and sung all over the country.

The catchiness of the simple melody (dum-dum, dum-dum... dum-dum, dum-dum... sing that out loud, you'll get it if you don't know the song) and the rare opportunity to speak humorously about the ugly side of death doubtlessly has guaranteed the ballad's survival into the modern era. Like most folk songs, there is no definitive version.

When I (Troy) was growing up, my siblings and I used to sing this song quite a lot – likely to annoy my mother – and there's a good chance that we invented some of our own lyrics to fit the tune. Anyway, this is the way we knew the song, growing up in the 1970s and early 1980s:

> You shouldn't laugh when the hearse goes by,
> For you may be the next to die.
> They wrap you up in a big white sheet,
> And bury you down in the ground six feet.
> All goes well for about a week,
> Until your coffin begins to leak.

The worms crawl in, the worms crawl out,
The ants play pinochle on your snout.
Your liver turns to a slimy green,
And your snot runs out like whipping cream.
You spread it on some moldy bread,
And that's what you eat when you are dead.

A folk singer named Harley Poe added a final chorus to the song that we never knew. I'm adding it here because I wish we had:

And this is what it is to die,
I hope you had a nice goodbye.
Did you ever think as a hearse goes by,
That you may be the next to die?
And your eyes fall out, and your teeth decay,
And that is the end of a perfect day.

We were strange kids.

GONE, BUT NOT FORGOTTEN

Remembrance Through Postmortem Photography

On January 7, 1839 an announcement was made to the world that would forever change how we view life, and death, through the lens of a camera. French artist Louis Daguerre presented photographic examples he had long been working to achieve and perfect to members of the French Académie des Sciences, sparking the beginning of a phenomenon few of the era could have anticipated.

The aptly named daguerreotype photograph, the first practical application of photography, was created on a polished silver-plated sheet of copper. This sheet was exposed to iodine vapors to sensitize it before being placed in a large box camera. Once exposed, it was treated with mercury fumes to develop and rinsed with salt water to set.

The resulting images were a remarkable advancement in capturing detail valuable to

LOUIS DAGUERRE,
INVENTOR OF
DAGUERREOTYPE
PHOTOGRAPHY

FIRST KNOWN POSTMORTEM PORTRAIT OF ELIZABETH ROYAL BY ARTIST JOSEPH BADGER, 1747

both artistic and scientific studies. Once the photographic process was revealed, the daguerreotype became almost immediately popularized, and the practice of photography spread quickly throughout both Europe and America.

Prior to this invention, painted portraiture was available only to those wealthy enough to afford it, leaving middle and lower classes to rely on images committed solely to memory. They had no permanent visual representation to refer to until the daguerreotype became well known. Its invention was not without complications, however, as many working in the trade seized an opportunity to profit from the desperation of the bereaved.

In his article *Memento Mori: Death and Photography in Nineteenth Century America* for UCLA, researcher Dan Meinwald notes:

"As a specialty item, a postmortem photograph was more expensive—sometimes considerably more expensive—than an ordinary portrait. In part, this had to do with the unusual requirements of its making, if only because the photographer had to come to the subject rather than the other way around. However, this by itself could not have justified the high price of a postmortem picture. Photographers, no less astute than other business people, were charging an extraordinary fee for a product desired with extraordinary fervor by their customers. Whatever the reason for the high fees, the commissioning of a postmortem photograph often involved an economic sacrifice."

From 1841 to 1860, an estimated 30 million daguerreotype photographs were taken just in America alone. Among these were images of the recently deceased. In the 1850s, additional photographic procedures arose, greatly decreasing the cost for pre and post-death portraiture. The ambrotype (portrait on glass), tintype (portrait on thin metal), and carte-de-visite (portrait on paper) would eventually become more widely used than the daguerreotype.

Today, these surviving post-mortem photographs are somewhat misunderstood, and often dismissed as macabre reminders of a time in history seemingly obsessed with death. If we take but a moment to glance into the past with an open mind and compassionate heart, it isn't difficult to imagine how valuable something like a photograph could be, especially to those who were not afforded the luxuries we ourselves so frequently take for granted.

The images, in truth, are anything but grotesque. In its infancy, photography was far less accessible than it has become today. Many people could not afford or did not think to have photographs taken while living, leaving the necessity for a visual record more important when death arrived to claim the lives of those most precious to them. The invention of the photograph allowed many the opportunity to remember and stay connected to their dead indefinitely.

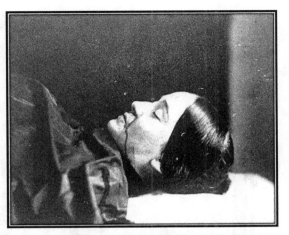

POSTMORTEM DAGUERREOTYPE OF WOMAN WITH BLOOD, CIRCA 1843
(THE BURNS ARCHIVE)

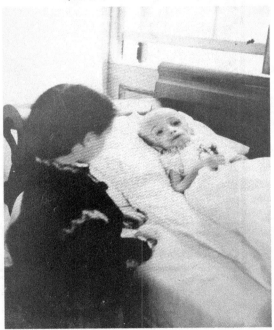

POSTMORTEM TINTYPE OF CHILD DEAD FROM DEHYDRATION, CIRCA 1885
(THE BURNS ARCHIVE)

POSTMORTEM PHOTOGRAPH OF INFANT POSED WITH NURSING OR
"MURDER BOTTLE" (THE THANATOS ARCHIVE)

When the first postmortem daguerreotypes were produced, little to no
effort was made to beautify the look of death. Illness was not easily disguised
on the faces and on the flesh of those who'd suffered a great deal before they

finally succumbed. Sickness claimed the lives of many but was especially rampant among children. As a result, postmortem photographs of children are most common.

As the practice progressed, attention was focused on creating a more peaceful or 'lifelike' image. When the situation allowed, the deceased was made to appear as though they had simply drifted off to sleep in peaceful repose.

Photo tinting was applied by hand, and the eyes of the deceased were often painted open to appear as though the individual were alive and well.

Many photographs of children included objects familiar to them, such as blankets and toys; others with flowers, or beside the family pet. Some children were posed with one of the earliest incarnations of the nursing bottle. Mothers of the Victorian era were thrilled with this invention, as it allowed their infants more freedom and ability to feed themselves. The nursing bottles were most often made of glass with a nipple attached to a rubber tube extending to the bottom of the bottle. In the days before sterilization and pasteurization (a heating process that kills harmful bacteria in the milk), many mothers unwittingly fed their children to death. Doctors did not endorse their use, but the convenience it provided was too great a temptation and their use were unfortunately continued. Over time, the bottles earned the gruesome but accurate title of "murder bottles."

THE MISREPRESENTATION OF FACTS

With information immediately available at our fingertips through internet search engines, blogs, and various informational sites, we can learn a great deal about most any subject in a relatively short period of time. It is unfortunate, however, that the internet is overrun with a great deal of information lacking any semblance of fact. It takes mere seconds to publish and perpetuate mistruths, and the result is irrevocably damaging.

This said, it must be mentioned that postmortem photography, while morbidly fascinating, was not the sole type of photography produced at the time. As death became more 'softened' and less obvious, photographs of the living inevitably made their way into the postmortem category. An individual sleeping on a sofa, for example, could easily be mistaken for a corpse. Without additional documentation to verify the individual in such photos as living or deceased, there is no way to properly identify or distinguish between the two with any real degree of certainty.

There are many researchers who have worked tirelessly to collect, study, and authenticate postmortem images to the best of their ability, but even their findings are subject to debate and criticism. A particular carte-de-visite

Text within the image:
Taken 9 Days after Death

Mother could not part with only daughter.

Miss Jeanette Glackmeyer Daughter whose above photo was taken 9 days after death

POSTMORTEM CARTE DE VISITE OF "GIRL DEAD NINE DAYS," CIRCA 1870 (THE BURNS ARCHIVE)

image (circa 1870) labeled 'GIRL DEAD NINE DAYS,' for example, is the subject of some debate. There are those who believe it to be a genuine postmortem example, while others claim it is a deliberate fake.

With the prevalence and accessibility of photo editing software, there are scores of people creating images that are obviously manufactured or digitally altered in some way, while others are less identifiable examples of photo manipulation, but are fraudulent nonetheless. The misrepresentation of history is a plague we unfortunately have no cure for.

Photographs including stands are an example of frequent mislabeling. These tools of the trade were rarely (if ever) used in postmortem photography. The purpose of the stand in photographs of the time was to hold a living individual in the desired position, prohibiting as much movement as possible. Should the subject move during the lengthy exposure time, the resulting image would appear blurry. If the subject were deceased, movement would not be a concern for the photographer, thus making the stand an unnecessary addition. Regardless, these images continually circulate under the guise that the presence of a stand undeniably identifies a

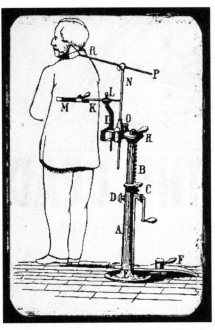

(ABOVE) AN ILLUSTRATION OF A
PHOTOGRAPHY STAND AND HOW IT
WORKED

(RIGHT) EXAMPLES OF PHOTOGRAPHY
WITH STANDS, MISTAKEN FOR
POSTMORTEM PHOTOGRAPHS

postmortem image. The misrepresentation of history, whether intentional or accidental, is a plague we unfortunately have no cure for.

Despite the often-disturbing imagery, genuine postmortem photographs unfailingly portray the human struggle with profound loss. Our mortality and inevitable deaths can be difficult to confront, but in truth there *is* love and beauty in the morbidity of these images, despite how little we recognize and appreciate it.

FACES OF THE DEAD

SPIRIT PHOTOGRAPHY AND HOW IT CHANGED AMERICA

One of the great movements in American history was Spiritualism, which was based on the belief that the dead could – and did – communicate with the living. Spiritualism came along at a time of great change in American history and took the entire country by storm. Séances began to be held in nearly every city in town and the spirit world seemed to be in constant contact with the land of the living.

Although it began nearly a decade before the Civil War, Spiritualism had faded in popularity by 1860. It was the massive number of deaths caused by the war that shocked and terrified Americans into a search for answers about what came after life had ended. Many turned to religion, while others embraced the idea that it was still possible to communicate with their lost loved ones. As detailed in an earlier chapter, interest in Spiritualism soared. But a large part of Spiritualism's appeal was not just that the living could talk to the dead – they might be able to see them, too.

The middle nineteenth century saw an amazing number of scientific discoveries that fascinated the public. With Spiritualism all the rage, it seemed inevitable that science and the spirit world would become intertwined. And with that, the practice of "spirit photography" was born.

The first anomalous photographs ever taken were assumed to be caused by unknown variables in the strange chemicals and new apparatus that photographers were then just learning to use. At the dawn of photography, it was nearly impossible to take photographs of people. With the exposure times of a half hour or more needed to impress an image on the

TWO ALLEGEDLY AUTHENTIC SPIRIT PHOTOGRAPHS TAKEN BY
WILLIAM MUMLER AT HIS BOSTON STUDIO

paper films and coated plates of the day, it was impractical to expect anyone to sit still for so long. It was not until improvements came along in cameras, lenses, photographic chemicals, and developing processes that exposure times were reduced to a matter of seconds instead of dozens of minutes. By this time, people were flocking to the portrait studios to have their images immortalized in time.

In those days, the photographer had to first prepare a plate by coating it with collodion, bathing it in silver nitrate, and then taking the photo while the plate was still wet. Each new exposure was an exciting event but imagine how excited W. Campbell of Jersey City must have been when he achieved what is considered to be the first "spirit photograph." At the American Photographic Society meeting of 1860, he displayed a test photograph that he had taken of an empty chair. There had been no one else in the studio at the time, but when the plate was developed, it showed the image of a small boy seated in the chair. Campbell was never able to produce any other photographs of this sort and, thanks to this, it would not be until the following year that the "real" history of spirit photography began.

On October 5, 1861, in a photographic studio at 258 Washington Street in Boston, an engraver and amateur photographer named William Mumler was developing some experimental self-portraits that he had taken and was startled to find that the image of a ghostly young woman appeared in one of the photos with him – or at least that was his story.

He was said to have recognized the young woman as a cousin who had passed away 12 years before. He later recalled that while posing for the portrait, he had experienced a trembling sensation in his right arm that left him feeling particularly exhausted. The photograph attracted great attention and it was examined by not only Spiritualists but by some of the leading photographers of the day. They all came to accept the fact that, as Mumler stated: "This photograph was taken by myself, of myself, and there was not a living soul in the room besides myself." Mumler was soon overwhelmed by public demand for his photographs and he gave up his regular job as an engraver to devote himself entirely to spirit photography.

William Black, a leading Boston photographer and the inventor of the acid nitrate bath for photographic plates, was one of the professionals who investigated Mumler and his methods. After sitting for Mumler in his studio, Black examined his camera, plate, and bath and kept his eye on the plate from the moment its preparations began until it was locked into the camera. After his portrait was taken, Black removed it from the camera and took it into the darkroom himself, where, as it developed, he was stunned to see the image of a man, leaning over his shoulder. Black was convinced that Mumler was the genuine article and could somehow entice the spirits to appear on film.

Others were, of course, not so sure.

Mumler had never been interested in the spirits, or Spiritualism, prior to his first alleged spirit photograph and his steep charge of $5 per photograph began to arouse suspicion that he was just in it for the money. He became the object of great controversy and eventually moved to New York, where he then began charging $10 for photographs. Predictably, the critics howled once more.

Mumler had many supporters, though. One of them was U.S. Court of Appeals Judge John Edmonds, who had originally come to Mumler's studio with the intention of exposing him as a fraud but left convinced that he could actually conjure up genuine psychic photos.

In 1863, Dr. Child of Philadelphia reported that Mumler was willing to allow him to thoroughly investigate the methods of his spirit photos and, as he said, find a rational explanation for the mystery. He permitted Child to watch all his operations in and out of the darkroom and allowed him to examine his apparatus. Dr. Child displayed the pictures made at the time, while he and several friends watched the entire process, from the plate

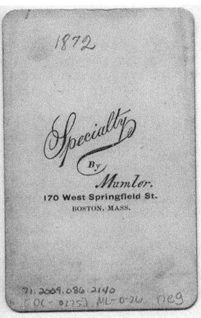

1872

Specialty
By
Mumler.
170 West Springfield St.
BOSTON, MASS.

71.2009.086.2140
[OC - 0225] ML-0-26 neg

MUMLER'S PHOTOGRAPH OF MARY LINCOLN, IN HER WIDOW'S WEEDS, IN WHICH THE SPIRIT OF HER SLAIN HUSBAND ALLEGEDLY APPEARED.

cleaning to the fixing. He took the precaution to mark each plate with a diamond before it was used and yet on each one of them was a spirit image. Child had failed completely to discover any human agent that was responsible for the formation of the spirit picture. Each of them differed considerably from one another and Child could not come up with a way to duplicate them.

Mumler's studio was frequented by many wealthy and influential patrons. Most of the time, the spirits that appeared on film were unrecognizable, but on at least one occasion, he produced a famous image that – legend has it – should have been impossible to fake. A lady who was heavily veiled and wearing a black mourning dress called unannounced one day at the studio. She gave her name as "Mrs. Tyndall," and asked to be photographed. Mumler later wrote, "I requested her to be seated, went into my darkroom and coated a plate. When I came out I found her seated with a veil still over her face. The crepe veil was so thick that it was impossible to distinguish a single feature of her face. I asked if she intended having her picture taken with her veil. She replied, 'When you are ready, I will remove it.' I said I was ready, upon which she removed the veil and the picture was taken."

It was only when Mumler saw the developed print that he realized the woman had been Mary Todd Lincoln. Behind her was standing the image of her late husband, Abraham Lincoln. This photograph – if genuine, and most likely, it is not – was perhaps the most astounding that Mumler produced during his career.

However, the "extras," as they came to be called, in Mumler's photographs did not astound everyone. After much controversy, pressure from city officials led to him being arrested and charged with fraud. But the testimony of several leading New York residents, including famed Broadway producer Jeremiah Gurney, who affirmed that as a professional photographer he had never seen anything like the images that were produced, led to Mumler being exonerated and his case dismissed.

Later, however, it turned out that the courts may have been a little too hasty when they dropped the charges against William Mumler.

According to an article in *Scientific American* magazine in 1902, Mumler may have been cleverer than anyone ever gave him credit for --- and a much bigger fraud. Experiments in duplicating spirit photos that were done long after Mumler was producing his controversial images discovered a simple way of creating spectral images that would have passed inspection by those who examined Mumler's plates and apparatus at the time. This method involved making a very thin positive image on glass that was the same size as the plate that was to be used in producing the spirit photo. The glass was then placed in the holder where the plate would later be placed, as well. With the glass in position, the plate could be inserted under the watchful eye of the examiner and the photograph produced. With the weak positive superimposed, the ghostly image would appear, along with the sitter, on the negative plate. In this way, the plates would never be tampered with and in examinations like those conducted by Dr. Child, his mark would appear on the plate that was used, and he would never assume that anything out of the ordinary was taking place.

Could this have been Mumler's secret? If we assume that fraud may have been involved with the creation of his photos, then yes, it could have been. But what about those photos that contained the images of loved ones that Mumler knew nothing about? Could his research have been so thorough that he delved into the private lives --- and photographs --- of those who made appointments so far in advance that he could obtain photos of dead relatives that would then appear in his spirit photographs? And what of those who came to him without an appointment and yet, their loved ones still managed to appear on film? Was it wishful thinking that the extras appeared to be so familiar?

Perhaps --- or perhaps not.

Other photographers, both amateur and professional, soon began to appear, eager to capitalize on the success of William Mumler. In America and Britain, new studios began to open, and the photographers began to call themselves "mediums," claiming the ability to make dead appear in photographs was just as relevant as those who contacted the spirits at séances. Spirit photography became wildly popular and literally thousands of dollars were made from those who came to have their portraits taken.

A SPIRIT PHOTOGRAPH TAKEN BY WILLIAM HOPE – HE WAS LATER CHARGED WITH FRAUD.

Typically, in spirit photographs, ghostly faces appeared, floating above and behind the living subjects. In others, fully-formed spirits would appear, usually draped in white sheets. Unfortunately, the methods of producing such images were simple. The fraudulent photographers became adept at doctoring their work, superimposing images on plates with living sitters, adding ghostly apparitions, and double exposures. The appearance of the fully-formed apparition was even easier. Many cameras demanded that the subject of the photo remain absolutely still, sometimes for periods of up to one minute, all the while, the shutter of the camera remained open. During this time, it was very simple for the photographer's assistant to quietly appear behind the sitter, dressed in appropriate "spirit attire." The assistant remained in place for a few moments and then ducked back out of the photo again. On the finished plate, it seemed a semi-transparent "extra" had made an appearance.

Other methods of obtaining fraudulent photographs were used, as well. Prepared plates and cut films were often switched and substituted by

ONE OF FREDERICK HUDSON'S
ENTERTAINING – ALTHOUGH
VERY QUESTIONABLE – SPIRIT
PHOTOGRAPHS

sleight of hand tricks, replacing those provided by an investigator. And while this might have fooled a credulous member of the public, sleight of hand maneuvers and instances of assistants prancing through photos draped in sheets did not convince hardened and skeptical investigators that the work of the spirit photographers was credible or genuine. However, in case after case, investigators walked away stumped as to how the bizarre images managed to appear on film. For every fraud who was exposed, there was at least one other photographer who was never caught cheating. More than a century later, many incidents with spirit photographs are as baffling now as they were then.

Unfortunately, that wasn't usually the case, though. Around the same time that William Mumler was going on trial for fraud in New York, a popular spirit photographer named Frederick Hudson emerged on the scene in London. Mrs. Samuel Guppy, a well-known medium of the day, brought him to the public's attention. A famous professional photographer named John Beattie eventually investigated Hudson in 1873. He carried out a series of experiments that were later published in the *British Journal of Photography*. At that time, Hudson was charging a steep fee for his photos, but only with the understanding that he could not be blamed if nothing unusual appeared, which often happened.

In his article, Beattie described how, with a friend, he had examined the glass room in Hudson's garden where the experiments were to take place, the operating and developing room with its yellow light and porcelain baths, the 10 x 8-inch camera with its 6-inch lens, and all the machinery involved. He also maintained that he had marked the photographic plate to be used and watched it being coated and prepared.

For the first photograph that Hudson took, using an exposure of about one minute, Beattie sat as the subject in profile to the background and Hudson's daughter (acting as the medium) stood next to him. No extra appeared in the photo. For the next experiment, Beattie wrote: "All was the same except that the medium sat behind the background. On the picture being developed, a sitting figure beside myself came out in front of me and between the background and myself. I am sitting in profile in the picture -- the figure is in a three-quarter position -- in front of me, but altogether between me and the background. The figure is draped in black, with a white colored plaid over the head, and is like both a brother and a nephew of mine. This last point I do not press because the face is like that of a dead person and under lighted."

Beattie continued: "In my last trial -- all, if possible, more strictly attended to then before, and in the same place relative to me -- there came out a standing female figure, clothed in black skirt, and having a white-colored, thin linen drapery something like a shawl pattern, upon her shoulders, over which a mass of black hair loosely hung. The figure is in front of me and, as it were, partially between me and the camera."

Beattie had initially assumed that Hudson was in some way faking the photographs, but now was no longer convinced of this. He was sure that the figures were not double exposures, had not been projected in some way, and were not the result of mirrors or even the result of images that had been manipulated onto the plates during the developing process.

What he did not take into consideration, though, was that the images could have been on the plates all along -- that the photographer had switched Beattie's plates for "trick plates." This seems to have been the standard operating procedure for many of the so-called spirit photographers of the day, as was described in the *Scientific American* article referenced earlier. Many spirit photographers, including a Mr. Parkes, who produced many psychic images, even allowed themselves to be observed while working on the plates. Parkes, for instance, had an aperture cut into the wall of his darkroom so that investigators could see inside while he went through the developing process. The problem was that the investigators had no idea just what plates he was actually developing.

In 1874, a French photographer named E. Buguet opened a studio and began a career capturing the spirits on film. Most of his photographs were of famous people, most of who claimed to recognize deceased loved ones and family members as "extras." This did not stop him from being arrested for fraud and tried by the French government. He admitted deception but even then, there were many who refused to accept his confession as genuine, claiming that he had been paid off by religious groups to plead guilty. In his confession, he stated that his photographs were created by double exposure. He would dress up his assistants to play the part of a ghost or would dress up a doll in sheet. This figure, along with a stock of heads, was seized by the police when they raided his studio. Buguet was fined and sentenced to a year in prison. Even after this, his supporters continued to insist his photographs were real. Reverend Stainton Moses, the famous medium, was convinced that at least some of Buguet's spirit photographs were authentic. He said that the prosecution of the case was tainted by religious officials, that the judge was biased, and that Buguet must have been bribed or terrorized to confess.

People simply refused to believe that any kind of spirit photography could be fake because they so desperately need it to be real. Spirit photography, like Spiritualism itself, provided an outlet for those who needed to mourn their dead. Unlike postmortem photography, which was discussed in the previous chapter, this was not a case of simply preserving the image of one who had passed on – this was capturing the image of a loved one who survived death in the next world.

It wasn't enough to simply remember the dead – we needed them to still be among us. And perhaps that makes it the most heartbreaking of all the customs that have surrounded America's obsession with death.

THE BEAUTIFICATION OF DEATH

THE UNDERTAKER IN AMERICAN HISTORY

Death grips the heart and mind of every living soul at one point or another. The emotional toll it takes can vary from person to person, depend heavily on individual circumstance, and last for varied lengths of time. Beyond the grieving, however, most Americans 'deal' with death in a matter of days, and at the behest of strangers seemingly more capable of handling the process than anyone outside of the modern-day funeral industry.

Until the late nineteenth century, death was experienced and handled almost exclusively within the confines of one's own home. Today, when the topic of the home-held funeral of the past is broached, it is not uncommon for people to remark on how strange and macabre a tradition that must have been before abandoning the topic altogether.

Many people (if not a majority) tend to be critical in their recollections, holding fast to the belief that today's methodologies provide a healthier, socially acceptable approach to dealing with death than those of the past. They do not view themselves as potential funeral directors (or dispositioners), even though preparing and caring for the dead was once a responsibility placed solely in the hands of the decedent's family. In fact, until the 1920s, it was still illegal throughout most of the country to remove a body from the home for any kind of funeral service.

The first 'undertakers' were not professionals called upon to whisk the dead away, chemically treat their bodies, or surround them with (or bury them in) material luxuries. They were women, and their only motivation in being "layers out of the dead" (also known as shrouders) was to properly honor and care for those they loved. These women would prepare the body for viewing by closing the eyes and mouth. Various orifices were plugged or blocked, and the internal organs removed and replaced with charcoal to slow decomposition.

Once washed and dressed, the body was placed into the coffin. If the weather required it, ice would be placed beneath it in large chunks, with smaller amounts placed around the body. This was a vital step, as embalming had not yet become mainstream and slowing decomposition was important while the body remained above ground.

The "wake" or period of time one's remains could be visited before burial, was held in the family parlor for a period of up to three days. It was during this time that family and friends remained close to the body to observe any lingering signs of life (if the aforementioned preparations had not taken place) before committing it to the grave, thus giving it the appropriate name.

The family members were often charged with the task of carrying the coffin on foot to the church for services, and then onto the cemetery where they themselves had dug the grave. Once the coffin was lowered inside, last remarks were offered before loved ones tossed a handful of dirt or straw onto the casket to symbolize a final farewell before personally filling in the grave themselves.

As the need arose, various individuals in the community were employed to provide specific services for grieving families. These consisted mostly of the carpenters who crafted the coffins, liverymen who provided horse-drawn hearses, and the cemetery sextons responsible for tolling the bells and occasionally digging the graves. Professional shrouders might also be hired to assist in bodily preparations. Businessmen began to recognize an opportunity to increase their profits by expanding the services they provided, and thus was born the first of the American undertakers.

COFFINS TO CASKETS

An enduring curiosity is what differences set apart the coffin from the casket. The coffin is made of a hexagonal design, wider at the shoulder area and narrow at the feet, earning them the nickname of "toe-pinchers." Caskets are rectangular, and often made of higher grade materials for enduring wear and tear. These two types are often used interchangeably, as the differences are minimal regarding function.

It became the goal of the undertaker to manage most if not all the planning and execution of the funeral, asserting himself as a necessary inclusion and gradually diminishing the family role in preparations and services. Merchants offered coffins for burial, provided from their collections on-hand or a catalogue from which the family could order.

Additional tasks included the supervision of the coffin as it was removed from the home and placed into the hearse, providing and arranging chairs at the cemetery, directing pallbearers, and remaining with the coffin until it was finally lowered into the grave.

Post-Civil War acceptance of embalming

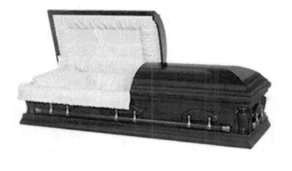

(TOP) AN EXAMPLE OF A MODERN CASKET

(BOTTOM) AN EXAMPLE OF WHAT WAS CALLED A "TOE PINCHER" COFFIN

resulted in partnerships between undertakers and embalmers, which began to outnumber hired female shrouders. With a larger role to play in arranging and performing funeral services, undertakers assumed the title of "funeral directors."

In 1870, Samuel Stein founded the Stein Manufacturing Company in Rochester, New York. By 1872, Samuel had applied for and been granted a patent on his cloth-covered "showcase" casket, featuring wood panels covered in velvet, Venetian lace-lined interior with both silk and satin accents, and handles made of solid silver. It was his exhibition of this high-end product at the Philadelphia Centennial Exposition in 1876 that became the standard for display in advertising caskets to the public. To further solidify their role as leaders in the emerging funeral industry, the Stein Co. also began the publication and distribution of *Casket*, a trade journal aimed at providing helpful business trends and merchandising options to the growing number of American funeral directors.

By the turn of the century, the couch casket became the popular option. The full couch casket featured a solid, one-piece lid that could be lifted for full viewing of the body, whereas the half-couch casket featured the lid in two sections, independently attached so the bottom half could remain covered and the top open for viewing. This casket design is still widely in use today.

DR. FRANCIS JULIUS
LEMOYNE, BUILDER OF
AMERICA'S FIRST
CREMATORY

CREMATION

The subject of cremation as a means for final disposition was not as widely accepted in the latter part of the nineteenth century as it has become today. This alternative to traditional burial, when first introduced to the country, often incited revulsion, fear, and even anger.

Dr. Francis Julius LeMoyne, a lifelong resident of Washington, Pennsylvania, was no stranger to the skepticism and hostilities many of his fellow Americans harbored regarding cremation. A graduate of Washington College, Dr. LeMoyne was a well-respected and trusted physician and civil rights activist well into the mid-1850s. As his health began to decline as he neared 60 years of age, he thought it important to downscale his medical practice in favor of dedicating more time and attention to research. Of particular interest to him was the conundrum of dealing with and disposing of the dead in a responsible and safe way.

LeMoyne personally abhorred the practice of burial and believed the methods at the time were harming his community. Embalming, while advantageous for the grieving during funeral services, polluted the soil in which the dead were buried, and the simple pine boxes used to house their remains did little if anything to prevent toxins from escaping into the groundwater they came into contact with.

Believing that cremation could eradicate much of the illnesses caused and spread by burials, LeMoyne proposed a crematory be built in Washington's public cemetery, but his requests were immediately and adamantly met with a resounding no from its trustees. It was then he decided to move forward with planning and erecting a crematory on his own land, with the help of fellow town resident John Dye.

The small structure measuring twenty by thirty feet was completed in 1876. Unassuming and absent of any frill, the crematory consisted of a quaint reception area and a smaller room containing the crematory oven LeMoyne had designed himself. The furnace was initially designed to be heated with coal, but a pipe was later added to allow the furnace to be heated by gas.

THE FIRST CREMATORY IN THE UNITED STATES, LOCATED IN WASHINGTON, PENNSYLVANIA

Many religious individuals considered his crematory and its use to dispose of human flesh "un-Christian" and grotesque. His attempt to combat the negativity by holding public meetings was only met with more resistance, and the people of Washington were largely opposed despite the doctor's attempts at educating them on the benefits of cremation. It would not be until he was 78 years of age in 1876 that Dr. LeMoyne would finally have the opportunity to cremate a man who had volunteered his remains to the process. The Baron de Palm, an immigrant nobleman from Austria, had fallen on hard financial times and became quite ill. Once he passed away, his body was sent to Washington on December 5, 1876 and was successfully cremated the following day at a cost of $7.04.

Dr. LeMoyne succumbed to diabetes and passed away on October 14, 1879 and became the third individual to be cremated at his establishment. In all, a total of 42 cremations were carried out until operations came to an end in 1901. Other crematoriums were built, but the practice did not become popular until well into the twentieth century.

America's first crematory still stands, nondescript but well preserved by the Washington County Historical Society on Gallows Hill in Washington, Pennsylvania.

MARKETING REMEMBRANCES

As mourning the dead in post-Civil War America evolved, so too did the number of services and products that businesses offered to the bereaved.

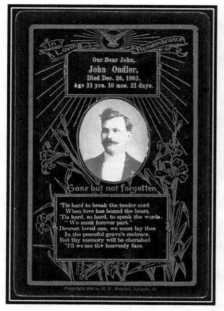 

TWO EXAMPLES OF MOURNING CABINET CARDS, PRODUCED BY THE
H.F. WENDELL COMPANY OF LEIPSIC, OHIO

Cabinet cards, or images mounted on heavy card stock, first featured portraits that families displayed at home in their drawing room cabinets. In 1881, several companies began marketing the mourning cabinet card to families who had placed obituaries in the newspaper.

Women were paid to collect obituaries from their local newspapers at a rate of one cent each, from which these companies would design and create a personalized card for the deceased featuring the appropriate birth and death dates along with various poems and symbology. This sample was sent along to the grieving families with the option to purchase additional cards by the dozen as they were, or with a variety of other options made available to them. If a photo was sent in with payment, it too could be included on the card.

H.F. Wendell and Company of Leipsic, Ohio sent the following poetically compelling letter to accompany the sample:

"DEAR FRIEND:

This is a bright, glad, beautiful world, fragrant with the odor of flowers, tuneful with the songs of birds, resplendent with the glories of earth and sea and sky, and yet its attractions now are, no doubt, unnoticed by you, for grim, merciless death has appeared in your midst and snatched from your companionship one of your loved ones. Your sky is hung with black and somber cloud curtains, your vision is o'ercast with the gloom of sorrow, and every sound that strikes your ear has in it a cadence of despair. Without the presence of that one who has gone before, the world, indeed, seems

This Cabinet Memorial Card

Is sent to you for inspection. Should you conclude to keep it, the price is 20 cents. In naming this price we do not mean to intimate that you are compelled to keep it. You are under no obligations whatever to keep it, but in case you do not send us the money for it, kindly return the card within twenty days.

In case you do not wish to keep the card, replace it within the large envelope, cross off your name, and return to us.

Should there be any errors in printing, return it to us with 20 cents in silver or stamps, state the correction you wish made, and we will send you another of your own selection it its place. We would be pleased to have your order. If you will send for one dozen or more cards, we will make no charge for this sample.

H. F. WENDELL & CO. - Leipsic, Ohio

We now make 4 cards for 50c; 6 for 65c; 8 for 75c; 12 for $1; 20 for $1.40; 25 for $1.75

AN INSERT SENT TO FAMILIES ALONG WITH
SAMPLE MOURNING CABINET CARDS

empty and cheerless to you, and in your heart there is a dreary, dismal, aching void.

The only consolation that is vouchsafed you is the sweet realization of the fact that your beloved it at peace. The one upon whom you have lavished your affection is now in that land 'where the weary are at rest.' Bending over the open coffin, looking at the folded hands, which will never clasp yours again in this world, gazing upon the closed eyes in which you will never more see your image reflected on this earth, your scalding tears fall as you realize that your earthly companionship with this one is forever at an end.

And, as stated before, your only consolation is that your heart's idol has heard the words from the Father's lips, 'Well done, thou good and faithful servant. Enter thou into the joys of thy Lord.' Your consolation is found in a consideration of the fact that your treasure is in heaven. The poor, worn frame will never more be racked with the agonies of pain. Suffering is at an end. But 'twill only be a little while until you will cross the dark river and join your companion among the hosts of the saved on the other shore.

And until then you will find solace in some such thoughts as the above, and in testifying to your faithful memory of the departed. In no more appropriate way can you express this fidelity of memory than by the possession of one of our elegant cabinet memorial cards. We trust you will pardon the liberty which we take in submitting to you for your examination a sample of these cards. You will observe that it is neat, simple, and attractive. The custom of commemorating the virtues of departed friends by means of memorial cards is not a new one. It has the dignity of age. It has existed for many years in Europe, and now it is common in all parts of the civilized world for the family of the deceased to send to each one of the *relatives and friends an appropriately inscribed memorial card. You will see that the enclosed card is suitable either for framing or for the album.*

Should you conclude to keep this card, the price is 20 cents. You can remit this to us at your earliest convenience. In naming this price we do not mean to intimate that you are compelled to keep the sample enclosed. You are under no obligation whatever to keep it unless you wish to do so, but in case you do not send us the money for it, kindly return the card within ten days.

If the sample is improperly filled out, or has been injured in the mail, return to us with 20 cents and we will gladly send you another in its stead. All the designs shown in our catalogue belong to us, and are fully protected by copyright. The cuts in our catalogue cannot possibly give you an idea of the real beauty of the cards themselves.

We have had long experience in this business and we feel perfectly justified in saying that these memorial cards are the most artistic and attractive ever gotten up. Trusting that we will receive your order, we are Yours most sincerely, H.F. Wendell & Co., Leipsic, Ohio."

The sale of these mourning cards flourished and remained a popular memorialization for the dead until production ceased in 1920.

DISCARDING THE PAST

As the funeral industry expanded and evolved, the need to establish its professionalism resulted in the formation of The Funeral Directors National Association of the United States in 1882. During its initial meeting, it was decided that the title of "funeral director" replace that of undertaker to 'elevate the occupation.'

In 1885, the nation's first fully functional funeral home was built in Pittsburgh, Pennsylvania. This business model provided funeral directors complete control of the process, from preparation of the body to coordinating memorial services. The responsibilities once nearly entirely those of the deceased's family were systematically moved out of the home and into the hands of local businessmen.

Around the turn of the century more and more funeral homes were built, and the family parlors began disappearing from homes to further distance death and dying from everyday family life, these parlors were referred to as 'living rooms,' as they no longer served as a sacred space in which to display and say farewell to the dead. Families became nearly entirely reliant on the funeral industry for assistance. Other terminology changed as well. Hearses became "funeral coaches", flowers "floral tributes", and ashes became "cremains", all to soften the harshness of the funeral experience.

AN EXAMPLE OF THE VICTORIAN PARLOR – A.K.A. THE "DEATH PARLOR." CUSTOM WOULD SOON HAVE THESE PARTS OF THE KNOWN BECOME KNOWN AS THE "LIVING ROOM"

These were not the only changes to take place, however. The once invaluable practice of photographing the dead to retain as keepsakes quickly declined in popularity during The Great Depression of the 1930s. These photographs were no longer viewed as tokens of love and remembrance, but reminders of death and sorrow that the American public no longer valued. Millions of postmortem photographs were systematically destroyed, and the dead pictured within them largely forgotten. As a result, the few that still exist today have become highly sought collectibles.

In the 1960s, flowers were so heavily marketed to funeral directors that over 60 percent of floral industry sales were attributed to sympathy flowers. They remain a staple of the average American funeral to this day, and as with any of the products and services offered through a funeral home, the markup on floral arrangements has risen exponentially over the years. Why? Simply because when it comes to a funeral, people are unwittingly led into believing such expenses are necessary.

THE HIGH COST OF DYING

FUNERALS IN MODERN AMERICA

"The cost of the funeral is the third-largest expenditure,
after a house and a car, in the life of an ordinary American family."

-Jessica Mitford, The American Way of Death Revisited

Before we begin to dissect the American death care industry, we must acknowledge two things; owning and/or operating a funeral home is a business, and as such, it is expected to make a profit. Secondly, despite the criticisms clearly laid out in this chapter, there are indeed people in the industry doing good, honest work for their clients and their families. We cannot hold every individual in the business accountable for the sins of the industry, but we can certainly become more aware of what is and is not acceptable, moral, and fair in hopes of inspiring change.

It is also important to note that while many families would like to be more intimately involved with the funerary process, many want (and often need) a funeral director to take over and make the necessary arrangements on their behalf. This is perfectly acceptable, of course, and it is not our intention to demonize every death care professional that assists them.

Over the past century, death has steadily moved from within the confines of the average American family home. Even when death occurs in the comfort of one's own bed, strangers are usually always called in to remove the deceased, store the remains, and prepare them for burial and/or cremation.

These services are marketed as not only necessary, but important for the grieving process, or achieving what most refer to as 'closure.' Upon closer inspection, however, it is hardly more than a financial transaction. An average American funeral can cost anywhere from $7,000 - $10,000 on up. When all is said and done, many families are left with little comfort and an exorbitant amount of debt, making the enormity of their loss even more difficult down the road. A payout on a life insurance policy may cover a great deal, if not all, of the funerary costs (and funeral directors are aware of this), but if more of the funds could be utilized to further care for the living left behind, it is worth being educated about the various options available before losing any unnecessary time and/or resources.

THE FUNERAL RULE

In April of 1984, the Federal Trade Commission (FTC) created and began enforcing the Funeral Rule, which was established to educate and protect consumers when dealing with a licensed funeral home or funeral director. This information is readily available on the FTC website (https://www.consumer.ftc.gov/articles/0300-ftc-funeral-rule), but for the purpose of including as much helpful information in this chapter as possible, we will include the rule in its entirety here as well.

The first line of defense in protecting yourself from deceitful or inadequate goods or services begins with knowing exactly what you are legally required to do, and what the funeral home you choose is required to provide you.

Under the FTC Funeral Rule, it is your right to:

1. *Buy only the funeral arrangements you want.*
You have the right to buy separate goods (such as caskets) and services (such as embalming or a memorial service). You do not have to accept a package that may include items you do not want.

2. *Get price information on the telephone.*
Funeral directors must give you price information on the telephone if you ask for it. You don't have to give them your name, address, or telephone number first. Although they are not required to do so, many funeral homes mail their price lists, and some post them online.

3. *Get a written, itemized price list when you visit a funeral home.*
The funeral home must give you a general price list (GPL) that is yours to keep. It lists all the items and services the home offers, and the cost of each one.

4. *See a written casket price list before you see the actual caskets.*
Sometimes, detailed casket price information is included on the funeral home's GPL. More often, though, it's provided on a separate casket price list. Get the price information before you see the caskets, so you can ask about lower-priced products that may not be on display.

5. *See a written outer burial container price list.*
Outer burial containers are not required by state law anywhere in the U.S., but many cemeteries require them to prevent the grave from caving in. If the funeral home sells containers, but doesn't list their prices on the GPL, you have the right to look at a separate container price list before you see the containers. If you don't see the lower-priced containers listed, ask about them.

6. *Receive a written statement after you decide what you want, and before you pay.*
It should show exactly what you are buying and the cost of each item. The funeral home must give you a statement listing every good and service you have selected, the price of each, and the total cost immediately after you make the arrangements.

7. *Get an explanation in the written statement from the funeral home that describes any legal cemetery or crematory requirement that requires you to buy any funeral goods or services.*

8. *Use an "alternative container" instead of a casket for cremation.*
No state or local law requires the use of a casket for cremation. A funeral home that offers cremations must tell you that alternative containers are available and must make them available. They might be made of unfinished wood, pressed wood, fiberboard, or cardboard.

9. *Provide the funeral home with a casket or urn you buy elsewhere.*
The funeral provider cannot refuse to handle a casket or urn you bought online, at a local casket store, or somewhere else - or charge you a fee to do it.

The funeral home cannot require you to be there when the casket or urn is delivered to them.

10. *Make funeral arrangements without embalming.*

No state law requires routine embalming for every death. Some states require embalming or refrigeration if the body is not buried or cremated within a certain time; some states don't require it at all. In most cases, refrigeration is an acceptable alternative. In addition, you may choose services like direct cremation and immediate burial, which don't require any form of preservation. Many funeral homes have a policy requiring embalming if the body is to be publicly viewed, but this is not required by law in most states. Ask if the funeral home offers private family viewing without embalming. If some form of preservation is a practical necessity, ask the funeral home if refrigeration is available.

The FTC also provides a pricing checklist to assist consumers in calculating the costs before hiring a funeral director for products and services. (https://www.consumer.ftc.gov/articles/0301-funeral-costs-and-pricing-checklist#Funeral_Pricing)

Making multiple copies of this checklist is helpful when contacting or meeting with various funeral homes, as it will allow you to compare prices and make the decision that best suits your needs as well as your budget.

FUNERAL PRICING CHECKLIST

"Simple" disposition of the remains:
- Immediate burial -
- Immediate cremation -
- If the cremation process is extra, how much is it?
- Donation of the body to a medical school or hospital

"Traditional" full-service burial or cremation:
- Basic services fee for the funeral director and staff -
- Pick up of body -
- Embalming -
- Other preparation of body -

- Least expensive casket (description, including model #) -
- Outer burial container (vault, description) -
- Visitation/viewing - staff and facilities -
- Funeral or memorial service - staff and facilities -
- Graveside service, including staff and equipment -
- Hearse -
- Other vehicles -
- Total   -

Other services:
- Forwarding body to another funeral home -
- Receiving body from another funeral home -

Cemetery/Mausoleum costs:
- Cost of lot or crypt (if you don't already own one) -
- Perpetual care -
- Opening and closing the grave or crypt -
- Grave liner, if required -
- Marker/monument, including setup -

EMBALMING - WHAT YOU NEED TO KNOW

EMBALM [əmˈbä(l)m]
Verb
To preserve a corpse from decay by arterial injection of a preservative.

Every state in the U.S. has a different set of legalities when it comes to dealing with the dead. However, as briefly stated in the FTC Rule, there are no states that legally require every body to be embalmed prior to burial. Most Americans assume that if a body is to be buried, it is legally required to embalm the remains first, and funeral directors are all too willing to continue allowing this assumption to bolster their bottom line.

Prior to conducting the research for this book, we admittedly knew very little about the practical application of this process in present day circumstances. We were aware of the details of its development and historical use, but the remaining knowledge we acquired had come from our own personal experiences in attending viewings or funerals of people who had been embalmed. It often presented the individual as a 'plasticized' version of themselves, along with making the skin and underlying tissues stiff and rigid to the touch.

Embalming someone involves the removal of present internal fluids and replacing them with chemicals to slow the decomposition process. Once a casket is chosen, consumers are actively led to believe this needs to be done for the deceased to be viewed in the best circumstance possible. This is untrue. Most modern funeral homes are equipped with refrigeration, which can store and help to preserve a body that is to be buried within a reasonably short period of time.

As most burials occur within three to four days following death, it stands to reason that embalming is not only unnecessary in many cases, but an additional expense that most do not need to commit to. However, a funeral home may refuse to provide a public viewing without first embalming the body, whether it is to be interred or cremated. One funeral home we spoke to stated, *"Embalming is required for public viewing. This is not a state law, but a company policy. We know that we will be able to make the individual look much better and presentable if we are able to embalm, even if cremation will be the final manner of disposition."*

The same company also stated that a private viewing, without the deceased being embalmed, was acceptable if the party attending said viewing consisted of less than twenty people. We are not altogether sure why the number of people viewing a body is significant, but many funeral homes have this policy in place to heavily encourage - and nearly force - their clients into paying for the service.

In our view, embalming a body set for cremation is akin to placing several hundred dollars in the hands of the deceased and sending it along with them to the incinerator; a complete waste. In addition, embalming can and often does alter a person's appearance dramatically all on its own. Do not be too quick to assume your loved one will look 'better' or 'more life-like' after they've been embalmed. Sadly, there isn't a process that can altogether make a deceased individual look alive when they are no longer living. The practice might make the funeral director's job and those of his staff a great deal easier, but it is not necessarily more effective or beneficial for the client.

The average cost of embalming services in the U.S. range anywhere from $200-$700 on up, depending on the geographic area and the size and condition of the body that is to be preserved. In Utah (which is the state we will be using as an example in this and additional chapters), funeral homes and mortuaries advertise the price of embalming at vastly different rates, which is puzzling when you consider that the time, tools and technique hardly differ from one funeral home to another.

THE EMBALMING PROCESS

Few Americans know that in its infancy, the practice of embalming was done in the decedent's home, attended closely by family members overseeing the process. Family involvement was not only expected, it was encouraged. Today, little is known about the process of embalming outside of the funeral home preparation room, which is not legally open to the public. If an individual requested access to attend the embalming of a loved one's remains, they would most certainly be denied. This fact left us with a sense of curiosity as to why this once common practice has now been hidden from public view, discussed very little, and is widely accepted despite a lack of knowledge on the subject.

What truly happens to a body when it is embalmed? The answer, in detail, is not for the faint of heart, but it is important (in our opinion) to know what really happens behind those preparation room doors when you entrust a body to a funeral director's care. Should you find yourself disinterested in these details, or believe you might find them disturbing or offensive, we encourage you to skip ahead and bypass this section altogether.

Once the 'intake' has occurred, and arrangements have been made to care for the deceased, the body is taken into a sterile, surgical room-like environment, stripped of any clothing, and placed on a gurney and/or table. The body is then 'bled out' by the opening of veins to drain the blood. Once this is complete, embalming fluid (consisting primarily of chemicals such as glycerin, alcohol, formaldehyde, borax, phenol and water) is pumped into the body via major arteries and/or veins. These include the jugular and subclavian veins, or the carotid and femoral arteries.

The eyes are then permanently closed with eye-cement and covered with caps dyed to closely match the skin tone. As the muscles in the face tend to relax following death, the mouth of the deceased is sewn shut to prevent it from falling or remaining open. A needle is pulled through the area between the upper lip and gums, exiting the left nostril and secured in place. If the showing of teeth is unavoidable, the teeth are cleaned and coated with dye-free nail polish. If the lips tend to drift apart, the embalmer might dislocate the lower jaw, drill holes in both the upper and lower portions, and then wire them together into the desired position.

The next step in the embalming process involves opening the abdomen and inserting a large, hollow needle connected to a tube (known as a trocar) into the body. It is then maneuvered throughout the chest and abdomen areas to remove bodily fluids, which are replaced by the embalmer's cavity fluid solution. The incision is then sewn up and the body is left to rest as the chemicals work to stiffen and dry the flesh. This is crucial to the embalmer, as his next duty is to prepare the body for viewing, and his canvas will need to be in the condition easiest for him to work with.

Each body presents a different set of challenges for the restorative artist, and therefore a various array of pastes, clays, cosmetics, and prosthetics are on hand to assist in making a body whole and as life-like as possible. Deliberate positioning in the casket (neither too high or too low), the placement of the hands, and carefully chosen lighting are all factors the staff must consider ensuring the perfect presentation.

PRE-NEED ARRANGEMENTS

Many people are attracted to the idea of pre-planning/paying for their funeral services well in advance to lessen or remove the eventual burden from family members or others charged with their care. This can backfire in a number of ways. In Utah, for example, there are no consumer protections in place for pre-need cemetery arrangements. Any funds the consumer places into the purchase of a plot, vault, headstone, and various other cemetery services can immediately be spent by the cemetery. If the purchaser changes their mind, they lose those funds. If the cemetery goes out of business, there is no way to recover the financial loss.

Pre-need funeral contracts must be guaranteed product contracts, meaning the funeral home cannot charge their customers any additional funds on the exact products and services they've ordered and paid for, regardless of when their death occurs. However, there are no legal protections in place to keep the funeral home from shady tactics such as declaring certain products are no longer available and a new (likely more expensive) alternative must be purchased. Tactics such as these protect the funeral home from financial losses due to market inflation.

Before signing any pre-need contract, be sure to read the fine print and research all state laws and regulations to protect your financial investment.

CASKETS - UPPING THE MIDDLE

Choosing a casket can be one of the most overwhelming and emotional parts of the entire funeral planning process. For the bereaved, it is a choice that not only reflects the tastes and personality of the newly deceased, it is an item many hope will adequately display the honor, love and respect they have for the individual who has passed away.

For the funeral director, however, it is something almost entirely different. Burial caskets are a high-ticket item, and perhaps the most lucrative one out of all the services and merchandise a client is likely to be presented with. As such, they require careful and deliberate presentation to make the highest possible profit for the company.

Grief plays an integral role in this transaction, and funeral homes know full well that clients are more likely to make an on-the-spot decision based on their emotional needs rather than fully considering their financial limitations. Funeral homes are routinely instructed through various publications, sales materials, and conferences on how to best up-sell their customers through careful wording, presentation, etc. When approaching and first entering a funeral home, we feel it only fair that the client be aware of the sales strategy, especially in such a difficult time of need.

There are dozens upon dozens of funeral homes listed in the state of Utah. When attempting to contact them to gain a bit more information on their services and associated prices, we found that very few were willing to communicate with us. We did not disclose the fact that we were researchers, we simply asked for assistance in availability and pricing. We were invited to visit several establishments in person but given little to no details via email or over the phone. This too is part of the strategy. If someone is looking to make arrangements, it is easier (and more ideal for the funeral director) if the bereaved sees the caskets and displays in person, as they are more likely to make a swift decision, fueled mostly by their emotions and less by the immediate availability of funds necessary for the purchase.

We found only one funeral home who had their casket pricing list available on their website. The additional lists we acquired were received after e-mail requests had been sent, some only after repeatedly contacting the businesses. If those employed in the death care industry were truly invested in the emotional well-being and healing of their clients, wouldn't the pricing for all their services be easily accessible and transparent?

Most Utah families typically spend an average of $2,500 for a casket, believing they aren't opting for a "cheap" one, nor are they going the most expensive route. They might be dissuaded by the funeral home's effort to either conceal their cheaper models or display them in the least attractive finishes and colors. There is a 'method to the madness' regarding these sales.

One funeral home sent a list consisting of fifty different casket models, from the highest priced ($9,254) to the least expensive ($595). Thirteen models were priced $3,000 and above, twenty-four models at and above $2,000, nine models at and above $1,000, and only four under $1,000. This pushes the customer toward purchasing a casket in the $2,000+ range, which is known as 'upping the middle,' and make no mistake, it is deliberate.

Another funeral home refused to provide a detailed list without an in-person visit, but mentioned their caskets ranged anywhere from $1,045 to a whopping $18,995. This would make their mid-range casket options around $9,000. With these kinds of numbers attached to the caskets, you can clearly see just how important these sales are to any funeral home. You'd be hard-pressed to find a funeral director who would encourage you to do your research, price-match, and go for a lower priced option.

According to the Federal Trade Commission, every funeral service provider is legally bound to accept any casket (or urn) provided to them, whether purchased online, at a local casket manufacturer, or anywhere else. It is also illegal to charge clients an additional fee to receive and/or handle a container purchased outside of the funeral home as well, though through clever re-wording, this fee is still applied in many cases.

For example, one funeral home's pricing list states, *"We welcome those individuals and families who have selected or obtained a casket from an alternative provider. To ensure our ability to provide excellent care and updated facilities to those selecting an alternative provider, an additional $500 will be added..."*

This sounds an awful lot like the 'handling fee' the FTC tries to protect consumers from having to pay. The purchase of a casket from another provider should not affect the funeral home's 'ability to provide excellent care,' so, in our opinion, this sort of policy is deceitful, and appears to be aimed more at protecting potential profit than it is to assist grieving families.

Another clever way of dissuading customers from an outside casket purchase is to offer service package discounts to those who purchase a casket directly. There are numerous fees lumped into these packages, some of which are renamed or listed in a different order, seemingly to protect establishments from their potential clients doing the math. The savings of a thousand dollars or more on a funeral package might *seem* advantageous, but if you are spending thousands less on a casket by buying one elsewhere, the so-called 'discount' the funeral home offers is really no discount at all.

Remember, you are under no obligation to purchase items or services you do not need or want. If a funeral home or director treats you or situation differently than he would have had you purchased a casket directly from him, your business should be taken elsewhere.

SEALER CASKETS - BUYER BEWARE

When making funeral arrangements for a loved one, a family might be presented with the option to purchase what is known as a 'sealer,' 'gasketed' or 'protective' casket. These hermetically sealed caskets are designed to protect the casket itself, though consumers are often led to believe they are ideal for protecting the remains from deterioration caused by outside elements such as air, moisture and bacteria.

You might be tempted to make such a purchase if you believe that your loved one's body will be protected, and natural decomposition delayed if his or her casket is sealed prior to burial. These caskets cost hundreds of dollars more than the un-sealed variety (though it costs the manufacturer less than $20 to make the seal), and believe it or not, accelerate the breakdown of human flesh.

In an article entitled, *What You Should Know About Exploding Caskets* by Josh Slocum, Executive Director of the Funeral Consumers Alliance, he states:

"...you can't protect a corpse from itself. While you're insulating grandma from the outside air, she could be stewing in her own fluids, turning into a slurry from the work of anaerobic bacteria. When the weather turns warm, in some cases, that sealed casket becomes a pressure cooker, and bursts from accumulated gases and fluids of the decomposing body. The next time relatives visit grandma, they could find her rotting remains oozing from her tomb in the form of a nauseating thick fluid."

The fact is that the body of a deceased individual is going to decompose, regardless of its housing, whether buried underground or placed in a mausoleum. It cannot be protected from its own natural processes. Cemeteries will often break these seals as a preventative measure, thus making the need for the 'upgrade' to a sealer casket completely unnecessary and a wasted expense.

BURIAL VAULTS - OUTER BURIAL CONTAINERS

The use of these containers, in which the casket is placed at burial, is not legally required by any state in the country. A vault's *primary* use is not to protect the casket. Many cemeteries require the use of burial vaults to keep the ground above the grave from caving in, either due to natural settling, or from the weight and pressure of heavy maintenance equipment passing over the grave.

As with caskets, vaults can be purchased with a variety of features. Standard and unlined versions (known as concrete grave boxes), for example, will keep the ground above the grave from caving in, but are not recommended by funeral directors as they are not designed to keep subsoil elements such as water from reaching the casket and damaging its contents.

What do vaults cost? Prices vary greatly from state to state, and manufacturers of burial containers rarely sell their products directly to consumers, making it nearly impossible to calculate the overhead a client is likely to be charged. A variety of lining options (plastics, steel, copper, or bronze) will determine the overall cost, along with any personalization the client wishes to add. The average price range for 'basic protection' is $1,000 or more to nearly $6,000 for 'premium protection.'

Sealer vaults are not what they appear to be. As with sealer caskets, sealer vaults work against the natural decomposition process. Air is unable to get into the vault, but it is also unable to escape it. This environment causes the remains to putrefy, as they cannot dry out. This is assuming that the seal - nothing more than simple weather stripping - holds. If the seal becomes compromised or damaged by mishandling, the vault will fill and leave your loved one left in a pool of rainwater.

It is important to note that, no matter the financial investment in a burial vault, it ultimately cannot entirely preserve what is housed inside. Spending more money might bring you some measure of reassurance and peace of mind, but the basic use and function remain the same as the less expensive alternatives.

WHAT YOUR FUNERAL DIRECTOR WON'T TELL YOU

Fact is, there are a whole host of options for individuals seeking alternatives to traditional casket and urn purchases. These options are not going to be presented to you at a funeral home, nor are they likely to be well-received by the funeral director you trust your loved one's services to. While it is illegal for a funeral director to charge you additional fees for handling an alternative container, interviews with individuals who have opted to provide their own reveal that this choice often directly affects how a grieving family is treated. Fees for other items or services have inexplicably inflated for these clients as well. Should a family encounter a home or director that is happy to work with them under these circumstances, that establishment certainly deserves their business.

The following are examples of various options available to you. This is not a complete list. Personal research is recommended before purchasing items and/or services through any provider.

Alternative casket/urn options:

- *Build your own.* A quick internet search will provide anyone with a desire to build their own coffin or casket a variety of downloadable plans. Casketplans.org is one such resource, with plans ranging from $19.95 to $39.95. They also provide plans for homemade urns for $14.95. If you are familiar with or have access to 3D printing, you can purchase plans for full-scale casket/coffin printing for as little as $4.95, with plans for casket hardware available as well. Depending on the size and design of the casket/urn you wish to build, there are dozens of free plan resources online.

• *Have one built.* Many individuals offer custom, affordable wooden caskets and urns as an alternative to those purchased through a funeral home. One such resource is Michael Scheetz of handcraftedcasketsandcoffins.com. Clients can request a custom design and arrange for freight shipping within the contiguous states. (International shipping is not available.)

• *Cloth-covered caskets.* Caskets made with solid wood frames, plastic liners, hand-sewn interiors and covered in cloth. Ideal for both burial and cremation. Available through covingtonbox.com. *Note: These caskets must be ordered through a funeral home or mortuary, though the cost will be significantly less than showroom caskets.

• *Biodegradable & environmentally friendly caskets, coffins and urns.* Finalfootprint.org offers bamboo, banana leaf, rattan and seagrass varieties.

• *Major online retailers of traditional caskets and urns.* Walmart.com, Costco.com and even Amazon.com all provide comparable casket and urn options often well below funeral home retail prices. Be aware that shipping costs may vary greatly between retailers.

CEMETERY FEES

Beyond the costs you will incur at the funeral home, it is important to know that most religious, town or commercial cemeteries set their own fee schedules.

• *Residential and Non-residential burial plots.* Those that lived outside of the city where the desired cemetery is located often pay a much higher price than those who lived within the city limits.

- *Opening & closing of a single or double plot.* Charges differ quite significantly for opening and closing graves, depending on their size. Weekday openings/closings are usually significantly less expensive than those taking place on a weekend or holiday.

- *Monuments & adornments.* Many cemeteries have restrictions in place for the size and type of headstone or monument, as well as additional adornments and plantings.

REGULATIONS VARY BY STATE

If you are planning a funeral, whether in whole or part, it is in your best interest to research the laws in your individual state. Becoming the "dispositioned," or the individual bypassing (and essentially becoming the funeral director) requires a more involved approach. For example, until recently, Utah state law required the involvement of a funeral director once an individual passed away, but this created a significant financial burden on families who wanted to make all the arrangements themselves, or that simply couldn't afford the funeral director's fee. That provision has since been reversed.

The most comprehensive and helpful resource we have found is a book entitled *Final Rights: Reclaiming the American Way of Death* by Josh Slocum and Lisa Carlson, wherein the laws of each state are clearly laid out for the consumer. Checking with your local state Office of Vital Statistics is also recommended.

IT'S YOUR FUNERAL

THE CHANGING FACE OF
AMERICAN FUNERALS

Although the average American funeral suits the needs and tastes of most (as it has become the 'socially acceptable norm'), many often prefer something less traditional. And while there are those who trust their close friends and family to make their final arrangements when death occurs, there are also those who prefer more control over their final disposition.

One need not be buried in a traditional casket or have their ashes sealed in an urn to be properly memorialized. None of us are obligated to follow the paths of those who have gone before us. You can spend as much - or as little - as your budget allows, and still have a service uniquely tailored to you and your loved ones.

In this chapter, we will introduce a variety of funerary options you may not have heard of, us know little about. Some of these options seem to have come straight out of a movie, while others are quaint, simplistic, and yet still appeal to one's unique sense of self.

Please note that the options listed below may be available through multiple providers and may not be available or legal in all areas. Your independent research is recommended.

AQUAMATION

This environmentally friendly option, also known as water cremation, or bio-cremation, is far less familiar than the traditional method. Through the process of alkaline hydrolysis, the remains of the deceased are immersed in a solution consisting of water and potassium hydroxide within a stainless-steel container. For four hours, the body remains in the solution which is kept at 200 degrees Fahrenheit until nothing remains of but a residual DNA-free liquid and the skeleton. The bones are then removed, softer and less dense after the soak, and are crushed into ash before being presented to the family of the deceased.

A green return to dust

A three-hour procedure, known as alkaline hydrolysis, mimics a faster, natural decomposition process, promising a more environmentally friendly alternative to interment or cremation.

The solution
92 gallons of water mixed with 4 gallons of potash lye, heated to 338° F on average, dissolves the body

Liquid
Is drained
It's 1,000 times less alkaline than at the start

Bone 'shadows'
Are soft and easily crushed into powder to return to relatives

Heating coil

SOURCE: Resomation Ltd.   AP

AQUAMATION PROCESS ILLUSTRATION
(ASSOCIATED PRESS)

For years, Aquamation Industries of Australia has been working on establishing locations throughout the country to provide this service to the public. According to their website, "Aquamation produces no toxic air emissions and uses a fraction of the energy of traditional cremation." In fact, it is said to use less than 10%.

Some find this method a bit gruesome, equating the process with 'boiling away the flesh' of their loved ones, and disposing of what remains by essentially flushing it down the drain. However, what is returned to the earth following alkaline hydrolysis is water, sugar, salts, amino acids and peptides, all of which make up the human body's original form. It is no less respectable than traditional cremation.

In the United States, this method of cremation has been utilized to dispose of human remains donated to science, as well as the remains of animals/pets, but it has yet to become a widely available or popular option within the American funeral industry. There are currently only four states that allow the use of alkaline hydrolysis to dispose of a human body, including Florida, Illinois, Maine and Minnesota. Ten additional states have legalized the process, but only as an option for the disposal of animal remains.

When asked why flameless cremation wasn't as prevalent, even in states where the practice is legalized, AquaGreen Dispositions, LLC of South Holland, Illinois noted that the equipment required for aquamation costs two to three times that of traditional cremation. They also noted that the American funeral industry has long set the standard for tradition, making it difficult for the population to embrace new options. This type of disposition will likely remain limited until the public becomes more aware and accepting of it.

Despite the cost associated with providing the service, AquaGreen Dispositions offers the transportation of remains, water cremation, urn, and necessary legal paperwork for the price of $1,795.00. Being environmentally friendly and cost effective makes aquamation an attractive choice for those in (or relatively close to) geographical areas providing flameless cremation. For more information or to arrange services, visit their website at www.aquagreendispositions.com.

BIODEGRADABLE TREE URNS | PODS

As green, or environmentally friendly options are becoming more and more popular, several businesses throughout the world have developed creative and unique ways to help put a loved one to rest.

Italian designers Anna Citelli and Raul Bretzel have developed a product called the Capsula Mundi - an egg-shaped bio-friendly capsule or urn made of starch plastics produced from natural renewable sources such as corn and potatoes. This product isn't just an urn, however. The cremated remains (also known as cremains) or ashes of an individual are placed inside. Once

LIVING URNS ARE WIDELY
AVAILABLE ONLINE

buried, a young tree (of the client's choosing) is planted above it. Over time, as the urn and its contents are subjected to subsoil elements, it becomes a source of nourishment for the growing tree, thus creating a living memorial of the deceased.

What if a loved one wished to be buried rather than cremated? Citelli and Bretzel ultimately hope to provide a larger version of the Capsula Mundi designed to encapsulate the body (post rigor mortis) in a fetal position. This capsule or 'green coffin' would also be buried with the desired tree planted directly above it. The idea is to create memory forests, which are essentially cemeteries without vaults, caskets, harmful manufacturing or embalming chemicals, and cumbersome tombstones. While a beautiful idea, the full-body pods are not yet available to the public. The urns can be purchased online through their website and are available worldwide. www.capsulamundi.it.

U.S. based company The Living Urn also provides a similar product, made entirely out of plant-based materials, and without adhesives or other toxic agents. Once the urn is purchased, it is shipped to the customer in an all-natural bamboo outer shell. A tree seedling is then chosen, whether through The Living Urn or from a local nursery. Cremains are placed into the urn, and are then treated with a product called RootProtect that, according to their website, "serves to offset elevated pH levels and dilute high sodium concentrations present in the ash..."

The urn is then filled with soil and planted in the ground with the seedling placed directly above it. The included wood chips surround the seedling, and help the soil below retain moisture for the tree (or other desired plant) as the contents of the urn provide nourishment for healthy growth. For more information, or to purchase The Living Urn, visit their website www.thelivingurn.com.

BURIAL AT SEA

You don't have to be a veteran of the U.S. Military to have a burial at sea, though the armed forces perform more of these services than civilians. There are numerous companies with a variety of options for you to choose from, should you wish to have your remains committed to the ocean after death.

There are three main types of burial at sea: ash scattering, casketed burial, and shrouded burial, each requiring a burial permit before services can be held.

A small fleet of vessels, whether motor or sail, are provided to the customer, depending on the needs, wants, and size of funeral party expected to attend. Some offer light refreshments for their guests, provide flowers, urns, and other items used during the reserved time out to sea. All faiths and their clergy are also welcome to attend and to perform the ceremony of their choice, if any.

For ash scattering, the vessel transports the funeral party several miles offshore. Once the boat reaches the desired destination, the ashes are dispersed, and the family is given some time for reflection before returning to shore.

Casketed burials are performed a bit differently. Once the desired casket is chosen, the crew coordinates with the chosen funeral home to prepare it for sea burial. The remains are respectively covered, and a drill is used to

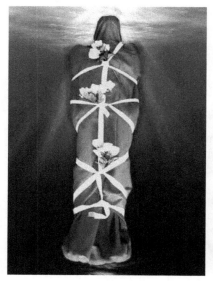

(LEFT) EXAMPLE OF A SHROUND USED FOR BURIAL AT SEA (KINKARACO)

(RIGHT) EXAMPLE OF A CASKET PREPARED FOR BURIAL AT SEA

create twenty 2" wholes throughout. Weight is added inside at the foot to assist its descent into the water. The remains are placed inside, and the casket is then closed and banded to prevent it from opening.

All full-body burials at sea must be completed in approved federal waters at least three miles offshore, at a water depth of 600 feet or more. When a body is prepared for a shrouded burial, the body is wrapped in natural cotton cloth, and secured with cotton banding. It is then placed into a special rental casket for transport to its destination, where the shrouded body is then released from the casket into the water.

For personal reference, or for future visitation to the burial site, families are often given the exact longitude and latitude GPS coordinates.

As there are several organizations on both East and West coasts, we recommend an independent review of what's available to best suit your needs.

BURIAL IN SPACE

Yes, you read that correctly. While it seems like something out of a science fiction film or novel, burial in space is a tangible - and surprisingly affordable - option for final disposition. While full-body services are not provided, sending one's cremated remains (or even just a DNA sample) into orbit is quite simple to arrange.

Celestis, the leading company providing these services, has been in business since 1994. They provide four memorial space flight options, including:

Earth Rise Service - $1,295+

Cremains or DNA are placed into flight capsules which are launched into space. The components of the rocket disengage, returning the capsules to Earth. They are then retrieved by helicopter and returned to family members as a 'flown keepsake.'

Earth Orbit Service - $4,995+

Families spend three days at the launch site with astronauts and other experts to celebrate the lives of those being sent into orbit. Once the rocket is launched with the remains or DNA on board, it will spend either months or years in orbit (depending on the specific mission) before eventually returning and burning up entirely upon re-entry. Families are also able to track the progress of each craft in orbit, to time and arrange additional memorial services, or simply to know when they're loved one is flying directly overhead.

Luna Service - $12,500+

With this flight, capsules containing cremains or DNA are launched into space and set on a mission to land on the surface of the moon, where they will permanently remain. According to their website, "Celestis Luna missions also permit - for the first time in human history - off Earth storage for DNA and digital data archives." When the moon is visible, families can look up and see the final resting place of their loved one in the night sky.

Voyager Service - $12,500+

Neither returning to earth nor landing on the surface of the moon, this mission provides a permanent and infinite journey into deep space for the cremains or DNA on board. The more adventurous of memorials, this is a fitting tribute to anyone with a passion for space exploration and adventure.

For more information, to make memorial spaceflight reservations, or to view all of those memorialized on past and upcoming missions, visit www.celestis.com.

CATACOMBO SOUND SYSTEM CASKET

For the "best in afterlife entertainment," Swedish company PAUSE has engineered a casket like no other. With a $35,000+ price tag, it certainly isn't

THE CATACOMBO SOUND SYSTEM CASKET (PULSE)

for everyone, but certainly appeals to the music lover with more than enough money to burn (or bury, rather.)

The CataCoffin, outfitted with two-way speakers, tweeters, subwoofer and amp provides the interred with a never-ending stream of music. With the CataPlay application, you can create your own unique playlist with Spotify. Your friends and family can also add music to your list, playing songs they think you might enjoy.

The CataTomb headstone functions as not only a grave marker, but also as a real time digital display of the song currently playing six feet under.

Getting your hands on this system might prove a bit difficult, but should you have the opportunity to visit the PAUSE storefront in Stockholm, you can always stop in for a 'live' demonstration.

Visit www.catacombosoundsystem.com for more information.

CRYONICS

When you're dead, you're dead, right? Perhaps not. According to the Cryonics Institute of Michigan, one can plan to cryogenically preserve their body as quickly as possible following clinical death in hopes of being revived by the doctors and medical personnel of the future.

In his book, *The Prospect of Immortality* published in 1962, author and researcher Robert Ettinger first introduced the concept of cryonics to the world. His further work eventually led to the creation of the Cryonics Institute in 1976, which housed the first full-operational cryonics facility in the world.

What exactly is cryonics, you ask? Once a clinical death occurs, the body is taken as soon as possible to be cooled to liquid nitrogen temperatures, arresting cellular decay, and preserving the body in a suspended state in hopes that future technology will not only allow life to recur, but that the patient will 'wake' with as much of their original memories and personality as possible, perhaps even younger and with more vitality.

There are currently over 100 patients preserved and stored at the Michigan facility, including Ettinger and additional members of his family.

If the potential of essentially being frozen and resurrected decades or even centuries from now appeals to you, a membership to the Institute is mandatory. While not the sole organization working with cryonics, they claim to be the most advanced in technology and process application.

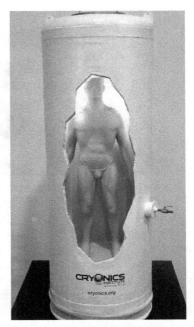

CRYONICS CHAMBER
(THE CRYONICS INSTITUTE)

A Lifetime Membership costs $1,250, which provides patients the opportunity to arrange cryopreservation for an additional $28,000. This can be covered by listing CI as the beneficiary on a life insurance policy. Additional family members can gain membership for $625 each, with no charge for children under the age of 18.

An Annual Membership costs an initial fee of $75 with a recurring annual charge of $120. Patients with an annual membership can arrange for preservation with the Institute for a fee of $35,000. Additional fees to be considered are initial preservation of the body and transportation to the Cryonics Institute provided by a licensed funeral director.

For membership and application information, visit www.cryonics.org

ETERNAL ARTIFICIAL REEF

With so many of the planet's natural coral reefs dying off and disappearing altogether, it is no wonder that ocean lovers everywhere are opting to help become part of the solution post-mortem.

EXAMPLE OF A PLACED AND GROWING
ARTIFICIAL REEF (ETERNAL REEFS)

An Eternal Reef is a memorial constructed of environmentally-safe concrete, designed to provide a new living habitat for various forms of sea life. Once an individual is cremated, their ashes are mixed with the concrete just before it is cast into the reef's design. Castings occur where the reef is to be placed, and all family members are encouraged to participate in its creation, though they are not required.

The reefs can be personalized by family members with hand prints pressed into the damp cement, along with any mementos that will not harm the environment. A bronze plaque with the deceased's details is placed, and the memorial is set aside to cure.

Once completed, family members attend a viewing, where they are given the opportunity to take pictures, create rubbings of the plaque, or write loving statements on the inside and outside of the reef.

When the reef is ready to be placed, families travel to the approved reef site by chartered boat, where the transportation vessel is waiting to place and dedicate the memorials one by one. Once placed into the ocean, the transportation vessel departs, and the family boat moves over the site to perform their personal dedications. Small tribute reefs are provided, which the family decorates with an assortment of fresh flowers, also provided during the dedication. These tributes are committed to the ocean as well as one last token of remembrance before returning to shore.

There are three options for the service, ranging from the largest size reef to the smallest.

Mariner Eternal Reef - $7,495
Size: 4' x 5' | 3800 - 4000 lbs.
Nautilus Eternal Reef - $4,995
Size: 3' x 4' | 1200 - 1500 lbs.
Aquarius Eternal Reef - $3,995
Size: 2' x 3' | 650 - 800 lbs.

The Eternal Reef Direct service is also available for those who wish to have their loved ones memorialized and placed in a reef but are not able or do not wish to personally attend the placement and dedication. The direct service is performed at a $1,000 discount from the full-price service for any size reef.

For more information or to make arrangements, visit www.eternalreefs.com

HOME FUNERAL | HOME BURIAL

Caring for the dead at home was once a familial responsibility. Relatives bathed, dressed, and spent time with their dead, handling most of the details themselves. This, of course, was only until the funeral industry took over. Home funerals have become increasingly more common in recent years, although most people aren't aware that it is even an option. Most states allow home funerals, though regulations may vary widely from one state to another.

If the concept of planning and conducting a home funeral is overwhelming, working with a funeral guide (not to be confused with a funeral home or director) might be ideal. These individuals help guide families through the process of filing the death certificate, suggest appropriate home care for the deceased, advise on transportation, final disposition and more. Funeral guides (or death midwives, as they are often called) must have limited personal involvement in a home funeral, however, as they are not licensed by the state and therefore cannot legally perform certain tasks.

In their book FINAL RIGHTS: Reclaiming the American Way of Death, authors Josh Slocum and Lisa Carlson note:

> Funeral directors, of course, have complained about death midwives, asking "Why don't they have to get a license before they haul bodies and perform wakes, just like I do?" Well, death midwives don't belong to an industry that has taken massive economic advantage of the bereaved, they don't lie about the legal or health necessity of embalming, and they don't manipulate the legislative system to shut down consumer choice.

Home burials are another matter and are only granted to those who obtain the necessary permits. These permits are most often issued to individuals whose land is located in rural areas, with restrictions on proximity to water and electrical sources. For a more complete description of state regulations regarding home funerals and burials, refer to FINAL RIGHTS, as it is an excellent resource.

LAB-CREATED DIAMONDS MADE FROM CREMAINS

LIFEGEM

While standard cremation is a popular choice, an individual's final disposition need not remain as ashes in an urn atop the family mantle or displayed on a shelf. For the past 15 years, U.S. company LifeGem has offered one-of-a-kind lab-created diamonds made directly from cremated remains, a lock of hair, as well as a combination of the two.

Once received in the lab, carbon is captured from the remains and/or hair and is then treated to convert the carbon to graphite. Once placed in the diamond press, the graphite is heated and pressurized, just as it would be in nature, until a rough diamond is formed. This process is considerably quicker than in nature, however, as the LifeGem diamond can be created in as little as six months (whereas natural diamonds can take millions of years.)

Once formed, the diamond is cut to the customer's specifications in either brilliant round, princess, or radiant cuts. They are professionally evaluated, laser inscribed, and shipped securely to the family once completed.

The diamonds LifeGem creates can be treated as any other, and treasured as a loose gem, placed into existing jewelry, or made into something designed to further memorialize the individual from which it was made.

Costs depend on size, color, cut and quantity desired and range from $2,690 to $24,999. For more information, visit www.lifegem.com

MUMMIFICATION

If you prefer to go the Ancient Egyptian route, you can forego the traditional funeral service and employ Summum, the world's only commercial mummification company, to preserve your remains.

Located in Salt Lake City, Utah, Summum offers modern mummification® to its clients wishing to be preserved in much the same way the Egyptians developed centuries ago.

Working with a designated funeral home, the body to be mummified is transferred to Summum's sanctuary following any funeral services they have provided. Once the body arrives, it is no longer accessible for viewing by

THE MUMMIFICATION PROCESS IS ALIVE AND WELL, SO TO SPEAK

family or friends. This is to avoid any undue interference when preparing and working with the body during the mummification process.

The body is disrobed and cleansed before an incision is made to remove the internal organs, which are also washed. Both the body and removed organs are placed into a bath of unspecified chemicals, where they remain immersed until the solution adequately penetrates the tissues.

Once removed from the bath, the internal organs are placed back inside the body cavity, and the incision is closed. The body is washed a second time, and an anointing oil is applied. Cotton gauze is wrapped around the body in several layers, followed by a polymer membrane to permanently seal them in place.

The completed mummy is placed and sealed into a Mummiform® (aka sarcophagus) specially designed and manufactured for the deceased, or into a full couch bronze or stainless-steel casket for internment. It is recommended that the Mummiform® or casket be placed in a mausoleum or cemetery where it will neither freeze or become overheated. This is to ensure the body remain in the best possible condition.

The cost for human mummification begins at $67,000. Larger or more complicated remains add to these costs. The Mummiform® or chosen casket is an additional expense, which can add tens of thousands to your final bill.

For more information on arranging mummification services, visit www.summum.org.

NATURAL BURIAL

Reminiscent of the days before the death care industry took over, natural or 'green' burials are making their way back into American culture as a more personal and environmentally-friendly funerary option.

GREEN BURIAL SITE

In the U.S., we bury excessive amounts of chemicals and materials used in traditional burials. According to Mary Woodsen of the Green Burial Council, the U.S. buries over 4 million gallons of embalming fluid (including over 827,000 gallons of formaldehyde), nearly 65,000 tons of steel, 20 million board feet of hardwood used for caskets, and nearly 2 million tons of concrete for vaults.

A natural burial not only significantly reduces costs, it also reduces the amount of potentially hazardous chemicals and materials going into the soil. The recent development of chemical-free embalming fluids - one made entirely out of essential oils - has been introduced as a more environmentally-friendly option than traditional embalming. Using non-toxic and biodegradable coffins, caskets and shrouds, natural burials ensure minimal disruption to the surrounding natural habitat.

Costs and hazards aside, many people opt for a natural burial because they feel an emotional or spiritual obligation to be returned to the earth from which they came. Most commercial and privately-run cemeteries require the use of vaults and caskets for internment, but there are locations where green burials are not only permitted but encouraged.

A helpful resource for planning a natural or green burial is a book entitled, *The Natural Burial Cemetery Guide: State-By-State Where, How, and Why to Choose Green Burial* by Ann Hoffner. It is available to purchase in its entirety, or by regional breakdown in both print and digital formats.

For more information or to purchase a copy, visit www.greenburialnaturally.org.

OPEN-AIR CREMATION | FUNERAL PYRE

Unfortunately, the option of having a natural, open-air cremation is extremely limited. Exclusively available in Colorado, The Crestone End of Life Project serves the residents of Sagauche County wishing to take a more natural approach to their cremation.

All faiths (or lack thereof) are respected, and project participants are on hand to support a family through the open-air cremation process, which involves wrapping the deceased in a shroud, placing the body on a stretcher, and laying it on a pyre above a half cord of wood before setting it aflame.

The details on costs, process duration, and transfer of remains post ceremony are not immediately available online, but contact information, a brief overview and photo gallery can be found at www.informedfinalchoices.org.

AND VINYLY...

If you're a music lover or happen to be an avid collector of vinyl records, this may be the option for you. Jason Leach's UK-based company And Vinyly has developed a unique way of preserving one's memory with music... by pressing their cremated ashes into vinyl.

Imagine becoming a literal part of your favorite album. When played, your ashes creating the little clicks and pops throughout; essentially 'you' merged with music.

PLAYABLE VINYL RECORDS CAN NOW BE PRESSED USED CREMATION ASHES

Leach will even make a preview album (sans you, of course) for approval beforehand, allowing you to see and hear the product you (or your loved one) will become a part of.

The records come in 7 and 12-inch sizes, in clear, color, or clear colored. You can choose to include personal recordings, your favorite music, or both, and even have creative say in the album and artwork covers.

For more information or to order a custom vinyl record, visit www.andvinyly.com.

BIBLIOGRAPHY

AMSLER, KEVIN – *FINAL RESTING PLACE*; 1997

BONDESON, JAN – *BURIED ALIVE*; 2001

BROWN, JOHN GARY – *SOUL IN THE STONE*; 1994

BURNS, STANLEY, M.D. – *SLEEPING BEAUTY*; 1990

-------------------------------------- – *SLEEPING BEAUTY III: MEMORIAL PHOTOGRAPHY*, 2011

-------------------------------------- WITH ELIZABETH A. BURNS – *SLEEPING BEAUTY II*; 2002

DAVIES, RODNEY – *THE LAZARUS SYNDROME*; 1998

DEATH: A GRAVESIDE COMPANION, THAMES AND HUDSON; 2017

DUKE UNIVERSITY LIBRARIES | DIGITAL REPOSITORY

FAUST, DREW GILPIN – *THIS REPUBLIC OF SUFFERING*; 2008

GAY, JOHN AND FELIX BARKER – *HIGHGATE CEMETERY: VICTORIAN VALHALLA*; 1984

JOLLY, MARTYN – *FACES OF THE LIVING DEAD*; 2006

HODES, MARTHA – *MOURNING LINCOLN*; 2015

ISERSON, KENNETH G. – *DEATH TO DUST*; 1994

JACKSON, KENNETH AND CAMILO JOSE VERGARA – *SILENT CITIES*; 1989

JONES, BARBARA – *DESIGN FOR DEATH*; 1967

KEISTER, DOUGLAS- *GOING OUT IN STYLE*; 1997

------------------------------- – *STORIES IN STONE*; 2004

KOUDOUNARIS, PAUL – *THE EMPIRE OF DEATH*; 2011

------------------------------- – *HEAVENLY BODIES*; 2013

------------------------------- – *MEMENTO MORI*; 2015

Meinwald, Dan – *Memento Mori: Death and Photography in Nineteenth Century America*

Meyer, Richard – *Cemeteries and Grave Markers*; 1989

Mitford, Jessica – *The American Way of Death Revisited*; 1998

Mord, Jack – *Beyond the Dark Veil: Postmortem and Mourning Photography from the Thanatos Archive*; 2014

Murphy, Edwin – *After the Funeral*; 1995

Permutt, Cyril – *Photographing the spirit world*; 1988

Pickover, Clifford A. – *Death and the Afterlife*; 2015

Quigley, Christine – *The Corpse: A History*; 1996

Roach, Mary – *Stiff: The Curious Lives of Human Cadavers*; 2003

Robinson, David – *Saving Graces*; 1995

Schechter, Harold – *The Whole Death Catalog*; 2009

Sickles, Megan – *Ashes to Ashes: America's First Crematorium*; 2009

Slocum, Josh and Lisa Carlson – *Final Rights*; 2011

Smith, Suzanne – *To Serve the Living*; 2010

Stannard, David E. – *The Puritan Way of Death*; 1977

Steers, Edward, jr. – *Lincoln Assassination encyclopedia*; 2010

Swanson, James – *Bloody times*; 2010

Taylor, Troy – *American Hauntings*; 2017

------------------------- – *Beyond the Grave*; 2002

Tebb, William and Edward Perry Vollum – *Premature Burial and How it May be Prevented*; 1896

Wilkins, Robert – *Death: a History of man's Obsessions and Fears*; 1990

Woodyard, Chris – *Victorian book of the Dead*; 2014

ABOUT THE AUTHORS

APRIL SLAUGHTER IS THE AUTHOR OF THREE BOOKS AND NUMEROUS ARTICLES ON GHOSTS, HAUNTINGS, SPIRIT COMMUNICATION, PSYCHICAL RESEARCH AND THE UNEXPLAINED. SHE WAS BORN AND RAISED IN UTAH, WHERE SHE DEVELOPED A LOVE FOR GENEALOGY AND AMERICAN HISTORY. AS AN ESTABLISHED ARTIST AND POET, APRIL ENJOYS ALL THE CREATIVE AVENUES OF HER WORK WHILE RAISING IDENTICAL TWIN DAUGHTERS ON THE OUTSKIRTS OF SALT LAKE CITY.

TROY TAYLOR IS THE AUTHOR OF NEARLY 125 BOOKS ABOUT GHOSTS, CRIME, AND THE UNEXPLAINED IN AMERICA. HE IS ALSO THE FOUNDER OF AMERICAN HAUNTINGS — GHOST TOURS, BOOKS, EVENTS, AND EXCURSIONS ACROSS AMERICA. HE WAS BORN AND RAISED IN THE MIDWEST AND DIVIDES HIS TIME BETWEEN ILLINOIS AND THE FAR-FLUNG REACHES OF THE COUNTRY.

Printed in the USA
CPSIA information can be obtained
at www.ICGtesting.com
CBHW061118101223
2545CB00010B/991